D1104882

Performing Asian America

In the series

Asian American History and Culture,

edited by Sucheng Chan, David Palumbo-Liu,

and Michael Omi

A list of books in this series appears

at the back of this volume

PERFORMING

ASIAN AMERICA

Race and Ethnicity on the Contemporary Stage

Josephine Lee

Temple University Press   Philadelphia

Temple University Press, Philadelphia 19122
Copyright © 1997 by Temple University
All rights reserved
Published 1997
Printed in the United States of America

⊗ The paper used in this publication meets the requirements of the American National Standard for Information
Sciences—Permanence of Paper for Printed Library Materials, ANSI Z39.48-1984

Text design by Mary Mendell

Library of Congress Cataloging-in-Publication Data
Lee, Josephine Ding, 1960–
    Performing Asian America : race and ethnicity on the
contemporary stage / Josephine Lee.
        p.   cm. — (Asian American History and Culture)
    Includes bibliographical references and index.
    ISBN 1-56639-502-x (cloth : alk. paper)
    1. American drama—20th century—History and
criticism.   2. Asian Americans in literature.
3. American drama—Asian American authors—History
and criticism.   4. Ethnicity in literature.   5. Race in
literature.   I. Title.
PS338.A74L44   1997
812'.5409035073—dc20   96-31621

CONTENTS

Acknowledgments   vii

1   Critical Strategies for Reading Asian American Drama   1

2   The Asian American Spectator and the Politics of Realism   34

3   The Chinaman's Unmanly Grief   61

4   The Seduction of the Stereotype   89

5   Acts of Exclusion: Asian American History Plays   136

6   Asian American Doubles and the Soul under Capitalism   163

7   Staging "Passing" on the Borders of the Body   189

Epilogue   217

Notes   221

Works Cited   231

Index   239

Photographs appear on pages 121–135

ACKNOWLEDGMENTS

Many friends, colleagues, and family members have supported me throughout the length of this project. I am particularly indebted to Michael Goldman, A. R. Gurney, Jr., Leyla Ezdinli, Randy Barbara Kaplan, De Witt Kilgore, Imogene Lim, Yuko Matsukawa, Mitziko Sawada, Ranu Samantrai, and W. B. Worthen. I also wish to thank Luisa Cariaga, Dennis Carroll, Tisa Chang, Chris Huie, Bob Hsiang, Corky Lee, Charissa Uemara, Roberta Uno, and Rick Shiomi for their indispensable help with information and photographs. David Palumbo-Liu and Janet Francendese provided sound advice throughout the process of revision and editing. My students at Princeton, California State University–Northridge, Smith College, and the University of Minnesota have given me valuable insights into the reading of these plays.

The initial research for this book was partially supported by grants from Five Colleges, Inc., the University of Minnesota Graduate School, and the McKnight Faculty Summer Research Fellowship.

I would like to thank all of those who by blood, relation, or spirit constitute the members of my extended family. I am especially indebted to my parents, Po Lee and Feng Ming Young Lee, and my sisters Jean and May for their continuing encouragement and care. Finally, I am most grateful to my husband, Kevin Kinneavy, without whose devoted efforts this book would not have been possible.

Performing Asian America

1

Critical Strategies for
Reading Asian American Drama

This book begins a critical examination of selected plays written by Americans of Asian descent. The works considered cover a diverse range of subjects and dramatic styles; my discussion teases out the shared strategies by which plays and playwrights make performance, dramatic form, and audience response inseparable from the meaning of race and ethnicity. As we shall see, such an examination necessarily engages with many pressing concerns, ones whose effects are felt outside as well as inside the theater. These concerns make it crucial for us to refocus our approaches to dramatic and literary interpretation in response to larger political questions about Asian American experience, identity, and action. Through the reading of these plays, we may gain insight not only into individual plays, but also more generally into the complex modes of action that these works employ and exemplify.

Before discussing such critical strategies, I will briefly summarize some significant history that will help to contextualize the genesis and production of these plays. The second half of the nineteenth century saw the first major wave of Asian immigration to the United States. Attracted by the economic opportunities provided by the California gold rush and westward development and spurred by civil unrest and famine in China,

Chinese immigrants came by the thousands. Their new lives in America were complicated by the acts of violence and institutionalized discrimination they soon encountered. White workers, threatened by economic competition from Chinese workers, lobbied for passage of the Chinese Exclusion Act of 1882, which restricted the immigration and naturalization of Chinese laborers and their wives.

Passage of the act did not stop early twentieth-century immigration from Asia. The need for inexpensive and industrious labor continued on plantations and railroads, and in the factories, mines, canneries, and farms of the West Coast states and Hawaii. Japanese and Filipino workers brought in as contract laborers soon faced similar restrictions. The impulse to stop Asians not only from entering the country but also from settling permanently gave rise to a host of laws restricting immigration, land ownership, and citizenship. The 1929 National Origins Act limited immigration from Asia to small numbers of exempted wives of U.S. citizens, students, ministers, and professors. Total immigration from Asia, which had reached nearly 60,000 during the period 1916–20, fell to 3,700 in 1936–40 and 2,300 in 1941–45 (Barringer 28).

Significant changes in immigration policy and law after the Second World War, although undoing some of the earlier restrictive policies, continued to reflect a pervasive fear of the "yellow peril." In 1943 the Chinese Exclusion Act was repealed, and foreign-born Chinese were declared eligible for citizenship; however, the annual immigration quota for China was limited to 105. In 1952 Congress passed, over President Harry Truman's veto, the McCarran-Walter Act, which gave all immigrants the right to apply for citizenship. Yet this act still established preferences for skilled immigrants and family members and maintained extremely limited annual quotas for Asian immigrants: 185 for Japan, 105 for China, and 100 each for countries of the "Asia-Pacific Triangle."

Nevertheless, the immediate result of the McCarran-Walter Act was a gradual rise in the number of Asian immigrants to approximately 20,000 per year for the years before 1965. In 1965 the Hart-Cellar Act abolished the quota system, establishing a limit to immigration of 290,000 total per year. Although it still limited the numbers of immigrants from Eastern Hemisphere countries to 20,000 per country (with certain family members of U.S. citizens exempted), the act allowed a great increase in Asian immigration, from 16,000 in 1965 to more than 100,000 by 1972 to more than a quarter million in 1989. Filipinos, Chinese (from China, Taiwan, and Hong Kong), Asian Indians, Koreans, and Vietnamese have been the largest groups benefited, although since 1975 significant numbers of Vietnamese, Cambodian, and Laotian refugees have also settled in the United States (Barringer 30–32).

In 1960, persons of Asian descent represented a mere one half of 1 percent of the U.S. population. By the year 2000 it is projected that Asian Americans, many of them native born, will account for about 4 percent of the total U.S. population (Takaki 5–6). This figure suggests a strong demographic basis for the felt presence of Asian Americans as active participants in a number of public arenas.[1] But the growing influence of Asian Americans has its foundations in political and cultural as well as demographic changes. Asian American activism, allied with other civil rights movements in the 1960s and after, has wrought important changes in the social fabric of American life. One significant aspect of these changes can be seen in recent cultural production; among their other endeavors, Asian Americans have been increasingly recognized for their contributions to the visual arts, literature, music, dance, and theater.

The new visibility of Asian American theater artists is part of a larger movement that has emerged in the past few decades: the escalating attention given to the political, cultural, and intellectual issues of race and ethnicity. Although plays by Asian Americans were written and performed earlier (notably in Hawaii), much of the current body of theatrical work has been produced or made available to readers only since the early 1970s. These works are now gaining more public attention. Recently, several anthologies of Asian American drama—*Between Worlds, The Politics of Life,* and *Unbroken Thread*—and new collections by David Henry Hwang, Philip Kan Gotanda, and Edward Sakamoto have been published.[2] Works by Asian American playwrights such as Jessica Hagedorn, Ping Chong, Diana Son, Brenda Wong Aoki, and Han Ong have also been included in recent anthologies of plays.[3]

To place these playwrights and their works into a grouping designated by national origin, ethnicity, or race is to imply that they participate in a common project: the reconsideration of identity as it is linked both to social representation and to artistic presentation. The playwrights whose works I discuss at more length in this book are well aware that they and their characters are seen as representatives of a group; at the same time, their plays problematize the categories of race and ethnicity. Both this self-consciousness about representation and the interest in redefining theatrical presentation define, I will suggest, a set of unique questions, preoccupations, and dramatic styles that mark these plays as "Asian American."

Insisting that drama by Asian Americans deserves a distinctive critical approach, or its own book, is somewhat risky, given the current climate inside and outside the academy and the theater. Increasingly, scholars, teachers, and directors are expanding their curriculum or changing their theater season to have a more multicultural emphasis. The inclusion of works by artists of color for "special" institutional recognition has drawn fire from those who charge that such a move promotes racial separatism. In a 1991 issue of *American Theater* on multicultural issues, significant space was devoted to Robert Brustein's condemnation of the "racial exclusionism" manifested in plays that are "committed to strict racial and ethnic orthodoxy, and the empowerment of disadvantaged people through the agency of culture" (Brustein 46). The so-called "ethnicity" school in literary studies argues a similar danger and urges that a marginalized literature neither should be singled out for exceptional attention

nor merits a group-specific methodology, for fear of promoting insider-
ism and fragmentation.[4]

These arguments underscore the importance of using care in how we
approach the performance and representation of race and ethnicity in the
theater. Race and ethnicity raise complex questions by challenging the
traditional criteria by which plays have been analyzed and valued. We can
no longer assume that the canonical classics can be evaluated according
to supposedly universal or objective aesthetic standards, with works by
artists of color added to the repertory solely to ensure political representation. These assumptions relegate art by marginalized peoples to the
status of add-ons to an existing canon. Further, it traps more progressive
academics into the politically misguided and functionally impossible task
of making academic canons fully "representative." Finally, it places artists
of color into the awkward position of speaking for others.[5]

In reality, preserving a more "universal" set of standards that would
allow us to avoid politics by focusing on presumably neutral aesthetics is
no longer viable in the face of current debates over race, gender, and class
differences. The old theories of genre, form, and response that erase racial difference and that separate art neatly into either political or aesthetic
dimensions are inadequate to the demands of new works: to their immediate topical concerns, the complexity of their artistic presentation, the
difficult questions of art and political representation that they raise. If I
argue for a more group-specific methodology, it is because a more nu-
anced and context-sensitive approach to understanding art is needed, one
that addresses not only individual works of art and artists, but also the
assumptions used in interpreting and evaluating them.

Now more than ever, we need ways of looking at drama and theater
that allow for a discussion of racial and ethnic as well as other differences. Perhaps the idea of the universal standard still persists in part
because critics have not developed adequate ways to discuss how theater
is a valuable or necessary practice. Thus, my aim is to suggest, within the

terms of this specialized study, how we might formulate a new poetics that would enable us to discuss more creatively the performance of race and ethnicity on stage. How are different ideas of what is Asian American inseparable from the interpretation of performance events? How do these plays work to construct race and ethnicity as theatrical values?

In this spirit, this book is organized around particular questions and issues rather than by playwright, genre, or chronology; it attempts to integrate interpretative readings with a set of theoretical topics and questions. I offer not only specific contexts for the interpretation of particular plays, but also a larger framework of questions within which to consider the staging of race and ethnicity.

Elaine Kim has pointed out that many critical approaches often treat Asian American drama and literature simply as illustrations of some off-stage sociohistorical reality (xv). Such approaches, as she insists, are somewhat problematic. First, they neglect the complex ways in which dramatic representation both reconstructs and is defined by its historical context: the complex interpretation of theater *as theater*. Second, they sustain essentialized racial categories, maintaining the assumption that ethnicity and race are natural essences that can be transparently reflected on the stage, rather than socially fabricated categories that are made through human performance. We must question the assumption that plays simply imitate a preexisting Asian American experience or identity, and instead describe how race is constructed and contested by theatrical presentation. The theoretical discussions formulated here try to resist readings of plays as mirrors of real lives, social behaviors, or historical events. Instead, they assume a complex negotiation of meaning by both performer and spectator, concentrating on the ways in which the events of the drama, character and action, and in turn playwright and reception are significantly racialized and ethnicized.

I purposefully avoid any attempts to create an alternative canon, to rank the individual masterpiece, or to assess the excellence of any writer.

Instead, I am concerned with the collective nature of the practice and meaning of drama. Less important than what an individual work might contribute to its author's reputation is what that work reveals about the shared assumptions and understanding of race and ethnicity: how and what these terms mean, and how they are presented on the stage. Further, by examining each play in the company of other plays by Asian Americans, we take the pressure off any individual work to be the quintessential Asian American play in some multicultural syllabus. Instead of trying to package a play as the representation of a singular Asian American voice, we are free to try varied approaches that foster comparisons and contrasts between these and other theatrical works.

Just as the idea of performance is crucial to studying race and ethnicity, so also is the reverse true. A study of theater and plays has much to offer current discussions of identity politics. The "liveness" or "presence" of theater suggests an immediate, visceral response to the physicality of race; the embodiedness of theater is experienced or felt, as well as seen and heard. The physical response of the spectator to the body of the actor complicates any abstraction of social categories. The theater does not let us forget that questions of racial difference concern our most basic gut reactions, experiences, and sensations. Literature and cinema or electronic media, as Ella Shohat has suggested, may be somewhat abstracted, divorced from the actual body.[6] Theater is less capable of a divorce from the body. Michael Omi and Howard Winant have recently challenged scholars to investigate how a racial ideology profoundly influences the conventions of behavior and engagement in the United States:

Rules shaped by our perception of race in a comprehensively racial society determine the "presentation of self," distinctions of status, and appropriate modes of conduct. . . . Everybody learns some combination, some version, of the rules of racial classification, and of

their own racial identity, often without obvious teaching or conscious inculcation. Race becomes "common sense"—a way of com-
prehending, explaining and acting in the world. (62)

Different manifestations of such a complex "racial etiquette" are distur-
bingly and profoundly investigated in the live action of the theater.

Toward a "Real Asian American Theater"

W.E.B. Du Bois's 1926 agenda for the Krigwa Players Little Negro Theatre
might well describe the ideal goals of a number of so-called "minority"
theaters today:

> The plays of a real Negro theatre must be: 1. *About us.* That is they
> must have plots which reveal Negro life as it is. 2. *By us.* That is they
> must be written by Negro authors who understand from birth and
> continual association just what it means to be a Negro today. 3. *For
> us.* That is, the theatre must cater primarily to Negro audiences and
> be supported and sustained by their entertainment and approval. 4.
> *Near us.* The theatre must be in a Negro neighborhood near the
> mass of ordinary Negro people. (Du Bois 134)

Yet any attempt to describe "a real Asian American theater" along these
lines is particularly complicated. Although certain people have undoubtedly been influential in initiating, enabling, or encouraging it, theatrical
activity by Asian Americans is not confined to any one specific theater, a
generation of playwrights, or a group of performing artists. Nor is there
necessarily one kind of audience or community involved in its reception,
interpretation, and meaning.

Thus it is dangerous to assume that "Asian America" can be fully expressed through a particular body of work, however diverse that body
might at first appear. Any contemporary critical study of Asian American
artistic production must be aware of the problems inherent in embracing

ideas of community and representation that are necessarily exclusionary. In fact, the term Asian America covers not only an extremely diverse population but one that is constantly changing. The 1980 U.S. Census included within its designation of "Asian and Pacific Islander Americans" six major groups—Chinese, Filipinos, Japanese, Asian Indian, Korean, and Vietnamese—as well as twenty-two smaller groups, the largest of which were Laotian, Thai, Cambodian, and Pakistani (Barringer 3). Yet critical overviews of published literature and drama by Asian Americans persistently erase parts of this picture. As Lisa Lowe points out, it is all too easy to skew the idea of "Asian America" toward certain kinds of experience by taking Chinese and Japanese American experience as representative—an approach that erases differences of gender, national origin, class, education, and age in favor of a totalizing "Asian American" identity (30–31). For reasons discussed later, this familiar pattern is unfortunately repeated in this book, for the majority of the plays considered were written by second or later generations of college-educated Chinese and Japanese American playwrights; dramatic works by Asian Indians, Pacific Islanders, Southeast Asians, and others are conspicuously absent.

This cautionary note leads us to consider how "Asian America" as articulated through theatrical participation might be less useful in describing a full range of real lives than in articulating imaginary or desired states of being and relation. If, as Abdul JanMohamed and David Lloyd suggest, "minority individuals are always treated and forced to experience themselves generically," that experience might in fact provoke not only a rebellious individualism but also an impulse toward community: "Coerced into a negative, generic subject-position, the oppressed individual responds by transforming that position into a positive, collective one" (10). The attempts of various playwrights, performers, audiences, and critics to make a "real Asian American theater" might reflect, if not an easily understood "us" in terms of a homogeneous community of ordinary Asian Americans, then at the very least an intensely imagined commonality shared by a number of diverse individuals and social groups. Theatrical activity by Asian Americans is intimately linked to the Asian American movement of the 1960s and after, in which an urgent call for political solidarity among minority groups took precedence over internal differences and a sense of collective identity was forged out of the experiences of groups with highly disparate backgrounds. Although a fully shared group identity is felt by many Asian Americans to be unachievable and perhaps undesirable, the legacy of the Asian American movement is a continuing emphasis on pan-ethnicity. These felt affinities and the imagined communities they produce can influence playwrights, I will argue, as much as the actual sites and logistics of production, audience, and reception do.

In some ways, the need for a new, more flexible understanding of the term Asian America, especially in theatrical performance, has come out of the common legacy of misrepresentation. As James Moy, Gina Marchetti, Darrell Hamamoto, and others have noted, American audiences have long had a fascination with viewing the "Oriental," whether in plays, musicals, and traditional Asian theater performances or through more vernacular forms such as movies and television shows, tours of Chinatown, or fair exhibits. The depictions of Asian Americans in these venues range from a vague "Oriental" exoticism to more complex and disturbing characterizations. Comic types such as Mark Twain and Bret Harte's Ah Sin—a wily and unredeemably "foreign" figure who spoke in gibberish—became popular in farce and caricature in the late nineteenth century.[7] The character of Fu Manchu, the "yellow peril incarnate in one man," was created by British author Sax Rohmer in a series of thirteen novels, the first published in 1913. Subsequently, in 1932, the character appeared in an MGM film starring Boris Karloff. Fu Manchu developed into a racial archetype that has maintained its popularity, resurfacing in comic book villains such as *Flash Gordon*'s Ming the Merciless and feature films such as *The Castle of Fu Manchu* (1968). The familiar figure of detective Charlie Chan, created by novelist Earl Biggers in 1925, is a self-effacing, polite, "domesticated" Asian who speaks in broken English despite his native-born status, spouts pseudo-Confucianisms, and exemplifies loyal service to a white superior.

Such stereotypes suggest a clear link between social tensions and cultural representation. As Gary Okihiro comments, both Fu Manchu and Charlie Chan present a complex blend of "feminine" and "masculine" attributes, reflecting a larger American anxiety over its relations with Asian countries internationally and with Asian Americans domestically (*Margins and Mainstreams* 142–45). More recent typing of Asian males as comic geeks, such as in the 1984 movies *Revenge of the Nerds* and *Sixteen Candles*, continues the trend set by the exaggerated characters Ah Sin, Fu Manchu, and Charlie Chan of ridiculing and disempowering the Asian American male. The ideology motivating the dissemination of these stereotypes of Asian American males—effecting a symbolic castration—is strongly tied to the historical immigration and antimiscegenation laws that prevented the immigration of Chinese women, thereby closing off options for marriage and procreation and creating large bachelor communities of Chinese and Filipino immigrants. It is no surprise, then, that the prevailing stereotypes of Asian women reference a white rather than an Asian masculine desire. The objectification of Asian women through these stereotypes of evil seductresses, "dragon ladies," geishas, or frail lotus blossoms in early plays, films, and books inevitably related to a white male protagonist. As Jessica Hagedorn points out, contemporary films from *The World of Suzie Wong* (1960) to *Casualties of War* (1989) continue to portray Asian women as "decorative, invisible, or one-dimensional" (79).

Just as these racial stereotypes influenced popular sentiment and fueled racism toward Asians by displacing the actual body in favor of the exaggerated image, so did white actors' portrayals of Asian characters on the theatrical stage pass for the real thing. C. T. Parsloe's "Great and Original

Creation of THE HEATHEN CHINEE" in the stage version of Twain and Hart's *Ah Sin* (1877) was praised for "truthfulness to nature and freedom from caricature" (Moy, *Marginal Sights* 25, 29). Parsloe's success undoubtedly led to the viability of actors playing in "yellowface," a tradition that was sustained in the forty-seven feature-length Charlie Chan movies in which the title character was played mainly by white actors, although his sons were played by Asian Americans (Wei 52). White actresses playing Asian women were equally popular on the stage and in film; Gina Marchetti notes that by playing the film roles of Asian temptresses, butterflies, or geishas, white actresses such as Mary Pickford or Shirley MacLaine could play roles that capitalized on a transgressive sexuality, thus allowing white women the power to subvert Western patriarchy (83–84, 176–201.) Unfortunately, even in these limited scenarios of feminist empowerment, Asian women were entirely overlooked.

Throughout the twentieth century, makeup books for the stage actor have provided instructions for how white actors should play the "Oriental," "Mongolian types," or "the Chinaman."[8] Although such instructions are no longer to be found in chapters titled "Exotics" or strategically grouped with makeup techniques for playing the "Hag or Witch," "Mephisto or Devil" (Liszt 42–43), or, more frequently, "minstrel" blackface, they are otherwise remarkably uniform. There is no longer an insistence on long fingernails, full body coloring, or the half-bald, half-queued portrayals of the "classic type," yet even recent makeup guides exaggerate and distort the features of the "Oriental" body through their directions and their illustrations.[9] These books invariably contain special details telling actors how to use makeup or sometimes a mask in addition to "appropriate hairstyle, costume, and Oriental mannerisms" in order to achieve "a believable Oriental appearance" (Bagan 143). These descriptions are often illustrated with caricatures or photographs of white actors in yellowface rather than of Asians themselves.[10]

The persistent performances of the all-too-familiar stereotypes of literature, theater, film, and television can be linked to a succession of anxieties felt on a national scale: a fear of the "yellow peril" contaminating the racial purity of an America ideologically designated for the "lovely White," the moral justification of overseas imperialism, and, later on, economic neocolonialism in the Third World.[11] But the discursive force of stereotypes is not restricted to a particular time and space but disseminates into a more amorphous and pervasive cultural vocabulary. As Edward Said suggests, Orientalism does not describe a specific Orient but instead is "a system of representations framed by a whole set of forces" (202–3). Although they are locatable in geographically and temporally specific anti-Asian sentiments, these distinctive stereotypes are often perpetuated without the accompanying critical and historical contexts that would render viewers more critical. In particular, musical works such as Gilbert and Sullivan's *The Mikado* (1885) continue to be presented as "classics."[12] Bruce McConachie notes that the success of "Oriental" musicals such as *South Pacific* (1949) and *The King and I* (1951) can be attributed in part to their enactment of theatrical metaphors that legitimated U.S. foreign involvement in Southeast Asia.[13] The highly profitable reincarnations of different versions of the Butterfly story, from David Belasco's *Madame Butterfly* to Alain Boublil and Claude-Michel Schönberg's *Miss Saigon* (1989), might well embody a "long line of Western misrepresentation of Asians, perpetuating a damaging fantasy of submissive 'Orientals,' self-erasing women, and asexual, contemptible men" (Yoshikawa 276). But critiques of these works have only just begun to appear, and they rarely accompany the frequent productions of these popular shows.

The legacy of the Oriental stereotypes has haunted Asian American performers. On the one hand, Asian Americans have performed and been acclaimed in a variety of roles and venues, including traditional Asian theater and opera, the "Chop Suey" vaudeville circuit, and nightclubs such as San Francisco's Forbidden City, as well as dramatic and musical theater.[14] Individuals such as the silent film stars Anna May Wong and Sessue Hayakawa or, more recently, television and film actors Keye Luke, Bruce Lee, George Takei, and Pat Morita have also achieved professional recognition and commercial success.[15] But for the most part, fame and fortune, if any, could be earned only by playing versions of a stereotype. The Rodgers and Hammerstein musical *Flower Drum Song* (1958), based on Chin Yang Lee's novel of the previous year, gave employment to a number of actors, both on Broadway and in the subsequent film version. The film was the first commercial film to feature Asian Americans exclusively in singing, acting, and dancing roles, and the talented Miyoshi Umeki, who won an Academy Award in 1957 for her role in *Sayonara*, played a starring role as Mei Li (Hamamoto 11). But, as Misha Berson notes, the characterizations of *Flower Drum Song* were not much of an improvement: "a wise Confucian patriarch, a China Doll vamp, a submissive, fresh-off-the-boat bride . . . familiar Asian stereotypes dressed up in new clothes" (xi).

Even as they recognize the limitations of these pervasively stereotypical roles, actors also acknowledge their economic dependence on them, as Philip Gotanda details in his play *Yankee Dawg You Die*. Although opportunities for Asian American actors have increased, even actors of a more recent generation—some of whom have distinguished themselves in striking and original portrayals—have subsequently found themselves once again relegated to theatrical invisibility in stereotypical roles. Casting practices still overwhelmingly discriminate against actors of color. Harry Newman cites a four-year Actors' Equity survey revealing that over 90 percent of all plays produced professionally during the mid-eighties had all-white casts (55). The pessimism expressed by members of the Asian American Performing Artists (formerly the Oriental Actors of America) in 1976 still seems pervasive. As one actress said, "I will never play Suzie Wong or a Vietnamese whore again. I want to play Blanche and Nora, Medea and Desdemona. I have a lot to contribute, but . . .

they won't cast me." Another expressed even more resignation: "If you have not worked for many months or years (as I have not), it becomes very difficult to make any artistic choices when you are hungry. . . . Unemployment runs out" (Y. L. Wong 14). Such desperation is clearly a factor in the continued reenactment of stereotypes. When Actors' Equity protested the import of British actor Jonathan Pryce for the role of the engineer in *Miss Saigon*, producer Cameron Mackintosh threatened to withdraw the show entirely, thus depriving a number of Asian American actors of potential jobs. The concerns of these actors in part convinced Equity to withdraw its protests, and Pryce took on the role.

One alternative to performing in traditional venues and in often stereotypical roles, was to create new spaces in which both the "Asian" and the "American" could be reimagined by Asian American actors, plays, and audiences. Frustration over the formulaic Oriental stereotypes and the lack of opportunities for nonwhite actors in Hollywood led to the establishment of the first Asian American theater company. In 1965, the Los Angeles company East West Players was formed by a group of Asian American actors led by the acclaimed actor Mako, who became its first artistic director. East West Players was followed by the establishment of other Asian American repertory companies such as Kumu Kahua ("Original Stage") in Honolulu, in 1971; the Asian American Theater Company in San Francisco, in 1973; the Pan Asian Repertory in New York, in 1977; and the Northwest Asian Theater Company (formerly the Asian Exclusion Act) in Seattle, in 1976. In the eighties and nineties a number of theaters also emerged in the Midwest, including Angel Island Theatre Company in Chicago and Theater Mu in Minneapolis. In addition to presenting works by Asian American playwrights, these companies bring to popular attention the talents of Asian American actors, directors, and designers, staging works by Shakespeare, Chekhov, and Ibsen with Asian American actors and working with Asian actors in intercultural productions.[16] These alternative theaters serve as the primary venues of performance for many plays by Asian Americans. In so doing, they serve an important symbolic function as specific sites of contestation and identity formation for their audiences.

Both these repertory companies and their productions were profoundly affected by the Asian American movement of the 1960s and 1970s, which drew awareness to the social and legal history of Asians in the United States, a history marked distinctively by naturalization policy, land laws, and immigration restrictions. As William Wei suggests, political reform based on a pan-ethnic identification was at the core of the movement's activism, which was galvanized by the civil rights movement and anti-Vietnam War protests:

> Among the last of the "ethnic-consciousness movements," the Asian American Movement has been essentially a middle-class reform movement for racial equality, social justice, and political empowerment in a culturally pluralist America. . . . The concept *Asian Americans* implies that there can be a communal consciousness and a unique culture that is neither Asian nor American, but Asian American. In defining their own identity and culture, Asian Americans bring together previously isolated and ineffective struggles against the oppression of Asian communities into a coherent pan-Asian movement for social change. (1)

Ultimately, Wei argues, it was the creation of "an inter-Asian coalition that embrace[d] the entire spectrum of Asian ethnic groups and acknowledge[d] their common experiences in American society" that allowed a new kind of theater and theater audience to be both imagined and realized (1).

One of the immediate manifestations of this inter-ethnic solidarity in the theater was the way it transformed the meaning of cross-ethnic casting. Pan-Asian casting has had a long history in Asian American theater; an example is the fiery performance of Korean American Randall Kim as

the Chinese American Tam Lum in the 1972 American Place Theatre performance of *The Chickencoop Chinaman*. In a pan-ethnic context, however, the practice of cross-ethnic casting is transformed: where it was
once used to perpetuate a myth of interchangeability ("all Asians look
alike") made notorious by indiscriminate Broadway and Hollywood casting practices, it now signifies the formation of a newer pan-Asian sensi-
bility.

Asian American political and cultural activism has historically been
rooted in local communities. As Michael Omi and Howard Winant note,
Asian American groups in urban centers have become galvanized in the
fight to preserve low-cost housing for community residents or to preserve
Chinatowns, Manilatowns, or Japantowns from the commercial transformation that would disperse longtime residents (104). One aspect of Asian
American theater that deserves more recognition is the community-based
theater group that comes into existence to address specific local issues,
such as the now-disbanded Asian American Tactical Theatre, which used
guerilla street theater to raise consciousness about issues concerning New
York's Chinatown (Y. L. Wong 17). Large urban centers with increasingly
diverse populations may now be home to several different Asian American theaters, including newer theaters such as the Silk Road Theater, in
New York, which focuses on Korean American issues, and Teatro Ng
Tanan (Theater for the People), a Filipino youth theater in San Francisco.
The emphasis on local communities continues to shape Asian American
theatrical performance even when theaters seek to appeal to a broader,
racially mixed audience. In some sense Asian American theaters avoid
stagnation because they are pressured to speak to local concerns, respond
directly to political events, and deal with changing demographics. Asian
American theaters are forced to cope with new questions about the nature of individual and collective identity; thus, the many different ways in
which "Asian America" can be conceived provide a tension that drives
theater practice. Productions such as *Peb Yog Hmoob: We are Hmong*

(1993) and *The Garden of the Soul* (1995), by Pom Siab Hmoob Theatre (formerly the Hmong Theatre Project, founded in 1990) in Minneapolis draw attention to the ways in which newer immigrants and refugees continue to change the definition of Asian American. Theater Mu's *Mask Dance* (1992, 1995) deals specifically with the concerns of adopted Korean Americans growing up in the small towns of Minnesota. Recent productions and readings of plays such as Elizabeth Wong's *Kimchee and Chitlins,* Karen Huie's *Columbus Park,* Brenda Wong Aoki's *The Queen's Garden,* or Chay Yew's *A Language of Their Own* have dealt with contemporary issues such as AIDS, homelessness, gang violence, and inner-city conflicts between Asian Americans and African Americans. Asian American theaters have also grown increasingly active in exploring differences of gender and sexuality within various Asian American communities.[17]

But Asian American theaters have not been the only venue for Asian American playwrights. David Henry Hwang's winning of a Tony Award for *M. Butterfly* in 1988 was greeted enthusiastically as mainstream recognition of Asian American drama. This acclaim somewhat obscures the fact that a number of notable productions by Asian American playwrights have taken place outside of alternative Asian American theaters. The first production of Frank Chin's *The Chickencoop Chinaman* took place in 1972 at the American Place Theatre in New York City, and Chin's *The Year of the Dragon* not only debuted there in 1974 but was also subsequently videotaped for PBS's *Theatre in America.* Performance and multimedia artists Winston Tong, Ping Chong, Jessica Hagedorn, and others identify more with New York–based experimental art collaboratives than they do with Asian American theater. Artists such as Chong sometimes openly resist the label Asian American.[18] Recently, theaters such as the New World Theater, in Amherst, Massachusetts, Mixed Blood, in Minneapolis, or the Group Theater, in Seattle, have regularly mounted productions of Asian American plays. By taking a comparative approach to works by playwrights of color, these theaters allow an even more radical reimagining of community.

A number of changes in the past few decades, including the political activism of Asian American groups, an increased visibility for artists of color, and the establishment of alternative theaters, have opened up new possibilities for redefining performance. At the same time, they have raised different questions about, and prompted new theatrical vocabularies for, performing race and ethnicity on stage. The imagined common ground of Asian America—as it is envisioned in the plays examined in this book—is not located solely in a resistance to racist stereotypes. Nor does it necessarily reside in the similar historical experiences of immigration, racism, or assimilation, or in a shared cultural background. Instead, these plays presume a more complex imagining of how "Asian American" is performed, individually and collectively. Although a theater performance always takes place in a specific time and space, the imagined audience projected by this theater, its range of identifications and concerns, cannot be limited to a particular region, group of people, or time frame. Frank Chin's Chinatown locales, Genny Lim's Hawaiian cane fields, and Wakako Yamauchi's Imperial Valley can have meaning for a variety of audiences in different places.

. In a humorous moment in *A Grain of Sand*, Nobuko Miyamoto's retrospective on the Asian American movement, Miyamoto enacts how Asian American activists had to find a proper radical chic in their dress, music, and dance steps in order to establish their political presence alongside African Americans and Chicanos. In *Turning Japanese*, third-generation Japanese American David Mura writes of his decision to learn Butoh dance, envisioning a reconciliation with his "essential Japanese-ness" through a new form of movement: "I suddenly realized that with my stumbling Japanese, perhaps the only way to break the barrier of language was to enter the culture through my body, through sight" (28). Both these episodes illustrate how racial or ethnic identity is deeply invested in particular forms of embodiment, the quest for the appropriate body or performance mode. In many ways, the common ground for Asian American playwrights exists in the questions raised about performing race and ethnicity, how to negotiate and reform "racial etiquette" in a changing society.

Within this negotiation and reformation, certain questions involving form and content recur. Asian American plays that differ considerably in time and geography can be startlingly similar in their dramatic preoccupations. For instance, some plays written in Hawaii in the first half of the twentieth century have affinities with mainland plays written after the Asian American movement, illustrating how Asian American identities might be both differently and similarly construed in particular times and places.

Hawaii's historically multiracial islands have a long history of Asian Americans, amateurs and professionals, writing and performing for the theater. Theaters such as the Honolulu Theatre for Youth (1955) and Kumu Kahua (1971) were preceded by many kinds of Asian and Asian American performance in Hawaii, including traditional theater, pageants, and history plays. Often, as in the case of Kumu Kahua and other Hawaiian theaters, the works are strongly defined by their location and time. Yet Hawaiian plays from even the early twentieth century address issues in ways that connect them with the later mainland movement. These performance strategies include the use of realism to depict the "authentic" situation of Asian Americans, the development of dramatic tensions centered on differences between East and West, and experimentation with devices such as the doubling of characters. These techniques suggest the emergence of a theatrical vocabulary that enables playwrights in very different contexts to talk about ethnic and racial differences. In this sense, the plays written in Hawaii prior to the Asian American movement might be thought of as the rightful dramatic predecessors of mainland works written decades later.

These plays preceded the larger consciousness-raising of Asian American activism in the 1960s and 1970s. Nonetheless, a preoccupation with the questions and tensions involved in enacting racial and ethnic difference is also paramount in these works. In 1947, Bessie Toshigawa's *Reunion* was mounted by the University of Hawaii Theatre Group; it was the first full production of a contemporary play written in pidgin. *Reunion* is concerned with the homecoming of World War Two veterans from the Japanese-American 442nd combat team. On one level it is a gently humorous play, full of local color, about the decisions faced by young men after their military service. On another level, it raises the issues that preoccupied later generations of Asian Americans: how these young men were to face changes in their particular community, the problems they experienced assimilating into mainland life, the effects of racism on their war experiences.

In a similar vein, Edward Sakamoto's *In the Alley* addresses issues that are as relevant today as they were at the play's first performance in 1961. Sakamoto's play provides a pessimistic sequel to Toshigawa's *Reunion*. As the play opens, a group of young men meet to socialize, drink beer, and complain about the lack of opportunities for them and their families. The playful aggression of their good-natured bantering and wrestling turns violent as Joe, a *haole* serviceman, wanders by with a local woman. Angered by the sight of the interracial couple, the men attack Joe. When Joe's friends retaliate, it is the innocent Jojo who becomes the scapegoat; his unconscious body is left alone on the stage at the play's end. The violence is presented most immediately as the result of misguided aggression and youthful bravado rather than as an act of systematic racism. Yet Sakamoto makes clear that the roots of these tragic acts lie in larger social issues—not in the individual characters, but in the environment in which they exist. The themes of Sakamoto's play—the anger of sons toward their ineffectual fathers, sexual jealousy, poverty—are inextricably linked to the dynamics of race. These are the very concerns that were taken up in the next decade in the groundbreaking works of Frank Chin.

What brings these plays together as Asian American is their common interest in questioning, by means of the theater, how race and ethnicity might be performed. This exploration entails a fusion of formal and thematic concerns that refuses easy distinctions between what is artistic and what is political. As Stuart Hall has said, "how things are represented and the 'machineries' and regimes of representation in a culture do play a constitutive, and not merely a reflexive, after-the-event, role. . . . [Q]uestions of culture and ideology, and the scenarios of representation—subjectivity, identity, politics—[have] a formative, not merely an expressive, place in the constitution of social and political life" (27). Asian American theater sees itself as part of a continuum of transformative political acts that contest rather than work within established forms of representation. Within these theater spaces, playwrights and performers have established alternative communities in which systems of meaning and signification can reinvent themselves.

What's "Asian American" About It? The Question of Inclusivity

The term Asian American not only highlights the tension of hyphenation, it also draws attention to its own incompleteness as a category. As Victor Bascara has suggested, Asian America is not accurately described as a diaspora of scattered people, but is better portrayed as an "archipelago with insular 'islands' differing not only in location, but also in historical circumstance and, therefore, differing in cultural/political concerns" (Bascara 6). Not only are there major distinctions to be made in terms of any of the constituent groups' history of immigration, country of origin, economic background, language, religion, and culture, but important differences also exist within ethnic groups in terms of gender, age, class, education, and other factors. As Barringer, Gardner, and Levin conclude in their study of 1980 census data, "Asian Americans do not represent a single block of persons about whom one can generalize easily" (320).

That, as Philip Gotanda puts it, "our culture is a live beast"[19] makes apparent a tension that will be inherent throughout the remainder of this discussion. On the one hand, it seems necessary to speak of a set of shared concerns, an imagined common ground where different theatrical events might produce symbolic meaning. On the other hand, to call a playwright, a play, or a theater Asian American inevitably conjures an image of Asian America as a coherent whole, promoting a dangerously simplistic "racial" category that erases diversity within itself. Although this book might disclaim a complete, comprehensive, or representative analysis of Asian American drama, any work on Asian America risks creating a monolithic and homogenizing category.

For the purposes of this study, I have used primarily printed material such as playtexts, reviews, histories, and literature. My justification for doing so is that the playtext is not only the most fixed part of the play-wright's work, it is also the only part I can share on an equal footing with the reader.[20] But by limiting myself to plays that are readily available in published form, I have had to exclude many theatrical and literary representations of "Asian America" that do not accommodate themselves to the formal literacy of publishing. To put it bluntly, "Asian American" is here construed as primarily Chinese and Japanese American, upper-middle class, college-educated, English-speaking, and heterosexual. Not explicitly represented in my study are the concerns of newer immigrants and refugees, as well as others whose life experiences do not fit this limited view of Asian America. Such a bias may have been influenced by the inseparability of Asian American theater from the larger political and cultural work of the Asian American movement, which from the beginning maintained strong ties with academic institutions and was dominated by second- and third-generation Chinese and Japanese Americans. Nonetheless, it is worth pointing out some of the ways in which the production of plays and the publication of dramatic literature may limit us to a particular view of Asian America.

By what process do the requirements of publishing constrain the development of dramatic literature and contribute to an artificial canon? As Roberta Uno has suggested, dramatic literature by Asian Americans has been a relatively recent development for practical reasons. Plays must be produced in theaters as well as written; their primary mode is performance rather than script (introduction, *Unbroken Thread* 4). This implies additional criteria in the selection process by which plays reach their public, introducing yet another level at which exclusionary practices can take place. Adding to the traditional elitism of modern and contemporary American theater is the pressure to conform to literary models that privilege language-centered, single-author plays that appeal to a broader, racially mixed audience. That published plays are aimed at English-literate readerships immediately excludes plays by writers with limited or no English skills (first-generation immigrants, for instance), or those writing primarily for a non-English-speaking audience. We might note that although characters with limited or no English have frequently been depicted, such as in Frank Chin's *The Year of the Dragon,* David Henry Hwang's *Family Devotions,* or Han Ong's *Mrs. Chang,* their authors are native speakers of English. The preference for language-centered performance scripts also negatively affects the publication of theater works that rely on movement, dance, or music, where the primary modes of action cannot be captured through verbal description. This point becomes especially meaningful when one considers the number of productions by Asian Indian and South Asian immigrant communities, such as Minneapolis's Theater Mu's 1994 *River of Dreams* (which featured works by Laotian, Cambodian, and Vietnamese writers and performers), that have been dance- and music-centered theater works. Similarly, the traditional relationships between playwright and theatrical company, which encourage a "finished" playscript—detachable from its initial performance venue and marketed to individual readers and theaters for re-production—do not allow for a more probing investigation of performances such as the many one-actor pieces by Asian Americans such as "Charlie" Chin, Amy Hill, Nobuko Miyamoto, Lane Nishikawa, Jude Narita, Nicky Paraiso, Canyon Sam, and Denise Uyehara.

Perhaps the most obvious way in which publishing norms control the dissemination of dramatic literature is that publishers of literature prefer authors who have already gained mainstream recognition. With the notable exception of Berson's 1990 *Between Worlds* anthology, published by the Theatre Communications Group, many of the collections of recent Asian American dramatic literature have been published by university presses and intended for a limited academic market. The only single-volume play that is currently marketed by a trade press is Penguin's edition of David Henry Hwang's *M. Butterfly,* which at the time of publication had already won numerous awards, including a Tony; Penguin has also subsequently republished a number of Hwang's other work in *FOB and Other Plays.* With such an emphasis on validation by mainstream theatrical institutions, it is not surprising that any claim that theatrical production can make for having value for a specific local community is discounted when plays are repackaged as "dramatic literature." Theater that is directed at specific communities—and much of the theatrical work by Asian Americans falls into this category—is automatically excluded by virtue of its topical nature. Vernacular forms of theater such as yearly shows, pageants, or displays in local Asian American communities are screened out in this selection process.

By making evident the limitations of studies such as this one, I hope to encourage other studies and publications to contest and build beyond, rather than reproduce, these problems. We must acknowledge the constraints that still exist at the level of dissemination of material. One obvious task is to publish or otherwise make available a broader range of dramatic works, as well as to acknowledge the limitations of what is currently promoted as Asian American drama, literature, and art. Such a critical dialogue is necessary, particularly at a time when such works are used as self-promotion or to establish a claim to pluralism in the theater season or academic curriculum. The danger of limiting "Asian American" performance to particular groups is accentuated when the inclusion of only one or two new plays in an anthology, a production season, or a reading list disguises itself as progress.

We also need to move toward a critical method that investigates the changing manifestations of what it means to perform—as opposed to simply be—Asian American. The rapid expansion and diversification of Asian populations in the United States renders suspect the notion of a monolithic Asian American experience or identity. Accordingly, this book cannot define what the quintessential Asian American play is or should be. Instead, I have attempted to outline some of the leading questions that we face in thinking about what is Asian American, and about what happens in the theatrical event. The plays I consider necessarily cover a broad range of subjects and dramatic styles. What they share are certain theatrical strategies that make issues of performance, dramatic form, and audience response inseparable from considerations of ethnicity and race. Traditional theories of theatrical presentation have not allowed for a discussion of how the perception of race and ethnicity affects cognition and meaning in the theater. In order to understand the emerging ways of constructing not only what is Asian American, but what is more generally racialized or ethnicized, I suggest that we begin by developing a more complex critical vocabulary and a theoretical position from which to talk about the theater.

Organization of the Book

I start this dialogue by discussing, in Chapter 2, how the use of realism by Asian American playwrights forces a reconsideration of theories of spectatorship in the theater. Feminist critics such as Jill Dolan are suspicious of realism's tendency to allow the spectator to become the unseen, privileged voyeur of theatrical scenes. For Dolan and others, realism seemingly protects a masculine spectator's privileged position of consumption, preventing the events of the drama from ever challenging his uninterrupted viewing pleasure in the feminine object. These terms—the masculine spectator and the feminine object—are easily translated into a critique of realism's portrayal of racial others, and in *Marginal Sights: Staging the Chinese in America*, James Moy paves the way for such a reading. Although he does not directly target realism, Moy does use a model of spectatorship similar to Dolan's, illustrating how a relationship of masculinized white spectator to feminized Asian object is preserved in a variety of artistic modes. Moy finds this guilty paradigm of Asian bodies "consumed" by white spectators at work not only in the use of Oriental stereotypes, but also in plays written and produced by Asian Americans. For Moy, viewing pleasure of this sort can only be victimization: Asians as the objects of the white gaze. There is no room for the Asian American spectator in this paradigm without making such a subject-position complicitous in its own oppression.

The positioning of imagined "ethnic" spectators, as suggested by certain plays by Asian Americans, complicates these binary viewing paradigms. The rigid model of the exotic Asian object, constructed for the pleasure and consumption of white spectators, affords only limited possibilities beyond simple recognition or refusal of racial and ethnic difference. Realism might in fact work in another way, by self-consciously countering stereotypical portrayals of Asians and teaching an audience how to see "real" Asian Americans. Moreover, the ways in which ethnic identification works in realistic plays are more complex than either Dolan's or Moy's paradigms allow. Two plays in particular, Frank Chin's *The Year of the Dragon* and David Henry Hwang's *Family Devotions*, illustrate how even within the confines of the fourth wall, realistic plays can complicate notions of a homogeneously "white" audience having power over the objectified Asian object. In *The Year of the Dragon*, this viewing relationship is made self-conscious by Fred's monologues and other moments that focus attention on the voyeurism of the audience and that openly deride the consumption of ethnic people by the tourist's gaze. In *Family Devotions,* several viewing perspectives are suggested, particularly through the figure of Chester, who is placed as an observer of the other characters. Moments of discovery in the play remind spectators of their exclusion from full knowledge and mastery.

For Asian Americans, dramatic realism is particularly potent, for it imagines the self as real and authentic and the audience as homogeneous and unified. But I do not end Chapter 2 with a celebration of ethnic solidarity, an idealized vision of Asian American theaters full of Asian American audiences. Instead, I find that Rey Chow's notion of the "ethnic spectator" is more useful, insofar as it allows for a more partial and tentative identification. This theorizing of spectatorship allows us to understand how audiences from highly different backgrounds can identify with characters, even those who sometimes take on a stereotypical and demeaned form.

In Chapter 3 I discuss how Asian American writers, notably Frank Chin, have adopted a violently masculinist stance to counter a perceived emasculation of the Asian male and the threat of extinction of the Asian American social body. The passionately patriarchal, homophobic, and sexist discourse that constitutes Chin's repudiation of the effeminate writer and informs his creation of the heroic outsider as Chinaman also drives his play, *The Chickencoop Chinaman.* I argue that the theatrical power of this play comes not only from its social commentary, but also from a Freudian fantasy of castration and rebirth in which Chinaman and black man are allied in their heroic struggle to transform bodily scars into marks of valor.

Chin is not the only dramatist to attempt such a redemption of the Asian American male. A later play, R. A. Shiomi's *Yellow Fever,* can be read in similar fashion, as a response to the symbolic emasculation of the

Asian male through historical racism and stereotypical representation. It
is also a play that, by translating the detective hero Sam Spade into Sam
Shikaze, envisions filmmaking as a means of making men whole. However, Shiomi's more playful handling of the terms of castration and scarring also marks a broader flexibility in this masculinist paradigm. The
play can be read not only as the realization of a desire, first articulated by
Chin's protagonist Tam Lum, to make a film that confers the normative
values of masculinity on the Asian Canadian male, it can also be interpreted as a fantasy that ultimately erases gender distinctions in favor of
ethnic ones. In *Yellow Fever*, castration is conceived as a historical
wounding that affects women as well as men. From this reading, I conclude that masculine identifications in recent plays by Shiomi and others
are often constructed within parodic and self-conscious contexts that allow more than one kind of viewer identification and spectatorial pleasure.

Chapter 4 uses two plays—Philip Kan Gotanda's *Yankee Dawg You Die*
and Hwang's *M. Butterfly*—to focus on a highly charged theoretical issue:
the reappropriation of Oriental stereotypes by Asian American playwrights. Earlier I suggested that theatrical realism might displace and
counter these exaggerated images. These two plays are more problematic,
however, in that they reproduce characterizations such as the grotesque
villain or the submissive tragic female, evoking rather than ignoring the
theatrical power stereotypes possess. Such works are either celebrated by
critics who believe that reproduction of the racist stereotype subverts it,
or decried by those who argue that repetition of the stereotype perpetuates the values of its ugly past. Homi Bhabha's formulation of the colonial stereotype as a fetish that reveals an implicit anxiety is useful in
resolving this critical conflict. For Bhabha, the repetitive and violent nature of the stereotype exposes the uncertainty in the power dynamic between the white self that seeks to imagine itself as coherent and its parodic "mimicry." From this perspective, Hwang and Gotanda create

versions of stereotype with exaggerated, undiminished powers. Far from defusing them into empty signs, the plays emphasize the overdetermination and pervasiveness of stereotypes. I suggest that whereas stereotypes cannot be reappropriated without evoking their racist history, their performances can nonetheless reveal the inner dynamics of a stereotype and suggest the potential for its disruption.

Both *Yankee Dawg You Die* and *M. Butterfly* use similar strategies. First, they rob the stereotype of its power to substitute for the natural or essential being and reveal it as a social construct, the product of specific historical and social circumstances. The stereotype becomes an enactment rather than a state of being; the characters are explicitly actors who either choose or are compelled to enact these stereotypes. This historicizing works to provide a specific context for these performances and reveals the anxiety inherent in the historic encounters that call them into being. The second strategy is to take advantage of the stereotype's inability to account fully for the body of the Other. A parodying of the stereotype in these plays makes obvious its inability to contain the excesses of the body. When the body of the actor is marked as "authentically Asian"—when an Asian stereotype is played by an Asian actor—the performance of the stereotype can become noticeably extravagant and hyperbolic. Finally, both plays openly acknowledge Asian Americans in the audience and play to their possible identification with Asian and Asian American characters, even those presented in stereotypical form. The two readings in this chapter consider the marketing of the stereotype to the public by unwilling actors and—a much more disturbing issue—the erotics of the stereotype.

Chapter 5 discusses the implicit agendas and strategies behind Asian American history plays and the relationship of those theatrical strategies to recent historical narratives about Asian Americans. Both history books and history plays participate in constructing ethnic and racial identity by strategically formulating the past. In this sense, no strict division between history as fact and theater as fiction is possible. Both are less reenactments of past events than a selective interpretation of details that reflect current impulses and tensions in the formation of Asian American identity.

For instance, the historian Ronald Takaki and others argue that Asian Americans have been singled out at significant moments as unassimilable; their exclusion was institutionalized by American naturalization policy, land ownership laws, and immigration restrictions. Dramatic histories also contest preconceived assumptions about America as the melting pot where immigrants assimilate by some natural and inevitable process, and instead draw attention to inequalities manifested in the social and legal history of Asians in the United States. Even though there are a variety of subjects for the history plays and a range of historical experiences of immigration and settlement, this impulse connects the histories and theatrical works. The action of plays such as Momoko Iko's *Gold Watch* and Wakako Yamauchi's *12-1-A* demonstrates that failure to assimilate is not so much the fault of a character's irreconcilable cultural differences, a stubborn refusal to let go of the old ways, as it is the inevitable result of exclusionary laws, institutions, and economic practices of a white-dominated America.

In the second part of Chapter 5 I examine how plays such as Hwang's *The Dance and the Railroad* and Yamauchi's *And the Soul Shall Dance* emphasize the close connections between Asian immigration and American labor practice. What is unique about the theatricalization of this history is its insistence on defining Asian American characters in excess of their pure functionality as part of the workforce. Characters are consistently portrayed, in their physical and emotional life, as not fully containable within the system that exploited them. The plays construct the "self" of the characters by emphasizing human action and experience in tension with the forces that seek to reduce them to laboring bodies, statistics, or profit margins. Finally, both written and performed history aim to create a sense of pan-Asian community, emphasizing common interests over disparate cultural backgrounds. These Asian American history plays emphasize the past as a site of collective formation, thus implicitly constructing the present performance as a moment of coalition-building. The theatrical devices and techniques used in the plays foster a sense of ethnic, pan-Asian, and intergenerational bonding, emphasizing the transmission of symbolic objects or knowledge from generation to generation and focusing on younger characters as the recipients of such legacies. Yet, as I suggest for Takaki's *Strangers from a Different Shore*, both written and staged history are not without their more problematic tendencies. I conclude Chapter 5 by looking at Darrell Lum's *Oranges Are Lucky* in order to see how a play might resist a tendency toward celebrating and mythologizing the heroic individual.

Asian American scholars have recently pointed to the tension between collective action and individual self-interest on the part of young Asian Americans, a tension that affects such issues as activism, affirmative action, and the myth of the model minority. As interpreted by some, individualism is historically encouraged by the larger capitalistic system, which seeks to divide and undermine potentially subversive alliances. Chapter 6 examines a trope common in both Asian American drama and literature: a violent doubling in which Asian American characters are pitted against their more Asian counterparts. This Asian American schizophrenia has received a variety of treatments in plays such as David Henry Hwang's *FOB* and Elizabeth Wong's *Letters to a Student Revolutionary*. Although each play performs and resolves this doubling differently, all call attention to the persistent divisions within characters who internalize the impulse toward individual success and repudiate a collective Asianness. The resulting tensions are indicative not so much of a split between Asian and American as of a rupture in a distinctly American system of values.

Chapter 7 considers the ways in which Asian Americans can be thought of as "passing," as moving between the demarcations of race described on the physical body. Instead of imagining fixed geographic or psychic spaces of self and other, theatrical boundaries that recognize and mirror preexisting differences, certain theatrical works by Asian Americans work toward a more fluid understanding of race and ethnicity. Beginning with a melodrama by Gladys Ling-Ai Li, *The Submission of Rose Moy*, I examine how plays inscribe racial and ethnic differences onto bodies, objects, gestures, and stage space. Velina Houston's *Tea* further explores the possibility of passing through cultural boundaries. Houston's staging of passing, both in the stories of characters and in the transformations of the actresses in the theater, reveals the preoccupation with "mixed" blood, intermarriage, and geographic transplantation that is central to many other Asian American plays. Chapter 7 concludes with readings of Ping Chong's *Kind Ness* and Jeannie Barroga's *Walls*. Although these two plays are quite different in structure and aesthetics, both challenge preconceptions about racial and ethnic difference as it is marked within the boundaries of space, object, and body.

2

The Asian American Spectator
and the Politics of Realism

The realistic play has dominated twentieth-century commercial and academic theater practice in America, dictating the shape and setting of the stage, the training of actors, and the kinds of plays that are written and produced. In the theater, realism prescribes both the style of presentation (a mimetic or "natural" mode of acting and staging) and the relationship between the staged performance and the audience. Recently, some critics have become increasingly skeptical of the politics of theatrical realism. Their argument is not so much with its formal or presentational qualities as with the more subtle coercion of perception that informs it. Although realism purports to be a faithful representation of ordinary life, it is in fact a more complex ideological practice, a manufacturing rather than a mirroring of some construct of "real life." Less important than how faithful or true to life the play is are the ways in which it constructs relationships between the spectator and the events occurring on stage, relationships that viewing communities must agree on as being "like life" and therefore meaningful. Recent reassessments of realism have been most critical of the ways in which realism calls not only for a particular level of detail in the theater set, props, and acting style, but also for a particular relationship between the spectator and the stage event.

If instances of modern dramatic realism, plays that pass for a reflection of preexisting reality, are increasingly regarded with suspicion or dismissed entirely as a species of political theater, then Asian Americans who write realistic plays are subject to the same kinds of criticism. The question becomes why Asian American dramatists choose theatrical realism, as so many have done, rather than the more overtly presentational techniques that have the potential to interrupt the illusion of reality and directly interrogate spectatorial privilege.[1]

As James Moy has documented in *Marginal Sights*, even so-called realistic American plays have frequently depicted Asian characters as exotic and spectacular. Such plays are chillingly reminiscent of the American Museum's 1834 display of Afong Moy as a "Chinese Lady," or P. T. Barnum's touring exhibits of "the Siamese Twins" or "Chang, Chinese Giant"; for a fee, spectators could view the presumably authentic bodies of these figures (Moy, *Marginal Sights* 12–15). Yet such an American tradition of looking at Asians as if they were curious objects seems dangerously reaffirmed in the details of staging and spectacle, the use of accent and vernacular, and, most important, the positioning of the spectator as subject in plays by Asian Americans.[2] Plays such as Frank Chin's *The Year of the Dragon* or David Henry Hwang's *Family Devotions* pose complex questions about how audience members as well as characters are ethnicized and racialized, hailed into complex subject-positions by the action of the plays. These two instances of Chinese American "family dramas" were both first produced for primarily white audiences in New York theaters: *The Year of the Dragon* at the American Place Theatre in 1974, directed by Russell Treyz, and *Family Devotions* at the New York Shakespeare Festival Public Theater in 1981, directed by Robert Alan Ackerman. They demand that we consider not only the paradigm of the white spectator and the objectified Oriental on stage—a model of oppressive viewing practices that is frequently evoked these days—but also how Asian American spectators might be positioned in diverse ways.

If Asian American dramatists ally themselves with a political agenda that seeks to subvert racism established within structures of representation, how do we account for the predominance of realism rather than forms influenced by Brecht or Artaud, which allow for a more explicit critique of the dominant ideology governing representation? If the "self" created in Asian American experience is by necessity fragmented, discordant, and divided, how do we deal with a work that shies away from postmodern experimentation with dramatic form and theatrical space? If Asian American differences, as Lisa Lowe has suggested, are marked by "heterogeneity, hybridity, multiplicity" (28), then how do we theorize these plays, in which the creation of Asian American characters relies on notions of a coherent psychologized self and insists on the "truth" and "naturalness" of the theatrical experience? From a theoretical standpoint, it would easier to focus on the more openly radical aesthetics of those Asian American theater artists who use more experimental modes (such as Jessica Hagedorn, Daryl Chin, Winston Tong, and Ping Chong); their sophisticated subversions of cognition and representation are more easily justified theoretically as revolutionary. However, not only do many Asian American dramatists still use dramatic realism as a basis for their work, many of their plays are praised or criticized on the basis of their "authenticity" and "realness" of presentation.

In short, we cannot simply dismiss dramatic realism as a mode of theater that so many dramatists and viewers have identified as "Asian American" and as political strategy. Let us turn these issues into a set of critical questions: How do Asian American dramatists rework the existing paradigm of realism to suit their own needs? What dimensions of their use of realism might be considered strategic and political? How must some of the existing arguments regarding realism, spectatorship, and power be revised when dealing with Asian American versions of theatrical realism?

One of the best-known critiques of theatrical realism is Jill Dolan's *The*

Feminist Spectator as Critic, which borrows the terms of Laura Mulvey's criticisms of classic cinema and its representations of women. Mulvey postulates that "[i]n a world ordered by sexual imbalance, pleasure in looking has been split between active/male and passive/female. The determining male gaze projects its fantasy onto the female figure, which is styled accordingly" (Mulvey 203). According to Mulvey, illusionistic narrative film in particular constructs "the image of woman as (passive) raw material for the (active) gaze of man" (208). If, in Dolan's words, Mulvey "concludes that the gaze, pleasurably, directed by the cinematic apparatus, is in fact male, and that cinematic representations are constructed for male spectators" (Dolan, *Spectator* 49), Dolan's project also seeks to describe the ways in which a certain subject-position, the "spectator," is brought into a gendered relation with a work of art.

At first glance, Dolan's adoption of Mulvey's paradigm of spectatorship, in which the male viewer is privileged with mastery and pleasure, seems somewhat detached from her criticism of realism. The connection becomes clearer when Dolan uses Mulvey specifically to critique Richard Foreman's Ontological-Hysteric Theatre, targeting Foreman's early work for employing the female nude "as a seductive image that Foreman can withhold, obscure, or offer at will" for the pleasure of the male spectator (Dolan, *Spectator* 50). Although Dolan says that Foreman's theater clearly cannot be categorized as realism, her critique of his work is related to her suspicion of realism as valid political theater. In Dolan's view, both Foreman's early work and realism are troubling in that they construct the theatrical action in such a way as to create a particular relationship between viewer and stage action. Dolan points out that for her, Foreman's actors "remain framed by the representational apparatus":

In fact, among all the theatre conventions Foreman discarded or attacked, his allegiance to the strict proscenium arrangement, with its convenient frame and distanced relationship between performers

and spectators, is the most crucial element in explicating the meanings constructed by his tableaux for the pleasures of the male gaze.
(*Spectator* 46)

For Dolan, Foreman is implicated in his preservation of the proscenium
frame, and in using such a frame to promote a gendered spectatorial
relation. As a "conservative force that reproduces and reinforces dominant cultural relations" (Dolan, *Spectator* 84), realism allows for even
more mastery on the spectator's part.

Others have adopted Dolan's critique of realism as the "insidious ideology of any representation that presents experience as truth" (Dolan, "Defense" 60), and also have adopted the model of an active masculinized
spectator holding the passive feminized object within his controlling
gaze. The audience of realism remains unacknowledged, hidden in the
darkness of the theater, but its very invisibility affords it a privileged,
authoritative position. The fourth wall becomes the dividing line between
theatrical presentation and audience consumption: "the aim of realism is
to produce an audience, to legitimate its private acts of interpretation *as*
objective" (Worthen, *Modern Drama* 17). This drama "*produces* 'reality'
by positioning its spectator to recognize and verify its truths" (Diamond
366). In the theater of realism, the stage performance erases the audience's presence; the spectator, "exiled from the field of the theater itself"
(Worthen, *Modern Drama* 15), becomes the unseen voyeur of theatrical
scenes. Erased and distanced, viewers are no longer aware of themselves
as specific viewing bodies.

Such a model of the spectator positioned to master the events of the
stage is the basis for an effective critique of many plays. But Dolan and
other critics who adopt Mulvey's paradigm of spectatorship in relation to
the stage neglect some of the drawbacks of this paradigm. Here we are
not concerned with comparing the technologies of classic cinema and the
dynamics of the stage, for, as Dolan points out, "Foreman's construction

of images cannot be parallel to that of the cinematic apparatus because he cannot control the spectator's gaze as carefully" (Dolan, *Spectator* 49). Rather, Dolan and others easily fall into the disadvantages inherent in Mulvey's model of gendered spectatorship.

Judith Roof has outlined some compelling reasons why Mulvey's model might be inadequate, and we can usefully extend her critique of Mulvey's paradigm to consider why a dismissal of theatrical realism using Mulvey's terms might also be flawed. Roof criticizes Mulvey's viewing paradigm on the grounds that it relies on a binary opposition of the masculine active spectator and the passive female object, and that this heterosexual model excludes discussion of other possibilities, such as lesbian spectatorship. The problem, as Roof sees it, is that according to Mulvey, "accounts for the operation of identification and narrative in film are welded to assumptions of heterosexual desire affixed to clearly and essentially gendered positions" (Roof 39). For Roof, the psychoanalytical basis for these models encourages the "concatenation of pleasure and mastery, seen as a masculine, active positioning created by an urge toward mastery enabled by a mechanism of visual disavowal" (39). Roof insists that viewer identification is much more complex, dependent not only on unstable distinctions between gender and sexual orientations ("While *gender* is one term, *desire* is another. No gender owns the look; no gender own desire for woman or for man" [50]), but also on flexible differences in race, class, age, and so on (52). While denying that cinema is a "free-for-all" or a "pluralistic leveling," Roof seeks to describe viewer identifications not permitted or accounted for by Mulvey's "rigid and binary and complementary system, reliant upon the premise of heterosexual desire" (39).

Not surprisingly, transferring Mulvey's paradigm of spectatorship to a critique of stage realism is subject to the same problems. Dolan's model presupposes a fixed viewing relationship, emphasizing the passivity of the objectified actor and the mastery of the spectator. This presumes that a

female spectator of an objectified female character, particularly as constructed in realism, is in an untenable position. Because she is always
forced to view herself as the powerless object of the gaze, any identification can only be a form of self-denial. A fixed viewing relationship between spectator and object, therefore, neglects a complex range of identi-
ficatory practices that might be affected by any number of factors.

This discussion of the nature of the viewing relationship, particularly
as it affects realism, can be extended to Asian American drama and its
versions of realism. It is quite easy to critique Asian American drama by
translating Dolan's terms to an ethnicized version of a masculinized white
spectator and a feminized Asian object. As formalized by the fourth wall
of realism, the model of the white spectator and an exotic Asian object
constructed for his pleasure and consumption seems quite persuasive.

Such a tactic is taken by James Moy in his recent study, *Marginal
Sights: Staging the Chinese in America.* Moy describes what he sees as the
persistent desire for the exotic Other and the subsequent commodifica-
tion of Chinese bodies, made into spectacles for the American public. He
distinguishes between serial and voyeuristic gazes, the former associated
with popular amusements in which "apparently authoritative series and
collocations of objects" were brought together "to create the *potential* for
meaning," and the latter the province of the "emergent self-conscious
literary elite" for whom Orientalized objects "served to affirm the authority of the onlooker" (8). In each of his provocative examples, drawn
from poetry, illustration, film, and photography, as well as stage plays,
Moy casts the Chinese "object" as that which is "fetishized" or "sexless,
and therefore harmless" (83) under the gaze of the spectator as masterful,
masculine, and white. Moy reiterates a binary and—if we read "fetishized" and "harmless" as suggestive of "feminine"—heterosexualized
viewing paradigm.

In reading the exaggerated stereotypes of Ah Sin and Fu Manchu,
Moy's paradigm is both useful and convincing. But it becomes problem-

atic as a generalization, insofar as it only accounts for viewing pleasure as the optical oppression of the feminized Asian actor by the masculinized white spectator. In trying to account for the mainstream theatrical success of both Philip Gotanda's *Yankee Dawg You Die* and David Hwang's *M. Butterfly*, Moy again uses the paradigm of Chinese bodies as "consumed" by white spectators: "marginalized, desexed, and made faceless, these Asian characters constitute no threat to Anglo-American sensibilities. Instead these figures provide a good evening's entertainment and then float as exotic Orientalist fetishes articulating Anglo-American desire" (*Marginal Sights* 125). Moy's reiteration of the oppositional and rigidly gendered viewing paradigm thus excludes or makes guilty any Asian American enjoyment of plays that employ exaggerated, stereotypical, or exotic Asian or Asian American characters. There is no room to maneuver Asian American spectators into this paradigm without making them accomplices in their own oppression. Any pleasure that Asian American viewers might take in theatrical spectacles marked "Asian" can, according to Moy, only be read as misguided and fraught with guilt, the product of internalized self-hatred.

Throughout *Marginal Sights,* Moy emphasizes the historical absence of real representations of Chinese and other Asian characters. His suggestion for reform centers on the production by Asian Americans of "authentic" self-representations, realistic characterization as a corrective for racist viewing practices. Moy argues compellingly for replacing exaggerated and stereotypical portrayals of Asians in the theater with more complex and detailed characterizations. These identifiably "real" Asian Americans would explicitly address the stereotypical construction of Asians that has dominated the American stage. Asian American realism would thus operate by using the stage to reform "reality," to counter how Asian Americans are often seen, and to teach audiences how to see "real" Asian Americans.

Jude Narita's one-woman show, *Coming Into Passion/Song for a Sansei,* seems to work along these very lines. Narita presents the most familiar stereotypes of theater, film, and advertising such as the Vietnamese dance-hall girl or the Filipino mail-order bride. However, instead of simply substituting for these clichés a more "positive" version of the Asian woman, Narita instead adds complex psychological detail to the initial stereotype; in her portrayals, these characters exhibit a capacity for resistance even as they are forced (by social circumstance) into recognizable patterns of behavior.

The political goal of such realistic representations is their mergence into a larger, mainstream vision of reality. The individual artistic vision executed in any play is not as important as the more general reproduction and dissemination of these versions of the real; the making of a masterpiece is less important than bringing about a cumulative change in the stereotyping patterns of theater, film, and advertising, a gradual reeducation of the visual eye in what is "real" and "natural." Yet the issue is clearly more complex than a kind of rough affirmative action plan for Asian American dramatic characterization.

Critics such as Moy call for realism as a solution to the racism of American theater and spectacle, yet at the same time they insist that the actual problem is ingrained in a long history of viewing practice. In Moy's words, "The extent to which socially conscious drama can emerge from the morass of the bourgeois perception of the world is questionable at best" (*Marginal Sights* 115). Implicit in this statement is the assumption that even "real" Asian American drama cannot confront a mainstream audience with enough force to change larger social perceptions; it can be effective only in a marginalized "alternative" space.

The fundamental problem that we return to lies in the positioning of white viewers as the masters of the feminized, passive spectacle and the difficult entrance of Asian American spectators into this model. If one adopts the viewing paradigm that Mulvey, Dolan, and now Moy all suggest, even the most sympathetic and realistic Asian American characters lose their political value once they have attracted the pleasure of the white viewer. This model of spectatorship encourages a rigid binary opposition; what is constructed on the realistic stage creates a sense of knowledge and mastery over the Asian body, manifested as a desire for the exotic, or perhaps today a liberal need to identify with an Other. At the heart of the problem is that realism is not a matter of characterization only, but an entire process in which viewers are coerced into accepting a particular vision of reality. Even though social problems are often at the heart of realistic drama, the emphasis on constructing an uncontested reality, as Worthen suggests, is problematic:

> Because realistic drama usually sees that world as an all-embracing "environment" . . . its social themes don't finally lead to a call for social change. Modern society may be a prison, but the liberation urged by realistic drama is imagined on the individual level; the character's search for freedom, value, and meaning leaves the world unchanged. Despite its critical stance toward modern society, realistic drama tacitly accepts the world and its values as an unchanging, and unchangeable, environment in which the characters live out their lives. (*HBJ Anthology* 375)

Within this model, Asian Americans can only participate through an angry but helpless witnessing of this dominant relationship between captive characters and their white spectators. Even the most sympathetic Asian American characters cannot compensate for being spectacles for consumption, victims of their part in a realistic play.

Or can they? In the following section, I suggest how we might reconsider the spectatorship of realistic plays by Asian Americans by assuming that the ways in which ethnic identification works in realistic plays are more complex than the model of masculinized white viewer and feminized Asian object can suggest. Even within the confines of the fourth wall, certain dramatic strategies can be drawn on to complicate the notion of a homogeneously white audience having power over the Asian object of scrutiny.

Like any theatrical realism, the realism employed by Asian American dramatists must be thought of in terms of acts calculated to produce particular relationships between performer and audience, theatrical constructions designed to pass for a preexisting true or authentic life. Thus it is easy to imagine Asian Americans writing plays that do what Moy suggests, satisfying the desire of a spectator to gaze upon and to know the "reality" of an exoticized Oriental Other. But to make this viewing paradigm self-conscious—to acknowledge openly the eye of the white spectator on the spectacle of the Asian—is to trouble its potential for voyeurism. David Henry Hwang does this in M. Butterfly, when his protagonist Gallimard explicitly tries to align the audience with the perspective of his "mind's eye," thus making us accomplices in his self-deceiving love for his exotic "butterfly." Hwang's play uses a presentational form of staging, incorporating opera and dance elements, a narrator (Gallimard), and characters who address the audience directly. But a subtle subversion of the white gaze can be seen even in plays that stay within the confines of realism's fourth wall. Certain plays can directly or more subtly call viewers' own differences into question, drawing attention to the constructed nature of the onstage "reality" and complicating the process by which audiences might feel they have access to the culture of the authentic Asian.

Frank Chin's The Year of the Dragon and David Henry Hwang's Family Devotions are two Asian American versions of what might be considered a staple of the realistic American stage: the family play and its familiar issues of generational differences, material versus spiritual success, and a male protagonist's search for identity. The Eng family in The Year of the Dragon, under the not so benevolent patriarch Wing Eng, must come to terms not only with Eng's impending death, but also with his abusiveness and hypocrisy. In particular, Fred, the eldest son, must deal with his frustration over a youth wasted in caring for his father and running tours of Chinatown for white tourists. Similarly, in Hwang's *Family Devotions,* Chester rejects both the upper-middle-class materialism and the overly zealous Christianity of members of his Chinese American family and instead finds himself allied with his great-uncle and his roots in the "real" pre-Christian China. For the most part, both plays seem to preserve realistic spectator–stage relationships. But both Chin and Hwang include challenges to the audience's invisibility, moments in which language and staging have the potential for a more fundamental and violent attack on realistic representation. They do so in a number of ways: by making any attempts at uninhibited "voyeurism" self-conscious and uncomfortable, and by setting up multiple perspectives in the play, embodied in characters who "gaze" on one another, thus reinforcing a sense of incomplete mastery over any knowledge or truth that can come out of viewing events.

The Year of the Dragon

As Ronald Takaki notes, throughout the twentieth century tourism has been a major source of revenue for the "gilded ghettos"—the Chinatowns of San Francisco, New York, and other cities. Chinese workers, forced out of the general labor market, found employment working in shops, restaurants, and entertainments that attracted white business by sensationalizing and exoticizing local life. Local residents, chambers of commerce, and business organizations promoted the redevelopment of Chinatowns and hailed the tourist industry as the solution to rampant unemployment (Takaki, *Strangers from a Different Shore* 245–51).

Frank Chin's *The Year of the Dragon* is dedicated to the memory of writer Louis Chu. Like Chu's novel *Eat a Bowl of Tea* (1961), Chin's play reacts to and plays against visions of Chinatown as exotic menagerie, parodying the romanticized Chinatown of works such as C. Y. Lee's

Flower Drum Song. The Year of the Dragon complicates a supposedly unseen and privileged spectatorial positioning by drawing attention to the
racialized nature of audiences and the conspicuous consumption of Asian
spectacles both inside and outside the theater. If the curious tourist seeks
in Chinatown a glimpse of the "real" Chinese, "a product that one can
buy, arrange to one's liking, and/or preserve" (Trinh 88), the strategy of
Chin's play is to address such presumptions directly, ridiculing the spectator who looks for the reality of Chinatown in stereotypes. *The Year of
the Dragon* seems to promise an insider's tour of Chinatown and a visit
with a "real" Chinese family, including witnessing their most private moments of infighting, eating, having sex, and defecating. However, in the
course of the play the voyeurism is made explicit and self-conscious, and
the knowledge gained through watching is shown to be painfully incomplete.

The play introduces a number of characters whose viewpoints suggest
to the spectator a means by which to enter the play. In addition to Fred,
the protagonist, several characters serve as commentators: Mattie, the
daughter; Ross, her white husband; and China Mama, Papa Eng's Chinese wife. Importantly, each is shown to have an unsatisfactory or partial
perspective on the action. Mattie, for instance, though trying her best to
explain her family to her husband Ross (and by extension to the audience), emphasizes both her sense of familiarity and of alienation. Returning to Chinatown after a fourteen-year absence, she is both insider and
outsider, commenting on what she sees and aware of being reduced to
the object of close scrutiny. In a telling moment, she suddenly realizes
what she looks like to her brothers: "[A]ll of a sudden I feel like just
another yellow girl on the arm of a Caucasian." Uncomfortable with her
family, Mattie pleads with Fred to leave Chinatown for Boston: "Out
there we'll be able to forget we're Chinamen, just forget all this and just
be people." Her brother Johnny points out the weakness of her hope that
ethnicity can be erased: "You have to forget you're a Chinatown girl to be

just people, Sis?" Mattie's perspective can be read as exemplifying the false notion of a generic spectatorship, making us aware of the danger of thinking that any group, including the audience, could be described as "just people," neutral, without race.

If Mattie's expressions of ambivalence mark her as "Mama Fu Fu," her husband Ross's viewpoint is even less desirable. Ross, who claims to be "more Chinese" than Mattie, takes on the perspective of the enlightened white spectator. His picture-taking in Act Two recalls the Western "objectivism" of both photographic art and dramatic realism. But just as the reality captured by Ross's camera is in fact painfully posed, so Ross's reliability as observer of this family must be questioned. Ross claims to have experience and authoritative knowledge of all that is Chinese American in the play, including racial hostility:

> *Ross.* Hawks hate me. Dove, Republicans, Communists, Democrats. Southern Whites. Freedom riders. Blacks. Chicanos, Indians, hardhats. Ecologists. The police . . . ! I'm Mr. White Male Supremacist. Middle Middle class American liberal Four Years of College Pig. So I'm used to hostility. (129)

But Ross's insistence that he is able to identify with the feelings experienced by Fred and his family and his protests that "I am not totally insensitive to Chinese like most whites are" are belied by his condescending remarks about Orientals and the "old ways."

Throughout the play, the limited perspective of each character individually exposes the fallacy of a single coherent point of view, a single kind of spectator. The play denies the existence of some unified reality in favor of a much less coherent set of perspectives. Each character's attempts to reflect on the situation are partial and inadequate, underscoring the impossibility of any attempt by the viewer to capture the totality of authentic experience through watching. Perhaps the most comprehensive view belongs to China Mama, Papa Eng's first wife, who sits stoically watching in the background of the play. Her position as silent observer reminds us once again that there are multiple perspectives on the action. At the same time, the play does not allow a fully sympathetic engagement with her. She can act only as a reminder, not a spokesperson, of the "authentic" Chinese viewpoint on the Chinese American family.

But one particular perspective on spectatorship is clearly implicated in the play. The tourist's perspective, which seeks to witness exotic Chinese in their real surroundings, is made explicit in Fred's monologues, which begin and end each section of the play. Fred's "tour" illustrates how the inhabitants of Chinatown, including himself, are reduced to freaks, objects to be exploited for this gaze. He uses different strategies to expose the voyeuristic, exploitative, and even pornographic desires of the tourist for contact with the "real" Chinatown. At first he speaks in a painfully exaggerated accent, parodying himself as stereotype. Suddenly he drops the phony accent, promising to "be me. Just me." But this move toward a more natural speech is revealed to be simply another ploy, a playing to the tourist's need for some semblance of authenticity, as Fred promises to take his tourists to the real Chinese restaurant "where I eat" and where the tourist can find "good home cooking and souvenir chopsticks." Each of Fred's speeches plays to the hunger of his tourists, their desire to experience sights such as the "Chinaman albino the color of Spam."

As the play progresses, Fred's colorful spiels become increasingly exaggerated, fantastic, and angry, exposing his impotent frustration over the viewing relationship of the white tourist's gaze and the exotic exhibit of Chinatown, what Chin once called a "game preserve for Chinese."[3] Both in his spiels and in the curses Fred mutters to himself, the theater audience is linked with the tourists Fred hates. The audience is implicated in its own watching, its own fascination with the sordid sights of Chinatown, as Fred addresses his tourist customers. Fred openly antagonizes the realistic audience and fosters the spectator's sense of alienation through making explicit the kinds of consumption that are taking place.

Significantly, Fred's speeches act as advertisement, most strikingly as a kind of "food pornography":

> Cantonese sweet 'n 'sour goes straight to your scrotum.
> Pekingese goo makes you dream in 3-D.
> Shanghai hash cures blind drunkenness and raises your
>   I.Q. six points!
> And the universal peanut grease
> of the Chinatown deepfry lights up
> every nerve of your body,
> from your vitals to your fingertips
> in a glittering interior chandelier
> glowing you up so nice and so warm. (77)

Acts of eating are central to the action throughout the play. However, the consumption of food is not only a nurturing and pleasurable activity, but one that can include the exploitative consumption of things Chinese by tourists. In Mattie's franchise, Chinese food becomes the commodity, mass-marketed and exploited for the white audience. In a larger sense, though, it is Fred himself who is fed on by all, not only by the tourist groups he leads but also by the members of his family. Oppressed by a father who rarely sustains him, acting as the breadwinner by putting Mattie through college, caring for his delinquent younger brother Johnny, and turning his own writing into aphorisms for cookbooks, Fred sees himself as privately and publicly devoured. Fred's difficulties with his writing and his identity have to do with his refusal to allow others to feed off him, not only whites, but also Chinese Americans. He is skeptical of those who may be interested in him only as fodder for their own academic agendas.

> I don't wanta be a pioneer. Just a writer. Just see my name in a book
> by me. About things I like writing about, and fuck the pioneers.

What've the old pioneers done for us, for me? I'm not even fighting nobody. I just have a few words and they come at me. "Be Chinese, Charlie Chan or a nobody" to the whites and a mad dog to the Chinamans . . . for what? To die and be discovered by some punk in the next generation and published in mimeograph by some college ethnic studies department, forget it. (117)

As the play progresses, it becomes painfully obvious that as spectators, we can enter into the play as sympathetic to Fred, yet remain incriminated along with the other consumers. In our watching of this play about Chinatown, we are also implicated in our desire for some experience of authenticity and realness. Fred's promise, then, to give the tourists access to some "special" food—and in turn, to give the theater audience access to the problems of his own psyche—becomes doubly loaded. Fred openly confronts the tourists with their own feelings of alienation; though hungry, they are afraid to eat the potentially unsanitary food of the Other:

> And now your eyes are inwards on your innards
> You're hungry, folks.
> Hungry! And afraid to eat anything here.
> I know the feeling . . . Bad feeling. (113)

Mattie's accusation that Fred himself is the "poison" is metaphorically true: Fred refuses to be consumed without causing his consumers, tourists and theater audiences alike, some pain. Fred's speeches become increasingly intense, even threatening, and his constant obscenities become more violent and provocative. As a character, Fred becomes less and less palatable as his anger becomes increasingly violent. Fred refuses to be easily digested, to become the easy victim of the gaze. Instead of going home happily sated with this vision of a Chinese American family, we begin to realize the indigestion of our own consumption.

In the final scene of the play, Fred is a grotesque figure dressed in white, the image of death as a Charlie Chan tour guide. This image moves the play toward theatrical expressionism, where Fred embodies the victimization of his environment. That environment includes the audience, now implicated in a system of viewing that reduces and oppresses Fred. Fred is clearly a commodity, sold to tourists, one of the freaks he describes. The audience (whether Asian American or not) is implicated in this final act of watching, poisoned by its own consumption of Fred's words. *The Year of the Dragon* allows us to witness Fred's experience but refuses to let us identify with his pain. It ensures that we can no longer sit quietly as the invisible consumers of some notion of Asian American reality but are instead forced to reexamine our own conditions of spectatorship.

Family Devotions

If *The Year of the Dragon* complicates and criticizes the voyeurism of the tourist's gaze, David Henry Hwang's *Family Devotions* (1981) promotes a different kind of watching—one that fosters the ideal of a collective and essentialized Chinese American identity, where, as the character Di-gou says, "the stories written on your face are the ones you must believe" (123). The family devotions performed by the characters are meant to extend to the audience as well, as theater partakes of the collective elements of ritual. At the same time, this desire for a shared sense of meaning is never fulfilled. Instead, the rites enacted in the play evoke a radical surrealism that accentuates the lack of connection between theatrical experience and audience, an unmet need for shared understanding and community.

The play itself undergoes a macabre transformation from gentle comedy to frantic and tragic ceremony. The curtain opens on a modern-day equivalent of the drawing room—the sunroom of the upscale Bel Air home of Joanne and Wilbur, where the extended family gathers to welcome Di-gou from China. The sisters Ama and Popo wait expectantly to see if their brother still celebrates their Christian faith, reciting to the younger generation the story of his childhood travels with their now deceased evangelist aunt See-goh-poh. Although the fundamentalist Christian attitudes of Ama and Popo are at first placed in comic contrast to the materialism of the younger generation of Chinese Americans, the conflict between different sets of spiritual values takes on a grimmer aspect in the second act of the play. After Di-gou reveals that he never really believed in the Christian God, Ama and Popo push Di-gou to testify in a round of "family devotions." Their insistence becomes urgent; they abuse Di-gou verbally and physically. The tone of the play shifts suddenly when Di-gou begins speaking in tongues; he reveals that See-goh-poh's evangelism was really a front, an excuse to travel and a cover-up for an illegitimate child. The truth of this revelation kills Ama and Popo. After the sudden death of his sisters, Di-gou seems to give himself over to the materialism of American life, exclaiming that his only desire is to drive "an American car—very fast—down an American freeway" (145). Apparently, the only one who is enlightened by this strange series of incidents is Chester. Through his contact with his great-uncle, Chester begins to recognize his roots in China. In the final stage direction, Chester stands where his great-uncle stood early in the play, and the shape of his face "*begins to change*," presumably to reflect his kinship to his great-uncle from China and his new-found ethnic connections.

Di-gou's revelation of See-goh-poh's past and the false basis for Ama and Popo's Christian faith is not hard to understand in terms of the dramatic tensions raised by realistic plays. Many realistic plays use the disclosure of a hidden truth as their central action. But even though we witness these events, no clear means of understanding the climactic revelation of Di-gou and Chester's final shape-changing is made apparent in the play. Some of the tension associated with these moments has to do with an ambiguous spectatorial positioning in the framing of these occurrences. The play does not maintain a clear window of access for the spectator, beyond revealing the falseness of Christianity in China or articulating the need for Chinese Americans, particularly those lost in the upward mobility of California living, to find their roots in the old country.

In fact, the entire play complicates any complacent sense of shared reality. There are already hints at estrangement in the opening scene as the objects that distinguish the family's upper-middle-class American normalcy—barbecue, microwave, tennis ball machine—go haywire, catch fire, explode, bombard the characters with tennis balls. As these objects take on a life of their own, the audience has no idea as to the cause of their possession. Similarly, when Di-gou and Chester, then Ama and Popo, speak in tongues, there is no collective understanding of these moments, only bewilderment.

Especially difficult are those moments in which the playwright establishes a bond between Di-gou and Chester. Although it is apparent from Di-gou's speeches that these two characters should be bonded together by a shared sense of what is Chinese, any sharing in this vision of collectivity is denied to the audience. Integral to the play are the ways in which Chester and Di-gou are spatially linked. In the beginning of the play, Di-gou first appears as a viewer framed in the glass door; later, he makes his entrance in the same way, first looking in on the scene through the glass. When Di-gou is beaten by his sisters, Chester watches helplessly through the same glass door. Finally, at the end of the play, Chester is framed by this glass as "*his face begins to change.*" Each of these moments serves to link Chester and Di-gou by suggesting that they are omniscient viewers as well as members of the family, standing both outside and inside the action. But if Chester's and Di-gou's perspectives seem to allow them more knowledge than the rest of the characters, it is a knowledge that they do not share with us; we are trapped outside the play by the frame of the stage and not allowed to share in their self-revelations.

For Chinese American spectators, the confusion can be greatest where we expect realism to show us the most.[4] The ending of the play in particular is left ambiguous. It is clear that as Di-gou's face becomes reflected in Chester's, we are meant to reach some understanding of how the faces of our own people, our families, our roots in China might still hold us. Chester, though assimilated, comes to share Di-gou's idea of a collective past, of roots, of family, and of "Chineseness." It is Chester is who is shown his face in the mirror-like back of his violin and told by Di-gou that

[t]here are faces back further than you can see. Faces long before the white missionaries arrived in China (*He holds CHESTER's violin so that its back is facing CHESTER and uses it like a mirror*) Look here. At your face. Study your face and you will see—the shape of your face is the shape of faces back many generations—across an ocean, in another soil. You must become one with your family before you can hope to live away from it. (123)

However, the speech calls only for a vague metaphorical connection, one that is not allowed to coalesce further. The attachment of Chester to his past appears to be less an attachment to a real China than to a nostalgic sense of the "Chinese," the imagining of community that is uniquely prompted his alienation in America. The moments in which Chester discovers his past heritage through his uncle, then, are those that might speak nostalgically to the Asian American spectator. Yet at the same time this powerful plea is never fully realized. The stage construction that transforms Chester's face into his uncle's leaves this transformation without the necessary exposition by which members of the theater audience might understand and share in it.

Perhaps the most striking similarity between some of Hwang's dramatic techniques and the works of his early mentor, Sam Shepard (one of the dedicatees of *Family Devotions*), is the likeness between Di-gou's speeches, Chester's final transformation, and Vince's speech in Shepard's

Buried Child. In Shepard's play Vince recalls having an experience like that we see enacted for Chester: driving down the highway, Vince imagines his face merging with his father's and his father's father's, embodying the patriarchal lineage. But these similar tropes work quite differently in the two plays, and this difference reinforces the complexity of the spectator's position in *Family Devotions.* In *Buried Child,* Shepard's transformation of Vince relies on the earlier establishment of recognition of an imagined "American" past, built on images of midwestern Americana that are echoed in the set and in the speeches of the characters: as Shelly, Vince's girlfriend from Los Angeles, points out, the house resembles the clichéd images depicted in Dick and Jane books or Norman Rockwell paintings. Vince's speech comes just at the moment of reclaiming ownership of this prototypically American house, at the climactic point when he gains the inheritance from his dying grandfather. By contrast, the transformation of Chester in *Family Devotions,* although it seems to suggest a similar reclamation of heritage, only highlights the dislocation of the Chinese American male. Chester's heritage, expressed through imaginative stage technique, is not given the definitive affirmation that Vince's is. Standing outside the glass door, Chester is denied access to the Bel Air sunroom, or to any stage space that is marked as his; his transformation remains unformed or unrecognizable.

Di-gou pleads with Chester that "The stories written on your face are the ones you must believe" (144). This reading of the Chinese American face through a mirror parallels one of the promises made by realistic drama, that through objective observation one can find the truth of one's own nature and own identity. Hwang's description of this play as "clearly autobiographical" (introduction, FOB *and Other Plays* xii) also stresses the need to find personal revelation through objective staging. But Di-gou's message cannot hold for us. The stage cannot act as a mirror that simply shows the truth of a collective relationship, configured by the roots of the past. The desire to return to China, to the knowledge of one's past, through the watching of the play, cannot be fulfilled; the play can only articulate this unsatisfied desire. Like Chin, Hwang also supplies us with multiple perspectives on the action, given by characters such as Jenny, the teenage daughter, and Wilbur, the Japanese American husband of Joanne. But their perspectives do not claim authority. Rather, these characters express a kind of dismay at not being able to understand, to interpret, to know what to feel. Jenny's reaction to the end of the family devotions may well be our own: "I don't understand this, but whatever it is, it's ugly and it's awful and it causes people to die. It causes people to die and I don't want to have anything to do with it."[5] Realism promises access, but here it pointedly denies us the goods. The moments of climax are not moments of revelation. Instead, in these moments the audience is aware of its exclusion from knowledge—not of facts, but of the revelations that these facts manifest—at the heart of the play.

The mixed critical reception of both *The Year of the Dragon* and *Family Devotions* gives us insight not only into the reported success or failure of the playwrights' craft, but also their ability to make spectators, sitting complacently beyond the proscenium, uneasy.[6] Both plays challenge the notion of the audience as invisible and privileged viewers. Instead, we are confronted by our own expectations of ourselves as an audience, and experience the severe dislocation of being reminded of our limited status as spectators. Such moments could be particularly jarring for some Asian American viewers if they expect unadulterated identification with and emotional sympathy for the characters, some totalizing vision of Asian American experience. Yet at the same time the dislocation from what is happening on the stage does not destroy the impulse of some Asian American spectators to identify with the play's characters and the situations presented. Although there are events in both these plays that work against a sense of mastery, of total identification, for either the Asian American or non-Asian American viewer, at the same time these moments support rather than oppose moments of sympathetic identification.

Such a statement seems a contradiction, and bears some explaining. If the model of the realistic spectator—placed in uninterrupted mastery over a passive feminized object onstage, and taking pleasure in his complete knowledge of that object—is no longer fully relevant, what other pleasures might Asian Americans find in a recognized "reality" onstage? I suggest that the desire for the authentic might be satisfied with a lesser degree of mastery, and spectators might identify with the reality in even grossly insufficient characterizations of Asian Americans.

The intense desire for stage presentation to validate, through public performance, a vision of authentic reality seems to spring from the desire for the solidarity of ethnic and racial identity. The desire for verisimilitude is reflected in Maxine Hong Kingston's description of her recognition scene while watching David Henry Hwang's *FOB*:

There—on the stage, in public—were our gestures, our voices, our accents, our own faces. It isn't sad scenes that bring the tears, but a realization of how isolated we've been and a wonder that our private Chinese lives and secret language can be communally understood. To see even one other person indicate "myself" by pointing to his nose makes me know I am not alone; there are two of us. But to be among an audience at a play—here are many of us. Here is a community. We become proud to the bones.

One of the happiest moments I have ever had at a theater was watching the young men in *FOB* pour hot sauce on their food and gulp it down in an eating contest. I myself had just written a scene about an eating race. To have a fellow writer who works an ocean and a continent away meet me at an intersection reassures me that there is a place called Chinese America and that I am seeing it with an authentic vision. (foreword, FOB *and Other Plays* vii–viii)

Yet this vision of Asian American theaters full of Asian American audiences recognizing their common authenticity and reality has never been achievable. The lure of realism for Asian Americans must be deeply connected to a much more fragile vision of community—and the desire for this envisioned community remains strong.

Realism holds the promise of public validation of a "real" self insofar as it appeals to a vision of performers and audience united in their recognition of common meaning. The power of realism, then, is that it allows audience members to see themselves as symbolically whole within the presentation of the drama. I suggested earlier that there is a tendency to read plays by Asian Americans simply as mirrors of a preexisting sociohistorical reality or experience. The most immediate responses to these plays often operate on the terms of "like me" or "not like me": Does this play reflect my life experience or doesn't it?

Yet rarely does a judgment of a play's reality depend solely on the degree of its imitation of actual life experience. The same impulse for self-recognition in the real persists in even less likely instances of identification. In Frank Chin's The Chickencoop Chinaman, the young Tam frantically projects his need for a Chinese American boy hero onto the unlikely figure of the masked Lone Ranger. The character of Vincent in Philip Gotanda's Yankee Dawg You Die serves as a role model for the young actor Bradley, despite his regular appearances in grossly stereotypical roles; Bruce Lee, Neil Sedaka, and even Godzilla are possible heroes in Bradley's imaginative life. In Women and Chinese Modernity: The Politics of Reading Between East and West, Rey Chow describes a similar reaction in her mother's response to the Bertolucci film The Last Emperor: "It is remarkable that a foreign devil should be able to make a film like this about China. I'd say, he did a good job!" (24). There is a world of difference between the mastery and dominance of the spectator's position in realism as modeled by Mulvey, Dolan, and Moy and what Chow paraphrases as her mother's response: "Still, that's me, that's us, that's our history. I see it in spite of the hand of the foreign devil" (24). Yet this description, too, relies on the recognition of a kind of reality even in versions of China made by foreign devils.

What can we say about this mode of Asian American reality, contented with less than total knowledge of itself and able to identify with the traces of the "authentic" Asian even in the most unrealistic or exoticized image? Some help comes from Rey Chow's concept of the "ethnic spectator," for whom the reality of art lies not so much in a recognition (or portrayal) of any real community as in a recognition of the fragmented, marginalized psyche. In Chow's description, the spectator is "ethnicized" in wanting to recognize in realism a reality that is "her own," in identifying with an ethnic or national history. For Chow, such "desires, fantasies and sentimentalisms," a certain "obsession" with the authentic and the real, may develop in response to the situation of alienation within Western culture. This is not simply nativism or a naive nostalgia for authenticity but a desire for wholeness that is fueled by a state of alienation and a sense of loss:

> We might say a response such as "Yes, that's me, that's Chinese" is a fetishizing imagining of a "China" that never is, but in that response also lies the wish that is the last residue of a protest against that inevitable "dismemberment" brought about by the imperialistic violence of Westernization. (Chow 25–27)

Chow's position allows us to understand how audience members can identify with characters quite different from them in gender, class, age, and experience. In addition, it sheds light on how the presence of the Asian body, even in a stereotypical and demeaned role, might provide a certain kind of pleasure for the Asian American spectator.

The constant pressure toward the real and the authentic accounts for the frequency with which Asian American readers call for a "true voice" or "our own stories." We should not underestimate the power of this desire, for it may be driven not so much by a naive need to see literal reality as by the desire to authenticate through public performance a vision of ethnic community hitherto erased from public view. The theater-goer who concludes, "that is authentic experience," may not be judging the play or player on the basis of its resemblance to any offstage reality; rather, she might be satisfied by the theatrical allusion to what otherwise remains unseen. Others, not finding this mode of identification, may cry out "but that was melodramatic and contrived" or "that was exotic and incredible" rather than "that was real."

I have approached the questions of Asian American spectatorship and identification through a discussion of a particularly slippery form, dramatic realism. If, as is sometimes the case, realism is construed as the spectator's confident, masterful relationship over the passive object in the frame, then Asian American realism is suspect, as other realisms are. But if Asian American spectators have a more tentative position in relation to the "reality" in front of them (perhaps by virtue of the ways in which certain plays—like *The Year of the Dragon* and *Family Devotions*—do not allow easy relationships to the real), a spectatorial position of mastery is an insufficient paradigm. Modes of authenticity and realness rely on a more complex identification, on viewers' needs to find themselves as whole in the constructed vision performed before them. That need comes out of the fragmented, traumatized situation of marginality.

In this constant return to the idea of the real, I acknowledge its power, however diversely articulated, not only among those identified as Asian American, but also those marginalized in other ways. In this sense, contemporary realistic plays and films by Asian Americans share some affinities with the peasant plays of the early Abbey Theatre, in Dublin, or the folk plays of the Harlem Renaissance, where the spectacle similarly fed a hunger for authentic or true experience and plays strategically positioned their viewers to create anew the image of community and identity. In this sense, we can better understand these particular versions of realism as the products of wishful thinking, a complex mimetic impulse that at once articulates the powerful impulse to find solidarity in shared experience and at the same time exposes the tensions and contradictions in these perspectives.

3

The Chinaman's Unmanly Grief

Contemporary Asian American critics tend to be somewhat embarrassed by Frank Chin's angry and misogynistic works. Some try to excuse Chin's sexism as idiosyncratic and personal; others label his work outdated (Cho 61). Even though Chin is still producing new work, there is a critical desire to associate him with the more unstudied, raw, and "youthful" period of Asian American writing of the 1960s and 1970s and those decades' "agonized temporizings" (Campomanes 56). Such responses, and the terms in which they are couched, suggest that Chin's work is only an aberrant phase in the otherwise "normal" maturational process of Asian American literature. These attempts to relegate Chin to history themselves reveal the still provocative nature of his work. Although Chin might rightly be placed within the context of the "cultural nationalist" period of Asian American literature, roughly congruent with the earlier phases of other minority movements such as the Black Power movement, we must resist too rigid a notion of development or evolution.[1] Chin's emphasis on the maligning of Asian American men not only by white racism, but also by the emasculating "honorary white Chinese American" female, still touches a raw nerve. His call for the redemption of Asian American masculinity has fueled the imagination of many new Asian American writers, and has also helped inform the current notions of an emerging Asian American canon, particularly in his influential work as a co-editor of *Aiiieeeee! An Anthology of Asian American Writers* and *The Big Aiiieeeee! An Anthology of Chinese American and Japanese American Literature.*

This chapter looks in some detail at Chin's most striking and influential play, *The Chickencoop Chinaman* (first produced at the American Place Theatre, New York City, on May 27, 1972, directed by Jack Gelber), and investigates its construction of Asian American male identity as a still pervasive communal statement. Although Chin has said that "The Chinese do not need a Freud,"[2] in *Chickencoop Chinaman* Chin does employ and rework classic Freudian paradigms in order to comment both on the ways in which Asian American men have been figuratively castrated by a white racist society and on the ways in which they must reclaim their masculinity in the face of this historical wounding. Ultimately, Chin redefines masculinity in terms of race, so that what signifies the true masculine cannot be separated from the Asian American; moreover, its signification demands the physical proof of such wounding, the "scars" which manifest on the body a history of denial.

The construction of masculinity in *Chickencoop Chinaman* sets the tone for later playwrights who work along the same lines, and the final section of this chapter considers one such example. R. A. Shiomi's detective play *Yellow Fever,* may be read as an answer to Chin's efforts to recuperate the Asian American male. In it similar tropes are evoked, including the idea of film as a medium dedicated to the recuperation of masculinity. Shiomi's open use of parody, however, suggests that such tropes should be read not as if they were representative of either the real or the ideal Asian American male, but rather as a public "fantasy," in Fredric Jameson's sense:

Fantasy is no longer felt to be a private and compensatory reaction against public situations, but rather a way of reading those situations, of thinking and mapping them, of intervening in them, albeit in a very different form from the abstract reflections of traditional philosophy or politics. (171)

In *Yellow Fever*'s playful treatment, the tropes of castration and redemption might be read less strictly than in Chin's work. The more flexible linking of ethnicity with gender in Shiomi's play offers an alternative interpretive position for those uncomfortable with Chin's versions of Asian American masculinity.

Although Freudian psychoanalysis has been criticized for being both insulated from cultural difference and universalist in its theories of subjectivity and self-formation,[3] these qualities in fact make it quite useful for analyzing the construction of "Asian American" in Chin's works.[4] *Chickencoop Chinaman* is easily read as a Freudian fantasy in which rational discussion cannot resolve deeply disturbing psychic events. Here, evoking Freudian paradigms becomes strategic, a way of insisting that the Asian American male's psychological self and identity are established in the same way as that of other males. By drawing on the familiar tropes of Freudian psychology—castration anxiety and the fetish—Chin also insists on the complex subjectivity of the Asian American male and his entitlement to a "normal" being and sexuality. At the same time, his intensification of these patterns of behavior reinforces the cultural differences evidenced in history: how the ways in which Asian Americans have been denied access to normalcy deeply affect the individual's self.

Chin's intense focus on the emasculation of the Asian American male reinvigorates Freud's description of the castration crisis. In its initial encounter with the woman's body and its visible lack of the male organ, the male child experiences a profound symbolic trauma. In Freud's paradigm, the male's fear of loss leads to behavior motivated by defensive, unconscious strategies of disavowal, repression, and projection. This castration anxiety is a "radical anxiety" against which are constructed "primary experiences of identity." The "consciousness of self" becomes intertwined with "processes of desire, sexuality, and fantasy . . . produced to counter against that founding anxiety and . . . always in dialectic with it" (Rosen 160). For Chin, the crisis lies in the compounding of this castration anxiety for the Asian American male by a historical racism that defines 'Asian' and 'male' as incompatible. To add to Freud's already rigidly heterosexual and overdetermined context, the Asian American male suffers from what Wong calls the "ethnicizing of gender": "the attribution of allegedly natural ethnic essences such as 'Chineseness' or 'Americanness' to 'masculine' and 'feminine' behaviors" (S.-L. C. Wong, "Ethnicizing Gender" 112–13). Because the construction of gender is inseparable from the construction of race, the Chinese American (and by extension, Asian American) male is doubly threatened, not only by the castration crisis that Freud described, but also by the historical racism imposed by whites fearful of seeing Chinese men as fathers. The preface to *Aiiieeeee!*, edited by Chin, Jeffrey Paul Chan, Lawson Fusao Inada, and Shawn Wong, notes that laws prohibiting Chinese women from entering the country and Chinese American women from marrying immigrants forced celibacy on Chinese men. Moreover, the stereotype of the Asian male appears to be another emasculating strategy enacted by white Christian societies, rendering the Asian male as "the alien . . . the image of white male sexual perversity" (*Aiiieeeee!* xxxi).

In the context of this castration anxiety and emasculation, the figure of the Asian American woman becomes doubly significant. In many works by Asian American men, the Asian American woman functions as a projection of male castration anxiety. Chin and his *Aiiieeeee!* co-editors frame her as the symbol of absence and lack, as the agent that threatens emasculation of Asian American men. In their view, her desire for white rather than Asian men must be read as an extension of the historical emasculation already in progress, in which "yellow" men are framed negatively:

The men are responsible for the civilization. The men are the masters. The masters of a perverse civilization are themselves perverts.
The women of this perverse civilization are helpless and hapless victims whose entire being and secret soul cry for escape and rescue
from this hateful civilization and culture. (*Aiiieeeee!* xl)

In marrying white men, Asian American women contribute to undoing
the patriarchal status of the "yellow man" and his position in the world.
Chin and his co-editors predict a certain "extinction" for Asian Americans, citing statistics indicating that large numbers of Japanese American
and Chinese American women marry "outside their race" (*Aiiieeeee!* xi–
xiii). The literary manifestation of this emasculation and denial of the
Asian American male's rightful place is the absent "love story." The only
Asian American writers to, in Chin's words, "lay a few words in praise of
yellow male sexuality" are "Eurasian women," who occupy a more ambiguous space than the threatening, castrating Asian American women,
whose desire for white men can only mean the absence of masculine
Asian men.

Chin's literary criticism strongly reiterates the threat of castration as it
is projected onto the feminine. Chin's essay, "This Is Not an Autobiography," characterizes both Maxine Hong Kingston and David Henry
Hwang as "ornamental Orientals" who are marked by their weak and
feminine use of autobiographical forms. Chin again evokes the terms of
patriarchal succession, repudiating those who have given up their Chinese literary fathers for Western ones: "Kingston's Chinese Americans are
really Greeks holding their eyes slanty with two fingers" ("Autobiography" 124). Kingston and Hwang are "feminized" in their mainstream
success: by adopting the "Christian" confessional autobiography, they
have married the white consumer. For Chin, the Asian American writer
must be masculine and his activity a form of man-to-man combat: "As a
rule of style and literary activity, it means the fighter writer uses literary

forms as weapons of war, not the expression of ego alone, and does not fuck around wasting time with dandyish expressions of feeling and psychological attitudinizing. The individual is found in the act of war, of not selling out, not in feelings" ("Autobiography" 112). Chin thus projects onto the literary world—and his own frustrations as an Asian American writer—the problems of the historical emasculation of the Asian American male. Chin's frustrations as a teacher are also part of a "natural" paternity he finds impossible; he is unable to pass down his legacy of knowledge properly to a literary son:

> Oh, I could couch this as advice to a young writer, if there were a young writer out there not anxious for a career faking it for fame as an Ornamental Oriental. Just one who wanted to know and didn't want their art to stand on faking yellow and making fog. . . . To fake the warm friendly teacher without a real and worthy student is to step into the role of one of the baldheaded faggot monks of ABC's "Kung Fu," and that's not the way we teach even willing and worthy students. ("Autobiography" 129)

The language of Chin's attacks, repeated in a number of articles, seems excessive and personal, as does his calling an old friend's decision to teach *The Woman Warrior* a betrayal ("Autobiography" 130). But again, we cannot read such remarks, particularly his famous denigration of Kingston's work, simply as a literary assessment. Rather, we must focus on the ways in which they express a larger pattern of disavowal and projection. Chin's rejection of feminized writers is less a comment on the quality of their work than on his construction of a psyche for the Asian American male, a psyche that is deeply rooted in fears of castration. Attacking the female and the feminized projects onto others the difference and lack the male fears for himself. Chin's construction of this psyche insists that within the traditional patriarchal and psychological models, Asian American males deprived of their manhood cannot help but lash

back in anger. Their anger—and its accompanying violent misogyny—
might in fact be a "natural" consequence of such emasculation.

The Chickencoop Chinaman

Chin's *Chickencoop Chinaman* plays out the intensified castration anxiety
of the Asian American male through potent theatrical moments of projection. The play constructs a fundamentally patriarchal world, where
normalcy is thought of in terms of the male order—fathers and sons—
and where any deviation from that order only intensifies its traumatic
experiences. The complex motivations of the protagonist, Tam, are fundamentally influenced by this symbolic castration and thwarted father-
hood. He realizes that as an Asian American male, he is damned in all his
attempts to realize himself fully; even his deeply felt emotion at this loss
is itself "unmanly" grief, unable to find adequate expression. This anger
and frustration come out both in his antagonism toward other characters
in the play and in his desire to make a film. Along with its deep sense of
disappointment, the play offers the possibility of a more positive resolution, namely, that the Asian American male might in fact construct his
own maleness by confronting the threat of castration, moving toward the
figure of the Chickencoop Chinaman, the mythical superhero described
by Tam in the play whose "punch won't crack an egg" but who at the
same time will "never fall down."

In the play, Chin racializes the Freudian paradigm of castration anxiety. The Asian American male's trauma is amplified by historical events
marking the absence of Asian American women and the emasculation of
Asian male immigrants. The play alludes to this history; in Chinese
American families, Tam recalls, there was "no juvenile delinquency . . .
because there was no kids." He later reflects on the loss of identity that
accompanied early immigrants, who not only were forced into celibacy
but had to become fictional "paper sons" in order to gain entry:

Our women born here lost their citizenship if they married a man
from China. And all our men here, no women, stranded here
burned their diaries, their letters, everything with their names on it
. . . threw the ashes into the sea . . . hopin that that much of
themselves could find someplace friendly. (26)

Out of these harsh conditions, the later generations of Chinese American
males are "unnaturally" or accidently born, or, as Tam declares himself to
be, "Created! Not born! . . . a Chinaman! A miracle synthetic!" Asian
American males, thus, are at a loss to account for their own existence.
That Tam's friend Kenji's mentions his childhood experiences in internment camps suggests that Chinese and Japanese Americans share a history of emasculation, and that in history lie the foundations for the anxiety that permeates the present of the play. Every event in this complex
play returns to these historical traumas as founding events of both psychological and social weight.

Foremost in the play are the responses of the characters to the many
fathers that are absent, disabled, or disfigured. Throughout the play, Tam
is confronted by the failure of Asian American men to be proper fathers.
His own children have been taken away by his ex-wife, Barbara. His
search for a father for Ovaltine "the Dancer," the black boxer who is the
subject of his documentary film, is derailed. His own biological father is
mentioned only once, half-jokingly: "Chinamans do make lousy fathers. I
know. I have one." But in a revealing pattern of acknowledgment and
denial, Tam can't help reminiscing about an old man, "a crazy old dishwasher." It is clear that Tam sees his own threatened emasculation embodied in the figure of the old man; he constantly denies him as "not my
father." Tam rejects the possibility of having been fathered, physically or
spiritually, by this immigrant Chinese, who is unmanned by his marginalized status. The old dishwasher is afraid of the white authorities,
cannot speak or understand English, and relies on Tam's care; he is un-

able even to bathe himself without Tam's assistance. But the very frequency with which Tam brings up stories about the old man testifies to a complex legacy of loss. For example, when asked by the young Robbie why he wears swimming trunks while bathing, he replies that it is a habit he picked up from the old man, who wore his underwear in the bathtub, afraid of "white old ladies peeking at him through the keyhole." Covering his genitals, the old man prevents ocular proof of his masculinity, suggesting also a lack of the male organ. Tam, haunted by a memory of the old man dying in his bath, a memory that reinforces the sense of physical danger, imagines a phallic image on the old man's dead body: "You could see his veins like snakes swimming in rosewater." He is momentarily lost in this image before he recollects, more matter-of-factly, "I helped him into his bath, and he died. It was just lights out." Both this vision of the old man and the fragmented, difficult way in which Tam tells it are revealing.

Kaja Silverman has commented that film derives its power from its ability to provide a substitute for a reality full of absences: "When a film covers over the absent real with a simulated or constructed reality, it also makes good the spectating subject's lack, restoring him or her to an imaginary whole" (10). The frequent allusions to film in the play seem to bear this out. Tam's intended documentary on the boxer Ovaltine looks to the power of the camera to create the literal proof of masculinity and paternity; in creating Ovaltine on film, he recreates himself in the image of a whole man. Thus he is desperately insistent that Charley Popcorn play the part of Ovaltine's "mighty daddy": "You gotta be his father. . . . You're all the fight he has left!"

The dream sequences in the play, like Tam's unmade film, are attempts to compensate for a missing psychic wholeness. Each of these dream moments, however, tantalizes him with the possibility of fulfillment, then ends with a taunting reminder of his figurative castration. The first dream sequence opens the play. In it, Tam engages with a "Hong Kong dreamgirl" who is twirling a phallic baton. The Chineseness of the girl promises that a sexual union with her will both affirm Tam's masculinity and return him to ethnic coherence:

> . . . these lips have had a hankering for servicing some of my Canton heritage in the flesh. But I've never been able to get close enough. Now you, my Hong Kong flower, my sweet sloe-eyed beauty from the mysterious East, I can tell that your little fingers have twiddled many a chopstick. Your smoothbore hands have the memory of gunpowder's invention in them and know how to shape a blast and I dare say, tickle a shot. Let me lead your hands. (6)

But she coyly retreats, and their union ends. In a second sequence, Tam's boyhood hero appears—the Lone Ranger, whom Tam now imagines as a Chinese American hero passing as white. Tam chooses the Lone Ranger because of the mask that hides his "slanty eyes," a mask that covers his Asianness and his symbolic lack of maleness. This heroic construction, now envisioned in the flesh, also fails him. The Lone Ranger turns out to be white, middle-aged, drug-addicted, lecherous, and racist. He responds to the writer Tam by shooting him in the hand, a symbolic maiming that disables Tam's ability to create artistic substitutions for his own inadequacy.

Tam's fluency with language, which often takes the form of sharp words that "rip" others, is also a response to his psychic wounds. For Lacan, the moment when the child enters language is also the moment of self-formation, in which the child realizes himself as a separate and distinct being. Lacanian readings of Freud suggest that the acquisition of language is linked to the traumatic moment when the threat of castration is perceived in the sexual difference of the mother. For Lacan, subjectivity is enabled when the child enters the symbolic order through such an experience of difference, simultaneously acquiring language and identity. Thus, in repressing awareness of female difference, the "patriarchal subject is constructed as a unified, consistent, but illusory identity—a 'self' whose words appear to give it control of a world to which it is central" (Gledhill 65). In other words, birth can be understood as a birth into language, the Lacanian moment of self-formation.

Significantly, Tam describes the moment of his "birth" as both immediately "linguistic" ("in the beginning there was the WORD! Then there was me!") and violently traumatic ("bloody" and "sordid"). The pains of birth are experienced again in the pain of separation, as the child realizes difference from the mother. Again, the scene of castration—the self encountering difference and separation, and the trauma of these occurrences—is intensified when linguistic differences further divide the child from the mother. The Lacanian emergence into language is rendered even more alienating, more violent, where ethnic as well as sexual difference plays a role in the formation of the self. In order for Tam to participate in the systems of symbolic exchange that make up the social order, he must submit to difference (and hence separation and castration) on two levels. The language of Tam's birth of "self" is English, yet on his lips it becomes the "motherless bloody tongue." His acquisition of English as a first language means that Cantonese, the maternal language, is lost to him: "I talk the talk of orphans." His connections to Cantonese are prelingual, experienced as the bond with the maternal body before speech.

Tam's speeches throughout the play refer to this scene of separation. For example, Tam describes his lack of understanding of his Chinese grandmother, who "has an ear for nothing but ancient trains in the night and talks pure Chinamouth you understood only by love and feel." The young Tam rejects his grandmother's link in favor of the "all-American" boy heroes of the radio. Substituting such figures as the Lone Ranger for the unsung Chinese American railroad workers (among them his grandmother's father), Tam says, "deafened my ear for trains all my boyhood long." Later, Tam compares his conversations with the old dishwasher in broken Cantonese—the remnants of a prelinguistic bond—with his ineffectual fluency in "Barbara's language": "With only foong, lawk yur, yit, lahng I had long deep talks with a man I remember to this day, but with all the fine pronouns, synonyms, verbs, adjectives, adverbs, nouns of Barbara's language I'm told I talk good, she left me on my birthday with nothin, it's all talk."

The cutting of the bond to the "mother tongue" in acquiring English speech is experienced as birth and as a castration; the two are inseparable. Tam finds it meaningful that Barbara abandons him on his birthday; the moment of his figurative castration (signaled by the loss of his children and his white wife) is also the moment of his birth. As a native speaker of English, Tam establishes his "self" through English, but speaking English emasculates him further, because it is the language of the dominant white culture that has emasculated Asian American men. Thus, Tam envisions his English, the speech of a castrated man, as infertile: "The buck and cluck of this child, your Chickencoop Chinaman gushes furiously. Like sperm. Numerously. Chug and thud, to conceive!" He never fully possesses English as his language: "No real language of my own to make sense with, so out comes everybody else's trash that don't conceive." In this context Tam's school nickname of "Tampax" or "ragmouth" has a stronger meaning, suggesting not only menstruation but also miscarriage, abortion, or unnatural birth.

Although Tam's "crazy talk" is unique to him, the psychological scars that he bears as an Asian American male are shared by the other male characters in the play. In this psychic economy, females embody the anxiety of castration, for they, threateningly, display the lack of a penis. In their visible difference, they serve as reminders of male vulnerability; they are thus both emblems of the castrated male and threatening emasculators. Men, particularly Asian American men, must recoup their masculinity by repudiating any similarity or affinity that might exist between them and that which is female. Often this is done by marking women with the visible signs of their own lack, pointing out what maintains their difference from men. *Chickencoop Chinaman* plays out this dynamic in the dramatic treatment of female characters, who are a constant source of anxiety. The Asian American male characters are both attracted to them and threatened by them, and thus the male characters frequently and violently mark the female characters with the comforting signs of difference.

The violent misogyny of the play enacts itself through a projection of "lack" onto that which is marked as female. Perhaps the most striking example occurs in the scene in which Tam and Kenji parody Helen Keller as a symbol of the "model minority," those who have overcome their racial "disabilities": "Helen Keller overcame her handicaps without riot! She overcame her handicaps without looting! She overcame her handicaps without violence! And you Chinks and Japs can too!" By mocking Helen Keller, Tam and Kenji distinguish themselves from the "sell-out" Asian American who has become "feminized"; and this difference is marked even more strongly by their exaggeration of Keller's struggling, incomplete language, and lack of sight and hearing. Such a parody allows Tam and Kenji to play out their fears of being disabled and emasculated; their psychic defense is to project the threat of their own loss onto Helen. But such a controlled "acting out" backfires later, when the Lone Ranger confides to them his lust for Helen Keller. The paradigm of white racist "love" for the "model minority" cannot be put to rest so easily.

If males project differences onto females, this act of projection is qualified by race. White women figure prominently in this economy of signification. On the one hand they have the potential to grant social status as well as sexual affirmation to Asian American men. On the other, they are particularly "scary" in their ability to threaten symbolic castration, reminding Asian American men of their inability to be real men by reversing traditional gender roles. Such women are envisioned as active rather than passive, powerful rather than weak, dominant subjects rather than objects of desire. Thus Tam recalls that the dishwasher was particularly afraid of "white old ladies peeking at him through the keyhole" while he bathed. Tam's former wife Barbara and to some extent Kenji's Eurasian friend Lee are both potential castrators. Lee directly taunts Tam with effeminacy: "All afraid of the pretty girls? But oh so anxious to do the right thing—avoid trouble—save face. Look at you so stoic, and that dumb little smile. Do ya talk in giggles too?" Her sexual experience is also a challenge; that Lee has had several husbands sets up an undercurrent of competition among the male characters. In particular, she plays off Asian American men against black men, accusing the former of making it "on the backs" of the latter.

Kenji and Tam both respond directly to their fears, defusing the "scary" qualities of "white women" by humorously exaggerating their body parts:

> Aww, man, if I'm going to go to all the trouble of mind to get a white girl, man, she's going to be all white. And tall. And giant, huge tits man. And blonde. The scariest kind of white girl there is, man, none of this working my way up for me. Blonde hairs all over her head. Tall . . . and tits, man like when I walk up to her and get my little nose stuck in her navel, man, and I look up at her belly, I feel like I'm on the road with you and see two Giant Orange stands across the road from each other. (28)

Through jokes, insults, and accusations, they mark Lee so as to neutralize her threat. Tam and Kenji recast her sexual experiences with husbands of different races as self-interested promiscuity; Tam accuses her of being a "one woman Minority of the Month Club." When she criticizes Tam ("I hate people making it on the backs of black people") Kenji retorts that "you made it on your back under blacks, and that's okay, huh?" But most important is the scene in which Tam recognizes Lee as part Chinese, citing the red in her hair as a giveaway. The hair becomes the mark that reveals her lack and removes her power to threaten them. The Asian

American woman is envisioned as threatening only insofar as she aspires to the power of whiteness. Through marking her with the sign of Asianness, she can be demoted to the status of the feminized Asian.

Another kind of emasculation is experienced not through language or personal relationships but in the fetishized object or body part. Freud describes the child who, in denying the female's lack of penis, substitutes a visual object, the fetish, in its place. The fetish thus conceals and at the same time marks absence.[5] The play also associates the Asian American male, already figuratively castrated and feminized, with the particular fetishization of objects that are "Oriental" in style. Thus the "Oriental" fetish marks the absence of masculinity in the Asian American male. Lee accuses Asian American men of substituting "culture" for "guts": "Watery paintings, silk, all that grace and beauty arts and crafts crap." Kenji responds violently to Lee's redecoration of his apartment, perceiving it as an attempt to "cover" him with fetishes: "Damn, you put me down! Bringin in this goddamn tatami grassmat Japanese bullshit and knockin the legs off the table. . . . we're not getting into no silk robes and walk around like fools for you!" White women in particular are accused of feminizing the Asian American male by seeing them in association with "Oriental" art and the lack of aggressive "masculine" sexuality. As Lee points out, Asian American men take advantage of the "stupid white girl who's been to a museum, some scared little ninny with visions of jade and ancient art and being gently cared for."

Most dangerous to this beleaguered Asian American male identity is the willing assumption of a fetish by the male himself. Tom, who is writing a book on "Chinese American identity," is assimilationist: "We used to be kicked around, but that's history, brother. Today we have good jobs, good pay, and we're lucky. Americans are proud to say we send more of our kids to college than any other race. We're accepted. We worked hard for it. I've made my peace." Recognizing that "in American eyes we don't appear as he-man types," Tom embraces fetishism in an effort to avoid accusations of homosexuality. For Tom, the only way to be accepted by whites within a heterosexual paradigm is to cover himself with the markings of the "female," to become the "ornamental Oriental." Tom's very body is a series of stylized and therefore fetishized poses, as detailed in Chin's stage directions: "*a very neat, tidy, uptight hip Chinese American. Longish hair, round steel rim glasses. He speaks self-consciously, styling his voice like others style hair.*" Tom's veneer of hip Orientalism, and the eagerness for acceptance behind it, effectively neutralizes his masculinity. Tam, who accuses Lee of rejecting Tom because "he didn't fulfill your lesbian fantasies," turns out to be correct: Lee considers Tom, her former husband and the father of one of her children, "not a man." He becomes "Uncle Tom" rather than a father to Robbie when Lee rejects his offer of reconciliation.

Chin's construction of the anxious Asian American male who is further threatened by the female can be located within the tensions of a particular period when the activists of the Asian American movement found themselves at odds with an emerging feminism.[6] Chin's creation of Lee, a savvy and intelligent woman, casts her as a menace that must be neutralized. Yet the overwhelming misogyny of the play—its portrayal of women as overprotective, child-stealing mothers or emasculating sex kittens—suggests less a preoccupation with the qualities of women than a focus on the thwarted desires of men. Again, Freud's paradigm of woman as the castrated figure has more to do with the psychic anxieties of men than it does with women. Similarly, homophobic remarks in the play— the fear of appearing "willowy" or "queer"—are more about how Asian American men are cast within the framework of castration than about gays. In this sense the physical dimensionality of Lee and "feminized" men such as Tom must be undercut in order for them to qualify as projections. What holds the play together is a sense of loss, or of the fear of being "cut," played out as theatrical action.

If the dynamics of *Chickencoop Chinaman* suggest that the anxieties facing the Asian American male are simply perpetuated without resolution, the ending can be read as a tragic reminder of this fact. Tam, deprived of his opportunity to create a father within the fiction of his film and chastised for his anger by Kenji, remains less than whole. At the end of the play he retreats into the kitchen for some "fast chopping." The implication that Tam is a cutter suggests that he himself has acted as an emasculator by projecting onto others the lack that he fears. However, another, more defiant and positive reading can be found for the play as a whole, in the transformation of the symbolic "scars" of castration into marks of a new manhood. This transformation is suggested in the ways in which the symbolic castration of the Asian male is extended to the black characters in the play. Charley Popcorn refers to Chinese as "yellow Negroes," and the entrances of characters at the end of the second act and beginning of the third act (first Tam is carried in on Charley's back, then Charley on Tam's) suggests an intertwined destiny. Chin suggests elsewhere that the relationship of the Asian American to the black man has overtones of competition; African Americans have been "cultural achievers, in spite of white supremacist culture, whereas Asian America's reputation is an achievement of that white culture—a work of racist art" (*Aiiieeeee!* 8).

Despite this apparent inscription onto another group of the lack felt by the Asian American male, there is a stronger thrust in *Chickencoop Chinaman* toward depicting Asian American men and black American men as mutually supportive figures whose masculinities complement one another. Kenji and Tam relate parallel stories in which Asian American men stand urinating next to black men; Tam refers to this proud moment as "the greatest piss we ever took in our lives." This act of male bonding takes on dual significance: it provides reassurance that masculinity and the male organ remain intact, and it confirms the difference between the male who possesses and the female who lacks. When Lee claims to be "one of the boys," she must be reminded that she is unable "to go out by the car and piss in the bushes."

In keeping with this dynamic of mutual affirmation, Tam fantasizes about the Dancer's stories of his childhood, which revolved around his childhood relationship with his father:

> *Tam.* You! I saw you as a bigger man, man, the way Ovaltine talked about watchin you strip off your shirt, and wash up out of a pan, outside the house. And how his eyes popped out when he was a kid, at your mighty back ripplin with muscles!
> *Popcorn.* Me?
> *Tam.* And the whiplash scars, how they made him cry, and how that made him sure, he'll be a fighter, a fighter down from his soul! (48)

But Tam is disappointed, as Popcorn denies both paternity and the scars of oppression that Tam imagines on him: "Whiplash never touch *my* back! You're sleepin, young man, Dreamin!" Popcorn even goes so far as to strip off his shirt and bare his back in order to show both Tam and the audience that no scars from whiplash and dogbite are present on his body. It is their absence that confirms that the relationship between Dancer and Popcorn is "business" rather than paternity, and proves Popcorn to be an inadequate father for Tam's film.

Tam's disappointment might seem paradoxical, for the scars that Ovaltine describes on his father's back are the marks of social castration for the black man, analogous to the emasculation of the Asian American male. Such marks would seem to confirm the problems of masculine identity that have maimed both black and Asian American men irrevocably; that Tam should become angry at their absence seems somewhat contrary to expectation. Yet Tam's frustration at not discovering the visible marks of a symbolic castration on Popcorn's back seems tied to the hope that the marks of castration on the father can be redemptive for the son. His film scenario suggests that the black man becomes the model for the Asian American male by undergoing social emasculation, only to produce a son who can become "The Champion of the World." These visible scars on the father become, in Tam's fantasy, the signs that urge the son to become stronger as a fighter. Such scars can become transformed into the marks of courageous persistence: the achievement of manhood in spite of racism. It is this story, this dream of redemption, that Tam hopes, and ultimately fails, to achieve on film.

Although Popcorn does not have the scars that are so crucial to Tam's myth, his encounters with Tam nonetheless do effect a transformation within the play, one that allows for the visible marks of castration to be reread as signifying nobility and heroism. Popcorn's account of his encounters with the old dishwasher is quite different from Tam's earlier memory of the old man dying in the bathtub. Popcorn recalls the old man insisting on paying to watch the fights and becoming indignant when he mistakenly believed he had been turned away. Tam's dishwasher becomes, in Popcorn's reminiscence, "The Chinatown Kid" who is "fierce, fierce!" Instead of focusing on the old man's frightened anonymity ("They were afraid of having names here. Afraid America would find 'em and deport 'em"), Tam now remembers the dishwasher wearing a "hat" that was "neatly brushed." Tam's memory of the old man as figuratively marked by castration is now transformed, readable in the same vein as the description of scars on the Dancer's mythical father. The old man's hat, like the scars, can be seen as a mark of his castration, another fetish substituting for and signaling the absence of his Asian manliness. Yet its being "neatly brushed" attests to the "dignity" that Popcorn insists he has. Each of these men, including the dishwasher, is in fact symbolically redeemed from his social scarring by a common interest in boxing. The play suggests that boxing might be an exercise in facing and overcoming the fear of being cut, in demonstrating courage when emasculation threatens.

This transformation enables us to revise our reading of the earlier image of Tam in the bath, which represented Tam's fear of castration, both acknowledged and denied in the hiding of the genitals. But the boxer-style swimming trunks that Tam takes to his bath are also, he tells Robbie jokingly, a superhero's "secret suit": "Whenever I see someone in distress I strip down to my secret suit, put up my dukes, and go swimming." This is one of many allusions in the play to the mythical "Chickencoop Chinaman," a figure envisioned as a superhero alternative to the Lone Ranger. Superheroes of comic books, television, and movies also undergo symbolic castrations, effected by catastrophes (Superman), accidents (Batman, the Incredible Hulk), or woundings (Spiderman), that strip them of their past identity and enable a painful rebirth into a creature of heroic power. This heroic scarring is a rereading of both Freudian castration and the historical emasculation of the Asian male. Asian American manhood is redeemed by the Chickencoop Chinaman, who reacts to the threat of castration with ingenuity and endurance—in this instance, with defiant and vigorous masturbation:

> When Chickencoop Chinaman have wetdream far from home,
> He cly Buck buck bagaw, squeezing off his bone. (29)

Toward the end of the play, Kenji announces that Lee will bear his child, establishing the promise of a future Asian American community in which a normative heterosexuality can be restored. If there is an optimistic note in the play, it is the hope of reconciliation, not just in the union of Lee and Kenji, but also in the ways in which Tam might rejoin them. This is suggested in the process by which the mythical Asian and Asian American male heroes—the dishwasher as "Chinatown kid," the "Chickencoop Chinaman," and, finally, the absent Railroad Grandfather—defy their castration and supersede the white heroes. At the end of each act, each Asian American character joins in a raucous cry for the Chickencoop Chinaman: "buck, buck, bagaw!" Even more important, Tam's final speech retells the story of the Railroad Grandfather, offering the possibility of redemption through paying attention to one's heritage: "Turn off them radios and listen in the kitchen!" The figure of the great-grandfather who works on the railroads is also symbolically bereft of wholeness; his absence leaves the Grandma "alone to roll cigars by herself," and when he returns he is marked with castration: "frostbit on every finger and toe of him and his ears and nose." Yet despite this troubled denial of paternity, reinforced by his death ("comfortable, comforting a little girl rolling counterfeit Spanish cigars"), his return to the family sets the tone for the ending of the play. Tam encourages the audience to "Ride Buck Buck Bagaw with me. . . Listen in the kitchen for the Chickencoop Chinaman slowin on home," asking us to join in expectantly for the return of the father figure. In trying to negotiate a masculinity for the Asian male within a system that has already rendered it impossible, the only possibility is to construct castration as enabling rebirth, transforming man into miraculous superman.

Yellow Fever

R. A. Shiomi's detective mystery *Yellow Fever* (first directed by Lane Nishikawa at the Asian American Theater Company and by Raul Aranas at the Pan Asian Repertory Theatre in 1982) can be read as an extension of the masculine desire for filmic realization shown in the earlier play by Chin. In *Chickencoop Chinaman*, Tam's making of a film compensates for his own felt lack of masculinity as an Asian American male. In the end, he gives up this project, promising Charley Popcorn that "you'll be part of a straight, professional fight film . . . not a word of fathers in it." If Tam's failure to make a film that would restore the father is disappointing, Shiomi's *Yellow Fever* steps into this void and fulfills this desire. Remaking Sam Spade into Sam Shikaze, the Japanese American detective who foils the murderous plot of the white supremacists, Shiomi evokes the fullness of filmic presentation, satisfying the terms left unsatisfied in Chin's plays. Although the tone is parodic and humorous, the questions addressed are more serious. Ultimately the film hero redeems Asian male masculinity, translating the terms of a white masculine private eye to eyes indelibly marked as Japanese Canadian.

The familiar characterization of the hard-boiled detective allows an instant affinity with Sam as he follows the clues and solves the mystery of the abducted Cherry Blossom Queen. As the plot develops along the lines of a conventional detective story, Sam as hero achieves mastery over the play's fictional fragmentation, thwarting the intricate plotting of Sergeant Mackenzie and Jameson and besting those who, like Captain Kadota and Nancy, have only a partial view of the puzzle. Importantly, the terms of the mystery in *Yellow Fever* are tied up with issues of racial tension: the plot of white supremacists to frame Chinese gangs and to spoil Captain Kadota's reputation and chances for promotion. Therefore, Sam's solving of the mystery suggests the victory and power of the Asian Canadian male to resolve the problems involved in racial difference and to bring about a satisfactory conclusion.

Several false leads also figure significantly in how race is constructed in the play. The openly racist Sergeant Mackenzie fantasizes about a "Hong Kong Tong Connection," imagining aggressive Chinese as threatening aliens, unnaturally perverted in their commercial and sexual dealings with women: "We all know how the Chinese like to trade in women." Mackenzie deals in blatant stereotypes, trying to pit Chinese against Japanese. Along with Asian gangs, both the Cherry Blossom Queen's "hajukin" boyfriend and the "Japanophile" Goldberg become suspects in the case. Although the boyfriend is quickly ruled out, Goldberg, whose Jewish name suggests some ambiguity and who considers himself a "Japanese specialist," remains a wild card to the end. The real kidnappers turn out to be explicitly marked both as raced—Scottish and Scandinavian—and as racist: Mackenzie, in league with Superintendent Jameson, and Pender-

son, "the Swinging Swede," who is motivated by the fear of "yellow fever," Asian Canadians as a "disease poisoning our bloodstream." At each
moment in the play, confronting a fragmented, incoherent story and con-
flicting information, Sam reduces all to an authoritative story that orders
and satisfies. Stage objects—hats, handkerchiefs, guns—become symbols
in the economy of masculinity; Sam correctly reads and uses them for his
own purposes. In the end, Jameson tries to shoot with a gun that lacks
ammunition; he has been tricked into symbolic impotence, outwitted by
those Asians whom he thinks to be less than men.

Like *Chickencoop Chinaman, Yellow Fever* works within familiar patriarchal, heterosexual patterns of narrative, extracting from them the dynamics of white masculine privilege without questioning how certain
other parties are excluded from it. The conventions of the private eye
detective story are preserved in terms of gender differences: the male is
the active agent, the female is the reminder of male virility or the lack
thereof. The plot relies on competition between white and Asian males.
The real target of investigation is not the Cherry Blossom Queen; she
serves only as part of the larger plot in which Mackenzie seeks to rid
himself of his partner Kadota and white supremacists seek to rid themselves of Asians in general. Other female characters are also relegated to
secondary roles. Rosie the café owner plays mother and nursemaid, sup-
plying Sam with missing pieces of information as well as feeding him.
Sam's ex-wife never appears, although she is discussed occasionally as
proof of Sam's manly disdain of creature comforts and material success.
The Chinese Canadian Nancy shows the most promise of being a real
character. As an Asian female "big-time" reporter, she fills the role of the
"classy dame." But her function as a snoop deteriorates into love interest
and helpmeet. She reassures Sam that he is still virile, "the guy that calls his
own shots," and she makes Sam "a decent bowl of juk" after an interlude
of love-making. After ensuring Sam's victory, she conveniently departs for
Toronto at the end of the play, leaving Sam's original world intact.

Alternative readings of the play, however, suggest that it reworks the terms of Asian American masculinity,as well as the classic detective film, more thoroughly. Viewed along the lines suggested earlier, some of the characterizations in *Yellow Fever* can support a more complex set of ambiguous identifications, ones that do not follow a strict detective story paradigm. The play does more than simply project evil racism onto a white enemy and heroism onto the Japanese Canadian. Rather, it works more subtly as a reminder of how Asian Americans should respond to situations that disempower them. It does so through acts of wounding and scarring that are analogous to Chin's staging of castration but at the same time are less rigidly gendered as masculine.

As in *Chickencoop Chinaman,* the masculine protagonist is deeply affected by a figurative scar that signals a symbolic castration. In *Yellow Fever,* such a scar is also part of the history of Asian Canada. Sam's opening monologue and the comments he makes throughout the play refer to an important historical moment, the internment of the Japanese during the Second World War by the Canadian government. Unlike the physical beatings from which he recovers during the action of the play, internment has left a lasting psychological scar on Sam. His comments throughout the play provoke a constant revisitation of the scene; he tells a jeering Mackenzie of the last time he took a vacation: "Thirty years ago. We all went to summer camp . . . in the winter."

The play casts the events of internment (and the racism that prompted them) as the source of a symbolic castration that can be felt across lines of gender, leaving effects that, to some extent, can be shared by non-Japanese Asians as well. The trauma of internment has left a visible mark on the entire Japanese Canadian community: "World War Two came and the government moved us out, sent us packing into the mountains, herded onto trains and dumped off in godforsaken ghost towns. . . . After the war it never was the same." Sam's inability to forget the traumatic incident, the wounding in the past, is also implied in the details given by Rosie of the old people of the community, such as the "ojisans [old men] living in hotels; so poor and lonely and stubborn." The troubles of Powell Street, "the ghetto," are located in the fractured and troubled past, in the gaps of knowledge surrounding a community split by a corrupt and racist government. Sam's solving of the mystery can be read as an attempt to piece together the gaps of this history, to confront the past. Certainly his desire to stay in Powell Street is tied to these memories: "Times have changed, now my nisei friends tell me I should move downtown, forget the past, and get a decent job. I just tell them I like the local colour." The alternative response is to suppress such a traumatic memory. Such a willed forgetfulness is embodied in Kadota, who denies his connection as "Nihonjin" with Sam until he needs his help. As the token Japanese on the police force, Kadota refuses to recognize the systematic racism around him and his own complicity with it; as Sam notes, "He was the kind that believed the camps were a blessing in disguise." Kadota's attempt to compensate for racism with hard work amounts to emasculation of a different kind. His failure to crack the case is linked precisely to his blindness regarding the government he works for, forgetting the ways in which it scars him again and again. Kadota realizes this only at the end of the play. When he finally learns the truth—that his own partner Mackenzie has been plotting against him—he is literally shot and wounded onstage.

In this interpretation, the character of the reporter Nancy, in her search for the perfect scoop, parallels Kadota. Nancy fails to see the facts of the case not so much because she is female, but because she is too young to remember the kind of overt racism that haunts Sam. Nancy is consistently surprised by and incredulous at the racist remarks of Mackenzie; she discovers for the first time the literal manifestation of such blatant racism. She is at first unconscious of her own classist and Orientalist attitudes, calling Powell Street "the ghetto." Sam accuses her, "Your kind only drop by when we turn out in kimonos," and he reminds her of her own limitations: "You're barking up the wrong tree kid. . . . You ought'a call the Gardeners' Association." As the Asian Canadian female reporter, Nancy is also in danger because she is seen as a pawn of the newspaper. The press is implicated for its historical participation in the paranoia that led to internment; Sam tells her, "We've been screwed by your kind before."

It is Sam's constant awareness of the scar—the internment that marks difference—that allows him to solve the case that the "token" Kadota and the "model minority" Nancy cannot solve. For the key to the case lies in remembering, keeping alive the consciousness of the wound made by the systematic racism of a corrupt authority. It is this historical trauma that connects Sam to the older community and affords him insider access to informants such as the eighty-two-year-old issei widow Mrs. Omoto, who "sees things nobody else does" but who would be discredited as a witness because she doesn't speak English.

The play, then, celebrates not only Sam's masculine prowess, but his service on behalf of a community. Although his fellow detective Chuck Chan chides him with "You run your business like a community service," the play clearly proposes this as ideal. Sam in turn commends Chuck to the audience: "He ran a classy operation downtown and still had time for the people over here." The play rewards the community of insiders— Rosie and other Japanese Americans whose collective knowledge is mined to solve the case. Moreover, the immediate Japanese Canadian community is extended as Chuck Chan and Nancy Wing join forces as allies, suggesting a larger pan-Asian collective. Their loyalties contrast strongly with Jameson's ease in betraying Mackenzie at the end of the play. Ultimately the failure of white supremacists is shown to be their failure to achieve community.

The play takes gleeful pleasure in defeating the "Sons of the Western Guard," who deem themselves "the saviours, the white blood cells, the first line of defense and the last hope of civilization!" But a more subtle lesson is also suggested: that such a victory comes only from vigilance and collective action. Those who have forgotten the racism of the past are at greatest risk of becoming victims of its resurgence. The Cherry Blossom Queen, the highly visible model minority, "some disco queen turned hakujin, hoping her crown would launch her into the mainstream modeling scene," is the easiest target for renewed anti-Asian sentiment. Her vulnerability is repeated in others, like Kadota, who sacrifices his sense for the hope of assimilation. In the end it is only Sam who, by constantly resurrecting the wounds of the past, can piece together the mystery to save them.

Earlier in this chapter I stressed the continued power of Chin's configuring of Asian American male identity and its accompanying tensions. His demand for the representation of Asian American males as fully figured heroic and intact sexual beings has left its mark on the plays of later writers. For instance, both Lawrence Yep's fast-talking con man in *Pay the Chinaman* and Alvin Eng's rapper the Goong Hay Kid, "the baddest dude . . . the defest C-town B-boy you ever saw," suggest constructions of Asian American masculinity based on similar principles.[7]

But there are also less obvious connections between what has been illustrated in this chapter and later plays by Asian Americans. Chin's play illustrates an extremely powerful trope: the scarring of the Asian American psyche as well as the physical body with the wounds of a historical racism. Shiomi's play *Yellow Fever* subtly shifts the construction of castration, implying that such a traumatic experience can be felt not exclusively and essentially by males but by a range of characters. Thus, this reading of *Yellow Fever* looks forward to the history plays to be examined in Chapter 5, plays about wounds of history as they are enacted for a variety of characters.

In an earlier chapter on the politics of dramatic realism, I asked for the admission of other models of the relation between spectator and play, models that would replace uniform perspectives with perspectives that are shifting and partial. I hoped to complicate notions of a single type of Asian American spectator and to suggest different possibilities of dramatic perception and cognition. In a similar vein, our responses to the plays discussed in this chapter cannot be distributed neatly along gender lines, in terms of simply identifying with characters as they are "male" or "female." In particular, Chin's work, however outdated or chauvinistic it may seem, complicates the idea of Asian American maleness more than it resolves it. In doing so, it asks for a complex rethinking of how gender, as inseparable from ethnicity and race, is reconstructed in the theater.

4

The Seduction of the Stereotype

A stereotype can be understood as the product of a historical relation of power. As I suggested in Chapter 1, the stereotype has become part and parcel of the exploitation and marginalization of Asian Americans, a means of justifying racist acts. Stereotypes in popular culture and art enact a violent dismemberment that focuses attention on particular body parts and features (in the case of Asians, eyes, noses, and hair, as well as skin) by highlighting or visually severing them from the rest of the body. This dismemberment preserves the fantasy of the oppressor's self as unified, coherent, orderly, and rational. As Homi Bhabha compellingly writes, "Black skin splits under the racist gaze, displaced into signs of bestiality, genitalia, grotesquerie, which reveal the phobic myth of undifferentiated whole white body" ("Mimicry" 92). Produced and sustained by such a demand, the stereotype then affects how the "Other" is seen within the systems of representation by which individuals and communities define themselves.

Stereotypes often outlast the specific historical conditions that first produced them. This longevity is no doubt due not only to the lasting impressions that such intensified and exaggerated signs produce, but also to the extent to which stereotypes bombard the sign system, leading to what Judith Butler calls an "oversaturation of the visual field" (17). As a consequence, the "racial etiquette" becomes conditioned by these grotesque images; the stereotype passes into common knowledge or becomes "fact" without contestation. In the trial of the four white police officers accused of the racist beating of Rodney King, the videotape of King being brutally beaten seemed irrefutable evidence of cruel and excessive force. However, when replayed frame by frame in the context of the courtroom, the videotape yielded another set of images altogether: the stereotype of the black man posing a threat to the four armed officers. As Butler notes, what seems to be authentic "seeing" is in fact influenced by the storehouse of stereotyped representations imprinted in memory, forming a visual field that is "not neutral to the question of race" but "is itself a racial formation, an episteme, hegemonic and forceful" (17).

Such a field of perception, of course, is more than simply visual; its histrionic perception is particularly relevant to the theater. When the racialized Other must deal with self-representation in the theater, the performative language he or she has recourse to is haunted by stereotypes, and this performative language is not only verbal but has to do with the language of the body as well. Because skin color is often associated with stereotype, the question of self-representation becomes remarkably difficult.

Until recently the history of Asian characters on the American stage was dominated by the repetition of stereotypes and their subsequent supersaturation of signification. Asian American performers and playwrights work in the context of this difficult legacy. I have already addressed one strategy used to highlight the damage inflicted by stereotypical representation on "real people"—insisting on an alternative realism that offers other means of representation and visibility. But a more difficult problem—the fascination with stereotype, even on the part of those who reject it—must also be given some thought. Stereotypes of Asian Americans are no longer simply the seductive images of the Orient rendered for consumption by white audiences. Instead, they have become woven into the complex fantasies Asian Americans have about identity, community, and gender. That Asian Americans enact Orientalized stereotypes is often interpreted as a form of misguided internalization of cultural oppression, as ideological brainwashing rather than a conscious decision or choice. But this only partially accounts for the complexity of responses when Asian Americans articulate an ambivalence about the desire felt for the body-as-stereotype.

Describing her participation in a protest organized against *Miss Saigon,* Yoko Yoshikawa notes her interesting response to the opening moments of the show:

> The opening number was dazzling—and loud. The musical opens in a brothel in Saigon, where prostitutes vie for the title, *Miss Saigon.* U.S. soldiers buy raffle tickets; Miss Saigon will be the prize. But I was not following the songs—this lusty dance of glistening legs and dark breasts, of ogling eyes and lathered lips in uniform mesmerized me. It pulled me in, as soft porn will. (277)

Although she is quick to add, "But I also felt sickened and alienated," there is remarkable ambivalence in this description. Yoshikawa recognizes that "the show was designed to seduce, flooding the sense with a 3-D fantasy," and although she emphasizes that such fantasy is "specifically targeted at a heterosexual western man's pleasure center," she herself, an Asian American lesbian, clearly also felt the pull of the performance, the seduction of the stereotype. This moment invites difficult questions. How do we understand this controversial impulse, this fascination with the excessiveness of the stereotype? How, moreover, do the performances of stereotypes manifest a unique theatricality, one that might in fact be employed by Asian American dramatists?

As I have suggested earlier, realistic plays operate to counter these exaggerated images by replacing stereotypical characterizations. But two other works by Asian Americans, Philip Gotanda's *Yankee Dawg You Die* and David Henry Hwang's *M. Butterfly*, employ a very different strategy; they illustrate the ways in which Asian American playwrights might incorporate stereotypes, using rather than ignoring their theatrical power. In *Yankee Dawg*, the two actors Vincent and Bradley enjoy as well as critique the stereotypical Hollywood roles for Asian men. In *M. Butterfly*, the spy Song dupes the Orientalist Gallimard into believing that he is a submissive "butterfly." Although both plays go to great lengths to make the playing of such stereotypes self-conscious, they also rely on their power and intensity.

Reappropriation of stereotypes is a dubious process, as is apparent from the critical reception of these two plays. Some critics applaud these plays' postmodern subversions of identity categories, others argue that the repetition of the stereotype necessarily promotes and perpetuates a racist history ingrained in representation. The relative commercial success of these plays has fueled this critical debate. Before reaching a commercial stage, *Yankee Dawg You Die* was first produced as a workshop performance by East West Players in 1986 and at the Bay Area Playwrights Festival in 1987. It subsequently premiered at the Berkeley Repertory Theatre in 1988 under the direction of Sharon Ott and has had numerous subsequent productions across the country. *M. Butterfly* was first produced at the National Theatre in Washington, D.C., and later opened on Broadway at the Eugene O'Neill Theatre, directed by John Dexter. In 1988 it won a Tony Award for best Broadway play, the John Gassner Award for best American play, and the Drama Desk Award for best new play. In 1993 David Cronenberg directed a film version of *M. Butterfly* starring Jeremy Irons and John Lone.

Although *M. Butterfly* has received more scholarly and critical attention than *Yankee Dawg*, the same interpretative strategies can be applied to both plays. Influential readings by Dorinne Kondo and Karen Shimakawa argue that *M. Butterfly* destabilizes rigid identity categories based on gender and ethnicity. Kondo finds that *M. Butterfly* "undermines a notion of unitary identity based on a space of inner truth and the plentitude of referential meaning" and allows ethnicity and gender to "become mobile positions on a field of power relations" (6, 7). Shimakawa argues that the play presents the actor Song as empowered in his adroit playing of many roles, to the extent that he "confounds *all* expectations, refuses to fit neatly into *any* Baudrillardian spaces" (361). Both critics applaud how Song, the actor and spy, exploits Gallimard's fantasy of the stereotypical Oriental woman as passive, seductive, and submissive, juxtaposing a "square" Gallimard and a "liberated" Song. Kondo concludes that Gallimard, trapped within categories, cannot appreciate the freedom offered by Song—the possibility of "different cultural possibilities, blurred boundaries, and rearrangements of power" (21).

What we must question in both these readings is whether the gendered, ethnicized stereotype, because it is not only determined but *overdetermined* by identity categories, can be treated as any other theatrical sign. Both Kondo and Shimakawa assume that a stereotype is compromised when its performance is made self-conscious—perhaps as a means of empowering the actor—and taken out of the realm of something that passes for truth. But can a stereotype be decentered—can its racism be neutralized—that easily? Such a concern is articulated in *Yankee Dawg You Die*, as the established actor Vincent claims insistently that his roles are only *acted*, that they mean nothing except in their consummate professionalism: "I never turn down a part." The younger Bradley disputes this claim, pointing out that in the case of the stereotype, the choice of roles does have immense social meaning: "Everytime you do any old stereotypic role just to pay the bills, someone has to pay for it—and it ain't you. *No.* It's some Asian kid innocently walking home. 'Hey, it's a Chinaman gook!' 'Rambo, Rambo, Rambo!'" Both Kondo and Shimaka recognize that the stereotype—a theatrical sign that is violently and rigidly oversignified—presents particular problems; both wonder, "Must one reinscribe stereotypes in order to subvert them?" (Kondo 27; Shimakawa 362).

James Moy has effectively argued that the stereotype always carries the weight of its ugly past. Moy finds both *Yankee Dawg* and *M. Butterfly* problematic precisely because of their reliance on stereotypes. Although seeming to "jar" their audiences, they use "disfigured" Asian characters to "represent or speak on behalf of the Chinese or Asians." He finds that although "both plays seem to be scathing indictments of the Western need to demean, stereotype, and psychologically control the Orient and its representations," their popularity is still testimony to the ways in which "the authors of these pieces have somehow managed to neutralize or deflect their explicit attack on Anglo-American sensibilities" ("Repositioning" 84). Moy criticizes these plays' lack of "authentic" representations and the absence of positive heterosexual male characters, and makes a compelling argument for why we should be troubled by the stereotypes that these plays exploit for their theatrical power.

We should not forget the very real and overdetermined nature of the stereotype as sign. It is not a simple matter to deconstruct stereotypes, as Hwang suggests he means to do by calling *M. Butterfly* "a deconstructivist *Madame Butterfly*" (afterword, *M. Butterfly* 95). At the same time, it is also insufficient to describe the use of stereotypes in these two plays as simply another version of exotic fare for white audiences. To understand their complex reappropriations, we must speculate further on the stereotype and the peculiar nature of its oppression. As Homi Bhabha suggests, stereotyping "is not the setting up of a false image which becomes the scapegoat of discriminatory practices" but rather "a much more ambivalent text of projection and introjection, metaphoric and metonymic strategies, displacement, overdetermination, guilt, aggressivity" ("Other Question" 33–34). I propose that rather than blithely dismissing the violent power of the stereotype as theatrical sign or setting it up as a "scapegoat," we explore this "ambivalent text" in more detail.

Homi Bhabha's formulation of the colonial stereotype as fetish is especially useful in reassessing these plays and understanding what is at the heart of the critical conflict they inspire. What is most useful about

Bhabha's characterization is his insistence that the "colonial stereotype is a complex, ambivalent, contradictory mode of representation, as anxious as it is assertive" ("Other Question" 22). Acts of stereotyping can be read not only as they straightforwardly enact a Eurocentric oppression of racial Others, but also as they are indicative of a more peculiar anxiety that arises from situations of contact.

For Bhabha, stereotypes originate in deeply rooted impulses of denial and disavowal; the racial stereotype as fetish, as opposed to the more private sexual fetish, is unique in that it is "recognised as 'common knowledge' in a range of cultural, political, historical discourses, and plays a public part in the racial drama that is enacted every day in colonial societies" ("Other Question" 30). He suggests that the violent excesses and incessant repetitions of the stereotype are indicative of this anxiousness, stemming from the deep instability of the colonial position, its "urgent need" to preserve distinctions, to play out differences between itself and "others." Thus, skin, as "a signifier of discrimination, must be produced or processed as visible" not just once but many times ("Other Question" 31). Bhabha opens up this reiterated confirmation of difference through recourse to stereotypes in the following way:

> As a form of splitting and multiple belief, the "stereotype" requires, for its successful signification, a continual and repetitive chain of other stereotypes. The process by which the metaphoric "masking" is inscribed on a lack which must then be concealed gives the stereotype both its fixity and its phantasmatic quality—the *same old* stories of the Negro's animality, the Coolie's inscrutability or the stupidity of the Irish *must* be told (compulsively) again and afresh, and are differently gratifying and terrifying each time. ("Other Question" 29)

The stereotype emerges from the anxiety of the colonial relation, where the white must continually disavow the native Other in the repeated dismemberment of stereotype. For Bhabha, the stereotype is always problematic for its users, because it exposes the uncertainty in the power dynamic between the white self that wants to imagine itself as coherent, and the Other, which to some extent eludes the full control of the master. This anxiety is manifested in both in the violence and the repetitive quality of stereotypes. Thus, stereotypes become performative acts in the service of creating and perpetuating the skin's "proof" of racial difference, which, much like sexual difference, must be constantly reiterated in order to quell a deeply rooted ideological tension. It is this tension, I argue, that gives the stereotype its uniquely powerful theatricality.

Bhabha's description of the stereotype suggests a means by which the Other invoked in the stereotype might turn the tables by accentuating the stereotype's anxiety, its implicit instability. Although stereotypes cannot be reappropriated without evoking their racist history, they can nonetheless reveal in their performances the inner dynamics of this history, which already suggest the potential for its disruption. To do this, one must highlight or foreground the anxiety inherent in the performance of the stereotype by overperforming its already exaggerated qualities, pushing violence into hyperbolic slapstick, or forcing its repetition until it becomes monotonous.

We can extend Bhabha's terms to examine more specifically who performs stereotypes of Asians and for what purpose. In the early development of "Oriental types" on stage, Asian actors were conspicuously absent; white actors developed a complex set of codes for the presentation of the Oriental Other. A certain anxiety is already apparent in the repetition of stereotypes such as Ah Sin and Fu Manchu; the representational control exacted over the image manifests the political and social tensions felt over contact with the "heathen Chinee" or the "yellow peril." These are larger social fears that must be assuaged by the constant reenactment of violent images. When the Asian performer takes over the performance of the Oriental stereotype, a much more uneasy dynamic emerges. The traditional seduction of the stereotype for the white spectator in its degradation of the threatening Oriental may in fact be to a great extent preserved. But the presence of the literal Asian body also has the potential to provoke another reaction, in its apparent excess of the role in which it is placed. There is an aspect of the performance that is no longer under full spectatorial control, that cannot remain a codified sign of the Oriental; the actor now embodies something else as well. Perhaps even the actor's skill in playing the stereotype might be threatening.

The response to the playing of the Oriental by the Asian or Asian American actor is also complicated when the spectator is Asian American. As I mentioned earlier, Asian Americans might experience the pleasure of self-recognition even in these limited roles. Jessica Hagedorn describes a vicarious identification with the tough Jade Cobra girls in Michael Cimino's 1985 movie *Year of the Dragon* as "defiant, fabulous images" who unrepentantly curse the protagonist, played by Mickey Rourke, for gunning them down. Hagedorn observes that, given a choice of only stereotypes—submissive, victimized Oriental flowers or aggressive dragon ladies—she would choose the latter: "give me the demonic any day" (74). This pleasure of recognition of the Asian body, even in the playing of stereotypes, is one that often confuses the reading of stereotypes strictly as racial oppression.

Thus, in the reenactment of the stereotype by Asian Americans, the initial anxiety of encounter is intensified. It is troubled first by the presence of the literal body of the Asian American actor, a body that threatens to exceed its caricatured role and its assigned function as projection. Second, it is unsettled by the declared presence of the Asian American audience, whose response denies the possibility of a monolithic "white" spectatorial position. The possibility of playwrights destabilizing the racial stereotype as a sign might well take advantage of this heightened anxiety and the vulnerability it reveals.

With this in mind, we can look again at the seemingly irreconcilable positions taken by critics of *Yankee Dawg* and *M. Butterfly*. Hwang's and Gotanda's versions of stereotype do deconstruct old versions of the stereotype—but through reenacting their repetition and violence, not through defusing them into playful or neutral signs. Far from revealing stereotypes to be without "real" effects, these plays emphasize their over-determined, literal, and pervasive manifestations. Seen in these terms, Hwang and Gotanda create versions of stereotype with undiminished powers. They reproduce them in all their ugliness, anxiety, and seductive-ness. But they also register an intensification of anxiety as the stereotype is performed by the Asian body. Rather than simply do violence to the stereotype, these plays expose what is already inherently violent in the performance of stereotype.

Both plays engage in similar strategies. First, they rob the stereotype of its power to substitute for the natural being and reveal it as a social construct, the product of specific historical and social circumstances. The stereotype becomes an enactment rather than a state of being, for the characters are explicitly actors, playing stereotypes by choice or out of compulsion. This is not a matter of neutralizing the power of the stereo-type by reducing it to "mere performance" ("I was only acting"). Rather, such historicizing works to provide a specific context for these perfor-mances, thus revealing the anxiety inherent in the historical encounters that call them into being. Second, both plays take advantage of the ste-reotype's inability to encompass the body of the Asian Other by overplay-ing the stereotype and thus revealing its inability to contain the excesses of the actor's body. Finally, both plays openly acknowledge the possibility of Asian American audiences and play to their possible identifications with even stereotypical characters.

Yankee Dawg You Die

By creating characters as working actors who discuss their craft, Philip Gotanda gives some historical context to the stereotypes that dominate the representation of Asians and Asian Americans in American theater, film, and television. Gotanda frames stereotypes specifically as the different actors' roles that Vincent and Bradley are compelled to take on. Several moments, such as the opening "marquee" in which both actors display themselves as leading men, are self-consciously stagy; in subsequent scenes the characters move quickly through different kinds of characterizations. Both the characters Vincent and Bradley (and, in turn, the actors playing them) demonstrate not only that they cannot be reduced to any one of these characterizations, but also that they are skilled professional actors, able to perform a variety of parts convincingly. Such a demonstration of skill reinforces that Vincent and Bradley fail to get major roles because of systematic racism in the industry, not because of their inability to play difficult parts. Their rational discussion about the history of these roles also helps contextualize these stereotypes. The idealistic Bradley experiences firsthand the discrimination still rampant in Hollywood, where color-blind casting is a myth. His eloquent criticisms set the tone for the play's castigation of Hollywood's practice of "Orientalizing" Asian American actors. Bradley and Vincent discuss at length both stereotypes and those productions that use them. As an example, Bradley rejects Mickey Rourke as a hero for playing in the pervasively anti-Asian movie *Year of the Dragon.*

Yet Hollywood stereotypes are not confined to discussion but come to life through the course of the play. Gotanda's use of stereotypes allows the actors moments of energy and vitality in the perverse enjoyment of these roles. It is in the performance as well as the critique of these stereotypes that the characters achieve their theatrical life. Gotanda recalls that the genesis of the play lay in the playing of a game with Eric Hayashi:

We got into a discussion about old World War II movies and soon found ourselves trying to remember our favorite "classic lines" the evil Japanese soldier would invariably hiss out in "Hollywood Orientalese." The one phrase that seemed continually to pop into mind was "Yankee dog you die." Whether that was ever really said or it was a kind of distillation of all those silly Sargeant Moto diatribes, I'm not sure. But we soon found ourselves locked in a raucous game of dueling stereotypes. Eric would say "Yankee dog you die" in thick Hollywood Orientalese, then I would say "Yankee dog you die" with an even thicker and more ridiculous accent, each continuing to challenge the other till our performances had reached grotesque proportions. In other words, our performances were now perfect for the portrayal of Asians in American movies. (79–80)

Significant moments in *Yankee Dawg You Die* point to a similarly exuberant overplaying of grotesque proportions. In the first part of *Yankee Dawg* the older actor Vincent replays a scene from his old song-and-dance days. He asks Bradley to join in, and Bradley, momentarily caught off-guard, does so. The presentation is clearly demeaning, but Bradley is "*swept along by the enthusiasm of Vincent*" into singing the outrageously stereotyped song with a chorus of "So Solly Cholly" in a high-pitched falsetto. For several minutes the two whirl around the stage, with, as the stage directions indicate, "*Vincent singing and tap dancing with Bradley in tow singing in a high pitched falsetto. Both are getting more and more involved, acting out more and more outrageous stereotypes.*" Bradley comes to his critical senses and angrily calls a halt to this playing, telling Vincent "You're acting like a Chinese Steppin Fetchit." The most deeply ambivalent, disturbing, and powerful moments in the play are those when the Asian American actors display a marked attraction for playing "Fetchits," and share with us as audience the thrill of being inside what is deeply shameful.

Gotanda both captures this shame and provokes an alternative reading of it, a reading that is centered on the body of the Asian American actor. If the field of viewing was traditionally saturated with white performers of Asian stereotypes, for the Asian American to perform at all is associated with the unnatural. Thus, even though Vincent's performances fall within the realm of crude Asian stereotypes and he is not allowed outside the role of the emasculated sidekick or villain (the only role in which he "gets the girl" falls prey to editing on late-night television),[1] his Asian American body has the potential to disrupt the field of what is "natural" with a certain illicit pleasure. Bradley's comment on seeing Vincent is telling:

> You know, Mr. Chang, when I was growing up you were sort of my hero. No, really, you were. I mean, I'd be watching TV and suddenly you'd appear in some old film or an old "Bonanza" or something. And at first something would always jerk inside. Whoa, what's this? This is weird, like watching my own family on TV. It's like the first time I made it with an Asian girl—up to then only white girls. They seemed more outgoing—I don't know—more normal. With this Asian girl it was like doing it with my sister. It was weird. Everything about her was familiar. Her face, her skin, the sound of her voice, the way she smelled. It was like having sex with someone in my own family. That's how it was when you'd come on the TV. (92)

This speech provides insight into the adulation of Vincent both by Bradley and within the Asian American community. The figure of Vincent performing, even as the hated stereotype, takes on great importance, signifying the potential for disruption of a performance field dominated by whites. Even though the role of the stereotype is familiar and detestable, the casting of the Asian body is enough to ensure a kind of welcome disruption, an illicit pleasure that sets up a key tension between stereotype and performer. It is only within this framework that we can understand Vincent's tribute to the performers of a past generation, who performed on the "Chop Suey Circuit." The fact that they performed at all, Vincent insists, is heroic; their performance of stereotypes must be interpreted in the context of their historical position as individuals lacking choices.

These performances by Asian American actors and the moments of complex identification implicit in them have implications for Asian American spectators as well as white ones. The play emphasizes a possible alternative to Hollywood, a community of theater and film run by Asian Americans. Gotanda suggests that the play was written as "my tribute to Asian American actors" (80). Bradley's initial success as an actor is enabled by Asian American theaters and independent filmmakers and their new recognition by critics, if not box offices. But the play also suggests that such a community began years ago; Vincent proudly tells how he and his dance partner were applauded by Anna May Wong and Sessue Hayakawa. Bradley's humorous monologue enacts the young man's wishful thinking that Neil Sedaka might be really "a goddamned Buddhahead"; he explains to the bewildered Vincent that the piece was written by a sansei playwright, showing "the need we have for legitimate heroes." The play emphasizes that the Asian American community not only produces its own work, but also sees and values the performances of Asian Americans differently. In this alternative setting a recontextualization of the Asian American body and its possibilities for performance—even for performing stereotypes—can take place.

This hyperbolic playing of stereotype is newly framed within the Asian American community. The Asian American actor's knowledge that he is playing to Asian American spectators accentuates the parodying of Oriental stereotypes. In playing the "Yankee dog you die" game, Bradley and Vincent overperform the already exaggerated qualities of the stereotype, pushing violence into hyperbolic slapstick. In Vincent's revisiting of his role as the loyal sidekick Saki, the tragic scene turns into hilarious exaggeration as it becomes obvious that both Bradley and Vincent have memorized each melodramatic gesture and cliché. Even if stereotypes begin as less than complimentary, they can be re-used against those who originate them as a source of oppression and marginalization; unpleasant though they may be, they provide a common vocabulary for the two actors, whose training is otherwise so different. Bradley and Vincent both enjoy their participation in an Asian American theater piece in which Godzilla takes the side of the young Asian American boy to stamp on the "fancy pants girl" who called him a "dirty Jap." In an interlude, Gotanda construes the actor Bruce Lee as a figure that promises masculine power within the Asian American body; Vincent, in the disciplined, graceful practice of tai chi, suddenly breaks into violent screams and kicks that physically articulate the frustration he feels.[2]

The play suggests that within the Asian American community, stereotypes might be reappropriated and their violence turned into humor. If stereotypes are histrionic ghosts, they can be turned toward revenge. However, this is not to say that a stereotype can ever be simply taken on as one of many arbitrary roles. The performance of stereotype is never liberating; it can never be separated from its historical racism, particularly when such racism is still rampant. To contextualize stereotypes as human constructions rather than essential beings, *Yankee Dawg* must insist on a division between the theatrical and the real, must insist that the actor has a coherent self distinct from the stereotype he plays. Gotanda maintains this distinction even as he gently parodies it; Bradley's improvisation recalls an acid trip in which he saw "cows that have a double life": "the dumb facade they show to the outside world and their true cow selves that they show to one another when they are alone." But the play also exposes Vincent's fallacy that his is a self that can remain untouched by social practice. In the play, boundaries—between actor and stereotypical role, between real and theatrical action—are consistently eroded.

The focus on boundaries is evident in Vincent's insistence that he does not want to be part of the Asian American community and in his arguments about the need for artistic freedom untouched by political correctness. He embraces the fiction of the actor as having a neutral body, able to perform "all the classics," and of the actor's freedom as an open choice of juicy roles. He further attempts to make distinctions between the roles he performs on stage and his offstage behavior, insisting to his lover Kenneth that as a "leading man," he cannot reveal his homosexuality. But Vincent's denial of what he feels to be his less than perfect profile ultimately leads to frustration and isolation. Even as he tries to preserve a distinction between the performing self and the private self, he is forced to the realization of his own exploitation, with the dream that he is being asked to "fuck" himself. Any argument that Vincent can make about an actor's freedom of choice in accepting roles dissolves as it becomes evident how little he himself has been able to choose; his policy of never turning down a role was born out of necessity.

The play exposes the fallacy that an actor's actions can exist in the realm of pure and universal art, separate from the politics that inform stage presentation. The dissolving boundary between theater and life is not abstract philosophy here; instead it is an everyday fact, one inseparable from the politics of race. The play emphasizes the trauma of the confusion of the real body with stereotypes disseminated through theater, film, and media by demonstrating how the self is immediately impacted by the stereotypical role. Bradley cannot separate the rehearsal of *Macbeth* from a murder he committed in the past in retaliation for a racial slur aimed at his girlfriend. Both Vincent and Bradley dream of their bodies being consumed, suggesting not only any actor's nightmare of selling his body as product, but the Asian American actor's specific anxiety over playing those roles made palatable to mainstream white audiences.

Through this relentless interchange of reality and representation, the play moves toward an affirmation of the actor's need to gain control of his own visibility—not to erase himself, but to reconcile self with role both physically and psychically. The merger of self and role, the erasure of boundaries, becomes evident in the transformation of the opening monologue as it is replayed in the closing scenes. At the beginning of the

play Vincent acts the villainous, heavily accented Sergeant Moto threatening a white American prisoner of war. In the closing scenes the monologue reappears twice, first as watched by Vincent on late-night television, then repeated at the end. But the final iteration of this monologue
becomes a different kind of performance altogether. Vincent gradually
drops his accent and begins to perform with *"great passion"* the same
words, turning them into a moving revelation of personal frustration:
"Why can't you hear what I'm saying? Why can't you see me as I really
am?" Moving from stereotypical role to revelatory statement, Vincent
places his acting ability in the service of creating a different persona for
the Asian American on stage, transforming a once stereotypical role into
a dignified, sympathetic character. The ending suggests a new fusion of
the self and the role whereby the Asian American actor is freed to inform
his stage presence with offstage experience. Vincent finally decides to
turn down the lucrative role of "Yang the evil one" in favor of working in
a low-budget film made by an Asian American director, a Japanese
American history "where I get to play my father."

The play's ending allows these characters only limited options, but a
choice nonetheless: to perform with integrity within the alternative Asian
American community, or to choose highly visible and well-paying but
despicably stereotypical roles in Hollywood movies. Although the ending
leaves Bradley's fate uncertain—desperate for work, he gets a nose job
and decides to take the monstrous role of Yang's son, "half Chinese and
half rock," in a high-paying science fiction film—it also evokes a community in the friendship between these two men, thus maintaining the
connection of Asian American actor and Asian American audience.

M. Butterfly

Vincent. You are walking along, minding your own business, your
head filled with poems and paintings—when what do you see com-

ing your way? Some ugly "rumor," dressed in your clothes, stagger-
ing down the street impersonating you. And it is not you but no one
seems to care. They want this impersonator—who is drinking from
a brown paper bag, whose pant zipper is down to here and flapping
in the wind—to be you. Why? They like it, it gives them glee. They
like the lie. And the more incensed you become, the more real it
seems to grow. Like some monster in a nightmare. If you ignore it,
you rob it of its strength. It will soon disappear. (*Beat*) You will live.
We all go to bed thinking, "The pain is so great, I will not last
through the night." (*Beat*) We wake up. Alive. C'est dommage. (*Yankee Dawg You Die* 90)

In *Yankee Dawg You Die*, Hollywood punishes both Vincent and
Bradley with its thirst for grotesque "rumors" and "impersonators" that
usurp the place of the actor both on and off the stage. At the same time,
the play optimistically suggests that performing the stereotype can reveal
the vulnerability of the system that produces it. Several of the playwright's strategies allow this to happen. First is the way in which the
stereotype is contextualized as "enactment" rather than "being" insofar as
the characters are presented as actors, compelled to enact the unnatural
stereotype. Even though performance is not necessarily considered a conscious choice, its divorce from "being" allows the possibility of critical
perspective. Second, the enactments of the Oriental stereotype by the
Asian body further trouble this performance of stereotype because the
Asian body has the potential to push the stereotype into excess or demonstrate it as one of many possible roles. Third, the play acknowledges
the possibility of the Asian American spectator, or an alternative community including people of color, to give new meaning and purpose to the
actor.

Each of these strategies is used in Hwang's *M. Butterfly*. The stereotypes of the play are self-consciously enacted by each of the characters;

moreover, the entire play is structured as a reenactment in Gallimard's imagination rather than a "true event," thus ensuring that perspective is even further mediated. The Asian American body of the actor is by no means conflated with the stereotypical role of the submissive Butterfly character; rather, the fluidity with which Song changes character suggests enormous power, a hyperbolic playing that again complicates the equation of Oriental stereotype with Asian. And because the Asian character is given not only the most interesting role, but also mastery over the gullible Gallimard, there is an implied appeal to the Asian American spectator. Song's slangy language in the play also seems to speak more directly and resonantly to an "insider" audience, answering directly some of the stereotypical assumptions about the Asian character. Song immediately throws cold water on Gallimard's assumptions that his body can pass for a Japanese woman's: "The Japanese used hundreds of our people for medical experiments during the war, you know. But I gather such an irony is lost on you." Song from the beginning dissects his own performance, outlining the terms that allow it to be Gallimard's "favorite fantasy":

> *Song.* Consider it this way: what would you say if a blonde homecoming queen fell in love with a short Japanese businessman? He treats her cruelly, then goes home for three years, during which time she prays to his picture and turns down marriage from a young Kennedy. Then, when she learns he has remarried, she kills herself. Now, I believe you would consider this girl to be a deranged idiot, correct? But because it's an Oriental who kills herself for a Westerner—ah!—you find it beautiful.
> *Silence.*
> *Gallimard.* Yes . . . well . . . I see your point . . . (17)

Inseparable from these strategies, however, is a disturbing emphasis on the attractiveness of the stereotype. Even in *Yankee Dawg,* Vincent and

Bradley describe the enactment of stereotypes in language rife with metaphors of illicit sexuality; performing the stereotype is an unnatural act
that holds a guilty pleasure. Watching Vincent on television is for Bradley
"like having sex with my sister." Yet Gotanda's *Yankee Dawg You Die*
depicts the marketing of these stereotypes to the public by unwilling actors. *M. Butterfly* more problematically emphasizes the seductive possibilities of the stereotype, not only for Gallimard but also for Song and
the other characters. *M. Butterfly* is much more explicitly about the
erotics of the stereotype, the fulfillment of desire through the performance of the image.

Examining the play as it parodies rather than perpetuates the stereotype yields perhaps the safest interpretation. The play does ridicule the
stereotype of the Asian woman as a submissive butterfly who sacrifices
herself for the cad Pinkerton, in the first-act summary of Puccini's opera,
Song's clever commentary, and the ironic staging of the first sexual
encounter between Song and Gallimard. However, these moments are
themselves interspersed with a more straightforward, and more disturbing, playing of stereotype. The first rendition of the Butterfly story, when
the characters lip-sync Puccini's opera, is clearly hyperbolic. Gallimard
translates the duet "The Whole World Over": "The whole world over, the
Yankee travels, casting his anchor wherever he wants. Life's not worth
living unless he can win the hearts of the fairest maidens, then hotfoot it
off the premises ASAP." Marc and Comrade Chin play their roles as
Sharpless and Suzuki without enthusiasm; Chin's version of covering the
floor with flowers is to trudge onstage and drop a lone flower. But their
humorous lack of enthusiasm for the illusion contrasts strongly with the
intensity of Song's acting. While the other characters openly exaggerate
the highlights of Puccini, Song in his exaggerated role remains, for the
moment, without irony.

Reading the play as a satirical reversal accounts for only particular
moments of the play.[3] Such a reading is itself unsettled by Gallimard's

asking for the audience's sympathy as an "ideal audience" and by showing us the substance of his "mind's eye": the emphasis is on rendering his
actions intelligible, not on dismissing him as stupid. Reading the play as a
pure parody is also dislocated by the framing of Gallimard's suicide as
tragic. The play seems to demand not only some sympathy for Gallimard,
but also that the spectators too experience the stereotype of the butterfly
as a seductive theatrical experience as well as something that we hold out
at arm's length. Although M. Butterfly deconstructs stereotypes, it does so
by evoking the power that the stereotype still wields.

To explore this reading of the stereotype further, we can think of M.
Butterfly as a work that not only directly parodies its fictional, theatrical,
and operatic forebears (for this commentary is only part of the play), but
also, in its incessant imitation of those forebears, speaks to the relentless
desire to see the stereotype recreated. The play explores how, for each of
the characters, human desire and the formation of selfhood are rooted in
stereotype. As we consider Gallimard's encounters with Butterfly, and indeed the other characters' location of desire in the stereotype, we become
implicated in these desires through histrionic perception.

According to Homi Bhabha, the colonial situation gives rise to a form
of "mimicry": "the desire for a reformed, recognizable Other as a subject
of a difference that is almost the same but not quite"("Mimicry" 86; emphasis in the original). The discourse that seeks to "normalize" the colonial state or subject produces the effect of imitation, but at the same time
it "mocks its power to be a model, that power which supposedly makes it
imitable." Because it "repeats rather than re-presents," the "diminishing
perspective" of mimicry exposes a certain anxiety inherent in the encounters that produce it. Any ability of the stereotype to "impersonate"
or stand in for a real body is troubled by the body's propensity to move
outside the realm of stereotype. The unsettling presence of the Other it
supposedly represents has the potential to disrupt the stereotype as the
partial representation that mocks its own attempts to imitate.

The successive parodic versions of the butterfly stereotype in *M. Butterfly* also suggest instances of "*trompe l'oeil*, irony, mimicry, and repetition" ("Mimicry" 85) of the colonial situation, even in their genesis. Hwang's play is based on a set of "originals" that are themselves varied in form: a novel (Julien Viaud, under the pen name Pierre Loti, wrote *Madam Chrysantheme* in 1887), a short story (John Luther Long's *Madame Butterfly*, written in 1898), a stage play (David Belasco's collaboration with Long, in 1900), and an opera (Giacomo Puccini's *Madama Butterfly*, written in 1904). In his description of his initial conception, inspired by the newspaper account of the affair between French diplomat Bouriscot and Peking Opera star Shi, Hwang says that he neither read the story nor saw the play or opera, but took the idea of the diplomat and the butterfly from a cultural stereotype: "speaking of an Asian woman, we would sometimes say, 'She's pulling a Butterfly,' which meant playing the submissive Oriental number" (afterward, *M. Butterfly* 95). When he heard Puccini's opera in the course of writing *M. Butterfly*, he was relieved that it seemed to suit these patterns precisely: "Sure enough, when I purchased the record, I discovered it contained a wealth of sexist and racist clichés, reaffirming my faith in Western culture" (afterward, *M. Butterfly* 95). No one original source for Hwang's play can be identified, but each bears a familial resemblance to the other versions, generating a mimetic discourse that seeks to reaffirm the differences between Western and Oriental. In fact, the many incarnations of Butterfly and Pinkerton implicitly reenact the continued situations of encounter and the anxiousness they hold for white Americans: the influx of Chinese as cheap, expendable labor, rivalry with imperialistic Japan, the threat of communism in Southeast Asia, military failures in Vietnam. Each new version, of which the musical *Miss Saigon* is only the latest, comes at a time when "Asia" as an alien and threatening entity must be publicly addressed as symbolic. White America's attempts to comes to terms with Asia produce a mimetic discourse that repeatedly performs masculine authority as the imperialist Pinkerton and inscribes feminine lack and difference on the decorated body and submissive actions of Cio-Cio-San.

In its staging of multiple enactments, Hwang's play overtly exposes the desperate need to stabilize the myth of what Song describes as the "submissive Oriental woman and the cruel white man." Hwang's play enacts these stereotypes not as a singular instance but as constant repetition, as seen in the imaginative fusion of recollection and fantasy by the imprisoned Gallimard: "Alone in this cell, I sit night after night, watching our story play through my head." But each time Gallimard reproduces Butterfly and her Pinkerton, it is as a set of "identity effects" that, in their failure to be imitations—"almost the same but not quite"—mock the very situations that produce them. Song's disruptive performances interrupt Gallimard's ideal performance. Thus, until the end, when Gallimard himself takes on the role of the suicidal Butterfly, he can only fail in his attempts at reiteration.

The play stages many scenes of contact where bodies are figured as amorphous and sexual and racial boundaries are permeable. What is significant is how each of these moments incites the characters to project on one another and themselves an identifying difference; such moments are clearly filled with theatrical anxiety often signaled by humor. Gallimard's story is traumatic because it reveals a threatening state of nondifferentiation. Early in the play, an assured, cosmopolitan trio at a cocktail party deride Gallimard's gullibility, his inability to recognize what is to them obvious: *la différence.* Yet, because the remainder of the play revels in gender's ambiguity rather than its obviousness, the three characters' facile dismissal of Gallimard's stupidity makes any complicity in their laughter more nervous than secure.

Hwang reiterates this anxiety when Gallimard revisits his youthful explorations of sexuality, first in turning down the fantasy of Marc's orgy in which a bevy of females strip and engage in anonymous sex in a pool, and then in describing Isabelle as his first experience of sexual intercourse. Gallimard's lack of desire in these encounters might have a number of explanations: his own insecurity, fear of aggressive females (as with Isabelle, whose orgasmic pleasure exceeds his), and perhaps, as David Eng suggests, a closeted homosexual preference for the male body.[4] But his disengagement is also linked to the description of these encounters as anonymous, impersonal, and lacking in difference. Marc's orgy, where it "doesn't matter whose ass is between whose legs, whose teeth are sinking into who," suggests faceless encounters of undifferentiated skin meeting skin. His lack of interest in Isabelle seems related both to her being a more active partner and to her undirected sexuality: Marc agrees that she is a "lousy lay," "there was a lot of energy there, but you never knew what she was doing with it." Both encounters, while marked as heterosexual, nonetheless fail to differentiate between kinds of skin, and therefore, for Gallimard, are erotically lacking.

For Gallimard, sexual desire and the erotic are based on specific differentiation on the basis of both gender and race. His desire for Song's Cio-Cio-San is precisely a desire to see himself as powerful in relationship to the female; later in life Gallimard is also put off by Renee's liberated sexuality and his wife's suggestion that he is infertile. But it also relies on more than a touch of racial differentiation. This seems maintained in his response to the fantasy striptease of women in pornographic magazines. Power conflated with gender may be claimed in pornographic magazines: "[M]y body shook. Not with lust—no, with power. Here were women— a shelfful—who would do exactly as I wanted." But even in this case, he loses his desire at the moment when she offers herself. Watching the imaginary woman, Gallimard gets a voyeuristic thrill, but at the same time he is impotent: "I can't do a thing. Why?" With the stripper, Gallimard's impotence suggests not only that he may be unable to take any sexual pleasure in women's bodies (an explanation not consistent with other moments in the play), but also another explanation: that the stereotype of the submissive woman as Caucasian is not enough as a fulfilling fiction. When Gallimard later does find some sexual pleasure in Renee's "picture perfect" body, he can only conceive of what he deems love in terms of the specific stereotype of Butterfly: a stereotype that is histrionic—fully embodied and live—instead of existing simply on paper, a relation of power fulfilled in all its colonial dimensions and contradictions. It is through the performance of this particularly loaded stereotype that he realizes himself. Gallimard conceives of his "perfect woman" as Oriental fetish, to cover his own fear of undifferentiation.

Here we are returned to Homi Bhabha's reading of the stereotype as a fetish, born out of a self protecting itself against the repeated reminder of sexual difference and the threat of castration. Bhabha aptly ties the sexual fetish to the colonial stereotype and racial differentiation. At the scene of the encounter, what is perceived as absent or lacking in the Other must be replaced by the symbolic markings of stereotype—parts of the body, clothing, skin, gesture. Like the sexual fetish, the stereotype says more about the colonialist's desire to repress his own traumatic fears than it does about any real lack on the part of the native. With each new encounter with racial difference, the colonialist's anxiety prompts him to mark and re-mark the body of the Other as stereotype, reducing the body to an image that serves to reassure him both of his own self-integrity and of the difference of the Other.

The Butterfly myth, through its sexual and racial dimensions, thus doubly satisfies the fetishist. The body is fetishized in order to mark both the feminine and a racial "lack"; it is eviscerated in order to affirm the whole, coherent self of the white European male. But it is not only the stereotype of the passive female as Butterfly that satisfies fetishistic desire. The characters in fact mark one another and themselves in a number of ways. In the play, the enacted performances of many different stereotypes become inextricable from the process of desire. Playing the stereotype becomes both a means of disavowing one's fears of symbolic castration (in a larger sense, the lack of wholeness and integrity of the self) and of marking the desirable differences of others.

Gallimard is attracted to his "vision of the Orient" with its "almond eyes" precisely because it is so strongly marked. He is not the only one who is so implicated, for the proliferation of stereotypes in the play is not limited to those of Asians. Minor characters are defined dramatically in this way, through a reductive fixation on clothing, gestures, and body parts. In a sense, the play invites the audience to make such gross generalizations as well. Hwang hits us over the head with a barrage of stereotypes—of heterosexuals and homosexuals, Orientals and cruel white men, divas, chauvinists, feminists, Communists, bureaucrats, socialites, and disco prowlers. Comrade Chin is reduced to "what passes for a woman in modern China." Renee deflates Gallimard's ego by describing the penis as "this little . . . flap of flesh," and describes the drive for dominance as a function of male insecurity: "The whole world [is] run by a bunch of men with pricks the size of pins." In reducing the male organ to a simple "weenie," of negligible biological as well as cultural value, Renee, too, evokes the reductive powers of the stereotype.

In this manner the play tempts us to conclusions that rely on simple identifications that invariably reiterate, reinforce, or draw on stereotypes, such as the submissive Butterfly or the gay stereotypes of the Caucasian homosexual or Rice Queen. The play tempts us to make formulaic equations—to conclude that Gallimard is just a homosexual, or Song is just a devious con man—even as the characters' actions and bodies exceed such formulaic limits. A statement such as Gallimard's final summation—"I am a man who loved a woman created by a man. Everything else—simply falls short"—exposes its own limitations, the complexities of behavior it cannot express. Yet at the same time the dramatic success of this moment and other such clever statements (for example, Song's "only a man knows how a woman is supposed to act") relies on our appreciating the neatness of the characters' observations, their memorable and easy witty categorizations.

Importantly, characters impose such stereotypes on themselves as well as on others. Moments of desire in the play are intensely marked as both gendered and racialized, and not only by Gallimard. Helga also sees in the Oriental butterfly a moment of desirable fantasy: "*She begins humming, floating around the room as if dragging long kimono sleeves,*" and asks Gallimard: "Did she have a nice costume? I think it's a classic piece of music." She describes Chinese men as sex objects performing martial arts: "Some of those men—when they break those thick boards—(*She mimes fanning herself*) whoo-whoo! "This reduction is sometimes satirized as humorous posturing; Marc leers at the women in the audience, assured that he is the object of their sexual desire: "Rene, there're a lotta great babes out there. They're probably lookin' at me and thinking, 'What a dangerous guy.'"

Most prominent among those who find satisfaction in the performance of gendered and racial stereotypes are Song and Gallimard. Their playing may be read to some extent as parody, insofar as their bodies exceed each role that they play. Yet at the same time, the emphasis is on the perfection of their playing and the ultimate satisfaction it affords. Song's acting demonstrates that the way to convince an audience that one is a woman, or even a transvestite, is to employ the stereotype, to accentuate "Woman" as an ideal that is both raced and gendered. Song uses not just one stereotypical role but a whole taxonomy of different raced and gendered stereotypes: the sophisticated, "liberated" Chinese woman desiring cafés and "bad expatriate jazz," the film seductress exemplified by Anna May Wong, the submissive Butterfly. In each portrayal, his constructions rely on a histrionic field of perception already oversaturated with images of Oriental femininity. Significantly, his performance of the Oriental woman is defined primarily through a manifested difference from other stereotypes of women as sexually aggressive, masculinized, and therefore threatening and unattractive: "But a woman, especially a delicate Oriental woman—we always go where we please. Could you imagine it otherwise? Clubs in China filled with pasty, big-thighed white women, while thousands of slender lotus blossoms wait just outside the door? Never. The clubs would be empty." Later, when Gallimard demands that Song strip, Song retaliates with a pointed comparison between his body and that of a Caucasian stripper: "So you want me to—what—strip? Like a big cowboy girl? Shiny pasties on my breasts? Shall I fling my kimono over my head and yell 'ya-hoo' in the process?" Gallimard finds erotic desire in the performance of Butterfly in terms of the body marked as Asian; he remarks to Song that previously the opera, with the lead "played by huge women in so much bad makeup," did not appeal to him, but he finds Song "utterly convincing."

What convinces Gallimard are first the accoutrements of enactment—makeup, robes, and gestures—and then, more strikingly, the body itself as it becomes fetishized as flesh. As Song tells the judge, to make Gallimard believe that he was a woman "wasn't that hard." Song becomes confident in his ability to make Gallimard want him with as little as "a simple shift and mascara." Testimony to this process is how Song can woo Gallimard even after he has finally stripped. The scene threatens the traumatic discovery of difference: a moment of intense anxiety is again built of the fear and projection of undifferentiation. This tension is resolved with Gallimard's anticlimactic laughter and his categorical statement, "Look at you! You're a man!" The anticipated moment of confrontation dissolves into his laughter as he and the audience register the biological "proof" of Song's masculinity. But more tension is forthcoming; the complicated sexual desire that Song's body can provoke is once again displayed as Song has Gallimard close his eyes and touch his face. Gallimard, his eyes covered, is drawn back into the relationship with the Oriental female: "This skin, I remember. The curve of her face, the softness of her cheek, her hair against the back of my hand." The moment suggests that desire can be brought on by fragmentation of the body: Gallimard, eyes closed to the reality of the penis, perceives Song's body once again as the Oriental female. But it also reinforces that the costuming that Song used to hide the supposed truth of his gender is not—and perhaps never was—necessary; the Asian body itself *is* the fetish, the object of desire. Even the tactile perception of skin is not neutral.

Both Song and Gallimard, it is suggested, are fully satisfied only by the stereotype. Song is thrilled to have his body serve as the fetish not only because he can dupe Gallimard, but because, as the play suggests, he himself realizes desire through playing this stereotype. Although Song suggests a moment of genuine transcendence, that sexual ecstasy might in fact dispense with those stereotypes that at first constituted sexual pleasure, he does not propose a means of articulating this relationship beyond "I am your Butterfly. Under the robes, beneath everything, it was always me." Moreover, the play moves quickly past this moment of transcendence to the restaging of stereotypes. Gallimard insists on love as only constituted by the stereotype, even when it ceases to offer him the relative position of power. Again, his choice indicates the strength of his desire, the necessity of having a Butterfly figure as the complex displacement of anxiety. He rejects Song as male and insists instead on the Butterfly of his imagination, which, lacking Song, he can only enact himself. Gallimard's half-laughing, half-sobbing response to Song's undressing can be seen as a simultaneous realization and projection of his own lack, one that sets the stage for his own transformation into the self-eviscerating Butterfly.

Thus, although there are several instances of highly theatricalized transformation in the play, ultimately the play only flirts with the possibility of freeing skin from its markings of race and gender. More striking is how the process ends with a definitive bodily *type;* perhaps the fascination with onstage transformations should be viewed as the fascination of marking, not unmarking, the body. But most disturbing about the play are the ways in which histrionic perception and stereotype seem inextricably woven together. If the seductive relationship between Song and Gallimard is based on their desire to play such stereotypes, an equally seductive bond is established between theater and audience, demanding that we not only see but feel stereotype in order to gain satisfaction.

Hwang describes his play as being about fantasy: "a lot of times we live our fantasies rather than our realities, and our fantasies can be motivated by things which are not politically sound" ("Conversation" 187). The play does suggest that it is not only the individuals who hold these opinions that are culpable, but also the situations of power that reinforce them. Gallimard appeals to the audience to understand the story "from my point of view. We are all prisoners of our time and place." Helga's nostalgia for her past life is likewise revealing:

> I never thought I'd say it. But, in China, I was happy. I knew, in my own way, I knew that you were not everything you pretended to be. But the pretense—going on your arm to the embassy ball, visiting your office and the guards saying, "Good morning, good morning, Madame Gallimard"—the pretense . . . was very good indeed. (*M. Butterfly* 75)

But the play also suggests that there is an aspect of fantasy that is not so easily contextualized, an erotic power that lies in the enactment of stereotype. Although any specific stereotype might bear a traceable relation to time and place, the desire to enact it, to escape into a world of fantasy, is less easily brought to light.

In this chapter I have tried to negotiate the possibilities of a perverse pleasure that might be felt by the Asian American spectator in the playing of the Oriental stereotype. It is easy to argue that what gives pleasure is the subversion of the stereotype, the disruption of the rigid hold over representation that takes place on a number of levels. But this position is complicated by Song's pleasure in his own performance: he is thrilled not only by his duping of Gallimard but also, the play suggests, by the fantasy of being loved as a butterfly. Such a pleasure makes it harder to imagine that our spectatorial pleasure comes from the thrill of subversion alone. Hwang's play confronts rather than denies the pervasiveness of the stereotype, in a way that cannot simply be explained as brainwashing or self-hatred, or even fascinated horror. The best we can do for a positive reading of M. Butterfly may be to conclude that the play uses both repulsion and attraction in sometimes contradictory ways. Unlike Yankee Dawg You Die, Hwang's play does not parody the stereotype in order to reveal a true, authentic self. Instead, "who I truly am" lies in the perfected playing of stereotype, the exaggeration of stereotype, or in the movement from one stereotype to another.

In speaking about the play, Hwang both emphasizes his use of stereotypes and offers his version of what might be seen as the play's hopeful message:

> M. Butterfly has sometimes been regarded as an anti-American play, a diatribe against the stereotyping of the East by the West, of women by men. Quite to the contrary, I consider it a plea to all sides to cut through our respective layers of cultural and sexual misperception, to deal with one another truthfully for our mutual good, from the common and equal ground we share as human beings. (afterword, M. Butterfly 100)

When this statement is read against the play, though, a certain doubt emerges. Even as Hwang insists that there is something beyond the myths of difference in "the common and equal ground we share as human beings," he also affirms that the play is about the world of fantasy (myths that have "oversaturated our consciousness"). But in his reappropriation of these myths, no true version of the story emerges to correct the stereotype; there is nothing aside from the endless imitations, which, particularly in the final performance of the butterfly by Gallimard, with Song as Pinkerton, are neither tragedy nor clearly parody. If *Yankee Dawg* works to construct the Asian body as something that can be seen through stereotype as real, *M. Butterfly* works in another way, through the repetition of acts that mock, in their very repetitions and subtle variations, the racist power that places them into being. At best, we can describe its threat as coming from "the prodigious and strategic production of conflictual, fantastic, discriminatory 'identity effects' in the play of a power that is elusive because it hides no essence, no 'itself'" (Bhabha, "Mimicry" 90).

The 1976 production by Asian American Theater Workshop (now Asian American Theater Company) of Frank Chin's *The Year of the Dragon*. Photographs by Chris Huie.

Art Lai as Sam Shikaze in Asian American Theater Company's 1982 production of R. A. Shiomi's *Yellow Fever*, directed by Lane Nishikawa. Photograph by Bob Hsiang.

John Wat as Sam Shikaze
and Margaret Jones as
Nancy Wing in Kumu
Kahua's 1992 production
of R. A. Shiomi's *Yellow
Fever*, directed by Jo
Scheder. Courtesy Kumu
Kahua Theatre Company.
Photograph by Jo
Scheder.

Gene Shofner as Sergeant Mackenzie, John Wat as Sam Shikaze, and Margaret Jones as
Nancy Wing in Kumu Kahua's 1992 production of R. A. Shiomi's *Yellow Fever*, directed
by Jo Scheder. Courtesy Kumu Kahua Theatre Company. Photograph by Jo Scheder.

Above. Theater Mu's 1994 production of R. A. Shiomi's *Yellow Fever*, directed by Marc Hayashi. Left to right: Francesca Carlin as Nancy Wing, David Tufford as Sergeant Mackenzie, Nelson Williams as Captain Kadota, Paul Juhn as Sam Shikaze. Courtesy Theater Mu. Photograph by Charissa Uemura.

Left. Nobu McCarthy as Mrs. Tanaka in East West Players' 1982 production of Wakako Yamauchi's *12-1-A*, directed by Saburo. Courtesy East West Players.

Dennis Dun as Ma and Art Lai as Lone in Asian American Theater Company's 1984 production of David Henry Hwang's *The Dance and the Railroad*, directed by Judith Nihei. Photograph by Bob Hsiang.

Dennis Dun and Art Lai in Hwang's *The Dance and the Railroad*. Photograph by Bob Hsiang.

John Cruz as Lone in New World Theater's 1985 production of David Henry Hwang's *The Dance and the Railroad*, directed by Roberta Uno. Courtesy New World Theater. Photograph by Robert Tobey.

Theater Mu's 1995 production of Genny Lim's *Paper Angels*, directed by Kim Hines. Left to right: Randy Minobe as Lee, Luu Pham as Chin Gung, Paul Juhn as Fong. Photograph by Charissa Uemura.

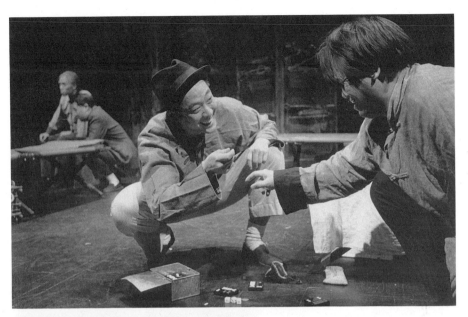

Above. Theater Mu's 1995 production of Genny Lim's *Paper Angels*, directed by Kim Hines. Left to right: Luu Pham as Chin Gung, Randy Minobe as Lee, Paul Juhn as Fong, Daniel Sach Le as Lum. Courtesy Theater Mu. Photograph by Charissa Uemura.

Left. Pan Asian Repertory Theatre's 1990 production of Wakako Yamauchi's *And the Soul Shall Dance*, directed by Kati Kuroda. Artistic/Producing Director Tisa Chang. Left to right: Carol Honda as Hana Murata, Roxanne Chang as Masako Murata, Dawn A. Saito as Emiko Oka. © Corky Lee/Pan Asian Repertory Theatre.

Above opposite. Smokey Leung as Grace and Dennis Dun as Steve in Asian American Theater Company's 1983 production of David Henry Hwang's *FOB*, directed by Judith Nihei. Photograph by Bob Hsiang.

Below opposite. Pan Asian Repertory Theatre's 1990 production of *FOB*, written and directed by David Henry Hwang. Artistic/Producing Director Tisa Chang. Left to right: Dennis Dennis as Steve, Stan Egi as Dale, and Ann M. Tsuji as Grace. © Corky Lee/Pan Asian Repertory Theatre.

Above. Pan Asian Repertory Theatre's 1991 production of Elizabeth Wong's *Letters to a Student Revolutionary*, directed by Ernest Abuba. Artistic/Producing Director Tisa Chang. Left to right: Caryn Ann Chow as Bibi, Keenan Shimizu as Chorus 2, Karen Tsen Lee as Karen, Mary Lum as Chorus 4, Christen Villamor as Chorus 3, and Andrew Ingkavet as Chorus 1. © Corky Lee/Pan Asian Repertory Theatre.

Above. New World Theater's 1991 production of Elizabeth Wong's *Letters to a Student Revolutionary*, directed by Nerfertiti Burton. Left to right: Fred Rowley, Theresa Wong, Mona Chiang, Peter Tamaribuchi, Ken Chu. Courtesy New World Theater. Photograph by Edward Cohen.

Above opposite. Asian American Theater Company's 1985 production of Velina Hasu Houston's *Tea*, directed by Judith Nihei. Left to right: Sharon Omi, Emily Cachapero, Amy Hill, Faye Kawabata, and Mitzie Abe. Photograph by Bob Hsiang.

Below opposite. Mount Holyoke College's 1991 production of Velina Hasu Houston's *Tea*, directed by Roberta Uno. Left to right: Leilani Chan as Chizuye, Anna Rima Diehl as Teruko, Ming Nagel as Himiko, Motoko as Atsuko, Sarah Underwood as Setsuko. Courtesy Mt. Holyoke College. Photograph by Fred LeBlanc.

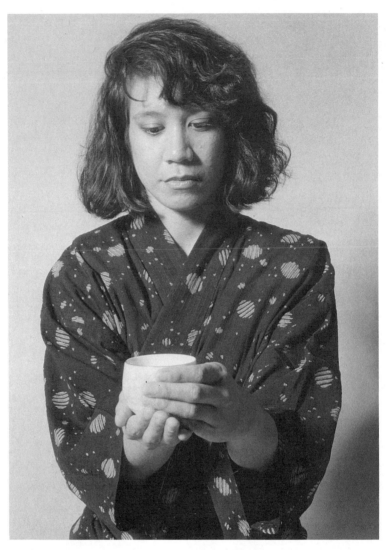

Margaret Jones as Himiko Hamilton in Kumu Kahua's 1991 production of Velina Hasu Houston's *Tea*, directed by Ellen Polyhronopoulou. Courtesy Kumu Kahua Theatre Company. Photograph by Suzanne Saylor.

James Roberts as Dave and Yoon Kim as Stu in New World Theater's 1991 production of Jeannie Barroga's *Walls*, directed by Michael Birtwhistle. Courtesy New World Theater. Photograph by Edward Cohen.

5

Acts of Exclusion:
Asian American History Plays

One cannot read or stage Asian American history without facing some fundamental questions about the construction of history. As Hayden White eloquently states in *Tropics of Discourse: Essays in Cultural Criticism,* history can no longer claim an epistemologically neutral space between "subjective" art and "objective" science:

> We should no longer naively expect that statements about a given epoch or complex of events in the past "correspond" to some preexistent body of "raw facts. For we should recognize that *what constitutes the facts themselves* is the problem that the historian, like the artist, has tried to solve in the choice of the metaphor by which he orders his world, past, present, and future. (47)

Glenn Omatsu rightly points out that the politics of the Asian American movement are inseparable from the writing of history. Crucial to the movement's activism over the past three decades has been the belief of Asian Americans that "ordinary people could make their own history by learning how historical forces operated and by transforming this knowledge into a material force to change their lives" (32). Yet this writing of their own history by Asian Americans could never be a simple unearthing of facts; rather, it had to be self-conscious about its metaphors of construction and the impulses behind them. If we assume that history is not the objective discovery but instead the "making" of the past, a directed project of reconstruction pressured by the impulses, desires, and agendas of the present, then it becomes impossible to make rigid distinctions between written history as "fact" and theater as "fiction." Strictly considered, both are less reenactments of past events than they are the interpretation of details in actions that reflect current debates about Asian American identity.

To reveal history's constructedness is not to rule out its power as authenticating. Asian American history is a history that knows itself as revisionist, and is explicitly in dialogue with already existing views of American history. The creation of a historical work—the writing of history by historians—no less than the performance of history in plays, participates significantly in the current construction of Asian American ethnic and racial identity. Both historical narratives and fictionalized history plays recognize that Asian Americans have their own vision of the past in America. The eagerness to write history points to the desire for an authenticating past that will support a communal future; within the enactment of the meticulous details of history are purposes that shape theatrical presentation.

This is not the place for a lengthy historical exposition, and I turn to Asian American historical narratives for a more limited purpose: not to reiterate the descriptions of history, but to tease out what forces direct the compilation and interpretation of such descriptions. Specifically, I will look at Ronald Takaki's writing of Asian American history in order to compare his agendas and strategies with those used by dramatists in writing history plays. Takaki's historical writing is particularly appropriate to consider here, in part because it seems uniquely theatrical in its presentation. As E. San Juan, Jr., suggests, Takaki writes a history that can be easily staged in current Asian American theater ("Beyond Identity Politics" 544). The terms of Takaki's writing of Asian American history, moreover, give us insight into the staging and characterization of particular Asian American history plays.

Takaki's historical writing and the plays considered in this chapter share the common impulse to contest an existing, traditional view of immigration and assimilation by illustrating how Asian Americans have at significant moments been excluded from the body politic as it is constructed in American immigration policy and law.[1] Such histories, both written and dramatized, construct an imagined community that is pan-Asian and transcends time, either in moments of collective action or in ties that connect characters. Takaki's history therefore serves as a touchstone for a discussion of plays in this chapter, for it outlines the strategies used in performing an Asian American past. These strategies include constructing an Asian American self in excess of its purely functional value as labor or immigration statistic. As we shall see, there are pitfalls as well as successes in envisioning historical processes by means of this transcendent, universal self.

The "Unmeltables"

First and foremost, the history plays examined here revise existing histories that show Asian Americans as problematically and willfully unassimilable, an exception to the "natural" process by which the United States absorbs its other aliens. In "Reflections on Racial Patterns in America," Takaki contests such assumptions, particularly as expressed in the work of Nathan Glazer. In *Affirmative Discrimination: Ethnic Inequality and Public Policy,* Glazer argues that the history of America is really one of an inclusive liberal society in which "men and women are judged on the basis of their abilities rather than their color, race, or ethnic origin" (220). For Glazer, the problems that arise reflect individual and temporary instances of prejudice rather than historically founded racism. Thus, in his view, programs such as affirmative action disturb the general consensus and progress of natural assimilation. Glazer bases his theory of an American ethnic pattern on three historical developments or "decisions," that

> first, the entire world would be allowed to enter the United States. The claim that some nations or races were to be favored in entry over others was, for a while, accepted, but it was eventually rejected. And once having entered into the United States—and whether that entry was by means of forced enslavement, free immigration, or conquest—all citizens would have equal rights. No group would be considered subordinate to another.
>
> Second, no separate ethnic group was to be allowed to establish an independent polity in the United States. This was to be a union of states and a nation of free individuals, not a nation of politically defined ethnic groups.
>
> Third, no group, however, would be required to give up its group character and distinctiveness as the price of full entry into the American society and polity. (5)

Although Glazer does recognize historical evidence of events contrary to these notions, such as slavery or the internment of Japanese Americans during the Second World War, he generally sees these events as temporary, occasional, and incidental occurrences, anomalies in the "major tendency to a greater inclusiveness" (17).

As Takaki points out, Glazer's theory of natural assimilation has important implications for current interpretations of race and the formulation of public policy. Glazer's interpretation of immigration history suggests that Asian Americans do not need collective action, that they can assimilate just as other groups have. Moreover, such success in assimilation should not be aided by affirmative action or other collective governmental policies; it is always naturally available in the process of individuals transcending their racial background and overcoming their past, even as they preserve their distinctive flavor or "group character" in a multicultural society. Such a view also erases racism as a collective or social problem, for it sees racial oppression only in terms of individual instances of prejudice and suppresses a reading of these events as a larger pattern of social injustice. Glazer's history, because of its emphasis on a natural assimilation of the individual rather than the necessity of collective action, lends itself to interpretations of Asian Americans as the model minority that can be held up to others coming from "failed" minority groups, such as African Americans and Latinos. Shelby Steele, for instance, in "The Memory of Enemies," an article published in *Dissent*, urges African Americans to take a more individualized view of their success and to look to the achievements of Asian American students in school and in semiprofessional positions as a model for such individualism: "Despite our collective oppression, opportunities for development can finally be exploited only by individuals. . . . Asians, Jews, West Indians, and others have found their avenues for development in the aspirations of their individuals who have approached American society with initiative, energy, and pragmatism" (331).

Takaki takes a diametrically opposed view. His arguments make clear the extent to which historians like Glazer have affected past and present public policies by constructing the past in certain ways. By minimizing or erasing instances of racially exclusionist forces and policies in American history, theorists like Glazer, Takaki claims, maintain the extent to which racial inequality still exists. "To diminish the significance of racial oppression in America's past and to define racial inequality as a problem of prejudice and limit the solution as the outlawing of individual acts of discrimination, as does Glazer, is effectively to leave intact the very structures of racial inequality" ("Reflections" 36). History can be read in Glazer's way only if we ignore all evidence of systemic rejection in the past, all details of U.S. policy regarding citizenship and suffrage. Takaki points out that U.S. law and policy have systematically excluded particular nonwhite immigrant groups from fully participating in the melting pot. These exclusionary laws included the first Naturalization Law of 1790, which

> specified that only free "white" immigrants would be eligible for naturalized citizenship. Clearly, this law did not allow the "entire" world to enter the United States as potential citizens or members of the body politic. Non-"white" immigrants were not permitted to be naturalized until the Walter-McCarran Act of 1952, which states that "the right of a person to become a naturalized citizen of the United States shall not be denied or abridged because of race. . . ." What is important to note here about the first naturalization law is the fact that it remained in effect for 162 years, or for a very long time. ("Reflections" 28)

Takaki notes that this law barred immigrants from Asia from becoming naturalized or holding property, thus rendering even more difficult the lives of Chinese migrant workers on the railway and Japanese farm workers in California. Takaki also insists that the history of suffrage shows the exclusion of both black and Native Americans on the basis of race. Most dramatically, Takaki counters Glazer's assumptions that all Americans would be treated as "free individuals," not members of "politically defined ethnic groups," who nonetheless would not be forced to give up their ethnic group identity.[2]

Takaki's writing of history focuses on discrimination in law and immigration policy as well as its effects on the experiences of Asian American and other immigrants of color. His accounts highlight the tension between instances when Asian Americans have been allowed to "count" as Americans (when they exemplified the success of the model minority) and when they have been marked as Asian. His reading of immigration history reinforces that, at least in terms of immigration policy, naturalization law, and suffrage, Asian Americans are bonded by their inevitable difference, the "different shore" whence they came. His careful detailing of historical events serves as a reminder that what Asian Americans face is "profoundly different from the experiences of European immigrants":

> They wore what University of Chicago sociologist Robert E. Park termed a "racial uniform." Unlike the Irish and other groups from Europe, Asian immigrants could not become "mere individuals, indistinguishable in the cosmopolitan mass of the population." Regardless of their personal merits, they sadly discovered, they could not gain acceptance in the larger society. They were judged not by the content of their character but by their complexion. "The trouble is not with the Japanese mind but with the Japanese skin," wrote Park as he observed American-white attitudes in 1913. "The Jap is not the right color."[3] (*Strangers from a Different Shore* 12–13)

I have suggested briefly how Takaki finds in history racial difference systematically deployed in U.S. law and policy, making the historical experiences of people of color radically different from the experiences of other ethnics. When we turn to the history plays written by Asian Americans, we are struck by the ways in which they emphasize such an argument theatrically, through their choice of setting and action. Although these plays cover a range of immigration and settlement experiences, a common impulse connects them: to demonstrate that failure to assimilate is due not so much to irreconcilable cultural differences of Asian Americans—that they are what Edward K. Strong called "unmeltables" in their stubborn refusal to let go of the old ways—as to exclusionary laws, institutions, and economic practices of a white-dominated America.[4]

Such exclusion is staged in different ways. First, Asian American history plays tend to be set in locales that recreate the harsh conditions of immigration and settlement, and to focus on specific moments demonstrating a history of systematic exclusion. These moments highlight immigration restrictions (Genny Lim's *Paper Angels,* which premiered at the Asian American Theater Company in 1980, directed by Amy Hill); the prohibition of land ownership (Wakako Yamauchi's *The Music Lessons,* first produced at the New York Shakespeare Festival Public Theater in 1977, directed by Mako, and Yamauchi's *And the Soul Shall Dance,* originally a short story published in 1974, first staged at the East West Players in 1977 and co-directed by Mako and Alberto Isaac); and labor conditions (David Henry Hwang's *The Dance and the Railroad,* whose first productions by the Henry Street Settlement's New Federal Theater and the New York Shakespeare Festival Public Theater were directed by John Lone in 1981, and Genny Lim's *Bitter Cane,* which received a staged reading at the Seattle Group Theatre and a workshop production at the Bay Area Playwright's Festival XII in 1989). In a sense, these plays can be thought of as dramatizing Takaki's argument in different historical moments, illustrating the impossibility of assimilation within America even as characters articulate an intense desire to be American or glorify America as a land of possibility. These plays contest mainstream views of a natural process of assimilation into an American melting pot by discussing those laws and policies institutionalizing racism and by enacting situations that highlight racial difference as codified in policy, law, and event. In these plays, the processes by which Asian immigrants were racially excluded perform themselves as history.

Two plays that deal with the internment of Japanese Americans during the Second World War—Momoko Iko's *Gold Watch* (which premiered at the Inner City Cultural Center, Los Angeles, in 1972, directed by C. Bernard Jackson) and Wakako Yamauchi's *12-A-1* (directed by Saburo at East West Players and Judith Nihei at the Asian American Theatre Company in 1982)—strikingly demonstrate how to perform this racial difference as a segregation that has been historically imposed on Asian Americans. The first acts in both plays unveil conflicts between first-generation Japanese American *issei* and their second-generation *nisei* children, setting up what could be read as a demonstration of the inevitable process of assimilation in successive generations of immigrant families. However, the subsequent action in each play reinforces that the inevitable and natural process of "melting" for which Glazer argues is not possible for these characters, even with the fervent desire of the younger generation to blend in. Through their symbolic actions and objects, the plays reinforce how the failure to assimilate comes not from a willful and stubborn clinging to the old ways but from exemptions made to the law during the Japanese American internment.

Set in the Pacific Northwest in the months immediately preceding internment, *Gold Watch* begins with a family conflict between Masu, a stubborn Japanese American farmer, and Tadao, his son. Tadao wants to play football, is ashamed of his father's accent, and has picked up from his schoolmates a casual racism directed against American blacks. Such a conflict could, of course, illustrate a cultural divide between young and old as the younger generation is assimilated into American life. But the play does not stop at illustrating these generational tensions. Father and son are linked by the tragedy of racism as the family loses its farm and possessions in their impending internment. They fight together against the common enemy, the faceless white marauders who raid the farm and kill the father. These acts ground the dynamics of the play in a specific interpretation of history, emphasizing the impossibility of assimilation not only for Japanese Americans but for all people of color. As Masu says to his son early in the play, "There are no black men around here. We are all 'ni-gas.' Everyone here."

In *12-1-A*, props, costumes, and action demonstrate in a more lighthearted way the Americanness of these characters; the flavor of 1940s America is evident in their dress, slang, and gestures. But the apparent assimilation of the characters is shown to be a myth that quickly shatters in the face of internment. The son Mitch, who at the beginning of the play is proud of his "American" accomplishments (a bowling trophy is prominently displayed throughout the play), gradually comes to understand the forces of exclusion and systematic racism after he leaves the camp on a work permit. He outlines for his mother and sister the contradiction he sees: "They wouldn't let us *in* the alleys, let alone bowl. Or the barber shops . . . or the restaurants. Can you believe it? And us breaking our fucking balls for their harvest—for *their* sugar—for *their* army! And for peanuts. Peanuts!" Mitch's education in his own legal and political difference, and his eventual transformation into a rebellious "no-no boy," characterizes the play's overall action. As the play progresses, it marks everything—including the bodies of the characters—with the awareness of an instituted and constructed difference from white America. The mentally retarded Harry's incessant singing of "Yes, sir, that's my baby" becomes, at the end of the play, a dirge played on the Japanese shakuhachi. Such moments reinforce the ways in which even willing characters cannot melt into the pot, and illustrate the historic institution of racial difference through American law and policy.

Creating Asian America, Past and Present

Takaki's history of Asian Americans promotes a pan-ethnic vision of an Asian American community. In *Strangers from a Different Shore: A History of Asian America,* he writes,

> We need to 're-vision' history to include Asians in the history of American, to do so in a broad and comparative way. How and why, we must ask, were the experiences of the various Asian groups— Chinese, Japanese, Korean, Filipino, Asian Indian, and Southeast Asian—similar to and different from one another? Cross national comparisons can help us to identify the experiences particular to a group and to highlight the experiences common to all of them. (7)

For Takaki, this history-writing project is aimed at forming collectives in the present; he describes the ideal community-building function of telling history: "And when the listeners learn about their roots, they feel enriched—members of a 'community of memory'" (10). This vision of an alternative nationalism for Asian Americans suggests Benedict Anderson's "imagined community" in which deep bonds transcend time and space and eclipse generational, cultural, and political divisions in favor of an ideal nationhood.

This drive toward a pan-Asian community is another aspect that Asian American history plays share with historical narratives. Both kinds of history writing are part of the strategic formation of a larger Asian American community from otherwise disparate groups. Although these histories acknowledge specific internal differences between ethnic groups, both historical narratives and history plays promote the idea of a pan-Asian community and underscore the need for collective action. In the act of witnessing a dramatized history is the implication that history binds present actors characters together through a sense of a common past.

What binds Asian American characters together in some history plays is their mutual exclusion by the white majority. As in Iko's *Gold Watch* and Yamauchi's *12-1-A*, David Henry Hwang's *The Dance and the Railroad* proposes racism as institutionalized rather than individual and suggests that necessary action can only be achieved through the solidarity of the Asian American characters. In its carefully choreographed movements as well as its narrative action, the play celebrates both the positive bonds that develop between the solitary Lone and his pupil Ma and the solidarity of the striking Chinese railroad workers. Significantly, the somewhat triumphant ending of Hwang's play departs from Takaki's historical account of the strike. According to Takaki,

> The Central Pacific managers moved to break the Chinese strike. They wired New York to inquire about the feasibility of transporting

10,000 blacks to replace the striking Chinese. Superintendent Crocker isolated the strikers and cut off their food supply. "I stopped the provisions on them," he stated, "stopped the butchers from butchering, and used such coercive measures." Coercion worked. Virtually imprisoned in their camps in the Sierras and forced into starvation, the strikers surrendered within a week. (*Strangers from a Different Shore* 86)

In Hwang's play, the railroad workers are victorious; even the standoffish Lone exults in their successful collective action: "We forced the white devil to act civilized." Rewriting the ending so that the strike is broken suggests the playwright's desire to see a positive outcome to the communal effort.

Like *The Dance and the Railroad*, other history plays use movement and choreography as well as plot and action to evoke a sense of unity. Many of these historical dramas use theatrical techniques to suggest that their events are more than just singular instances of oppression and that the formation of a pan-Asian collective is a necessary charge. The emphasis on several actors working as an ensemble—whether as a subtle aspect of the realistic intimacy of a play like *12-1-A* or as a more heightened theatrical effect such as a chorus—might suggest the same. The careful, even ceremonial blocking of actors in parallel action, gesture, and language called for in Velina Houston's *Tea* suggests a pan-Asian and, in this case, a specifically gendered solidarity. Even a primarily realistic play such as *Gold Watch* uses distinctive choral effects in the second act, where the Japanese American community meets in a "church meeting hall": Iko suggests that "*the theater itself can be considered the hall, with the actors at strategic points in the audience*," creating the sense of a community that extends to include the audience.

The staging of these Asian American history plays emphasizes the past as a site of collective formation, thus implicitly constructing the present performance as a moment of coalition building. Other theatrical devices and techniques foster an ideal of ethnic, pan-Asian, and intergenerational bonding, emphasizing the transmission of symbolic objects or knowledge from generation to generation and focusing on younger characters as the recipients of such legacies. Although the passage of time and the traversal of geography might be sites of psychic rupture, the plays more usually focus on building bridges, making connections with past events, people, and locales. Such connections are maintained even when conscious links are not. Objects such as Masu's watch in Iko's *Gold Watch* symbolize the passage of a spiritual legacy from father to son. Physical experience also becomes part of this transmission; examples include the actor's art in Hwang's *The Dance and the Railroad,* and Emiko's dancing as witnessed by the young Masako in *And the Soul Shall Dance.* In Lim's *Bitter Cane,* the dead father and living son are connected through the prostitute Li-Tai, whom they both love. This remarkable coincidence must be read not only as the stuff of melodrama but as infused with a particular idea of history: a fantasy of connectedness, where the son comes to bear home the bones of the father. In many Asian American plays that do not take place in a historical past, the past inserts itself as a lesson taught to audiences; the means include railroad speeches in *The Chickencoop Chinaman,* immigration stories in *FOB,* and the aging actors of the Chop Suey circuit in *Yankee Dawg You Die.* Again, history is performed as ever present, as a link with the past, allowing the Asian American spectator a sense of intimacy with an imagined community that bridges the ruptures of time and space.

Subjectivity and Excess: The Emotional Self as Strategy

Takaki's *Strangers from a Different Shore* uses the personal statement and the authentic human experience as testimonials to the truth of history. In this sense the book seems especially "theatrical." Takaki's approach—to create a subjectivity by means of artifact, or to leave room for suggestive speculation about the "selves" of these people—is an explicit maneuver to counter a more reductive view of history:[5]

> To answer our questions, we must not study Asian Americans primarily in terms of statistics and what was done to them. They are entitled to be viewed as subjects—as men and women with minds, wills, and voices. By "voices" we mean their own words and stories as told in their oral histories, conversations, speeches, soliloquies, and songs, as well as in their own writings—diaries, letters, newspapers, magazines, pamphlets, placards, posters, flyers, court petitions, autobiographies, short stories, novels and poems. Their voices contain particular expressions and phrases with their own meanings and nuances, the cuttings from the cloth of languages. (*Strangers from a Different Shore* 8)

The same emphasis on oral history as a way of preserving the past, or on personal history as a form of literature, has begun appearing in other recent Asian American publications.[6] There seems to be a particular urgency to give "subjectivity" to characters who might otherwise be an invisible part of the American labor force.

Historians and sociologists have recently stressed the connections between the immigration Asian American workers, their exploitation in the United States, and the economics of labor.[7] In a similar vein, the oppression of Asian workers in Hawaii and California forms the backdrop for plays such as Hwang's *The Dance and the Railroad* and Lim's *Bitter Cane*. One character describes the dehumanizing situation on a sugar plantation this way: "The seasons pass without fail. Each day follows the next. You plant, you cut, you harvest, you haul, and you don't ask questions. Like a dumb plow ox" (*Bitter Cane* 171). But what is even more interesting about the plays is that the exploitative labor situations are theatrically eclipsed by the emotional relationships developed in the plays. In *Bitter*

Cane, the incestuous love plot draws attention away from a more straight-forward exposition of exploitation. In *The Dance and the Railroad* the plot revolves around the railroad strike, but the main action theatricalizes something quite different—Lone's performances of traditional Peking Opera techniques and the growing friendship between him and Ma.

In the words of Royal Mead, secretary of the Hawaiian Sugar Planters' Association, as he testified before Congress in 1910: "[T]he Asiatic has had only an economic value in the social equation. So far as the institutions, laws, customs, and language of the permanent population go, his presence is no more felt than is that of the cattle on the ranges" (Okihiro, *Margins and Mainstreams* 155–56). What is unique about the Asian American history plays I have discussed is their emphasis on creating a particular subjectivity for the Asian American character, one that exceeds or stands outside of "economic value in the social equation." Emotional relationships and human bonds insist on human desire as that which cannot be contained, thus constructing a subjectivity that does not fit into an economy in which the "labor of colored bodies is reduced to abstract exchange-value (the cash-nexus) and wasted away" (E. San Juan, Jr., "Beyond Identity Politics" 558). The characters thus refuse to be held within a system that seeks to exploit and reduce Asians to the value of their bodies as labor. Such a mode of construction also emphasizes the individual's resistance to the reductiveness of certain kinds of history. If previous accounts turned Asian Americans into nameless and faceless data, mere points in a scheme of American economic development, these plays write another kind of history. They construct Asian American selves by emphasizing human action in excess of its purely functional purpose, as more than a statistic of labor or immigration. What is erotic, lyric, and personal fills these plays and creates a subjectivity that exceeds history as a series of numbers and dates. In each case, historical fact and statistic are made more complex because human experience is shown to be irreducible to economics.

Genny Lim's *Paper Angels* bears a close reading in this regard. In the play, Lim dramatizes the results of the Chinese Exclusion Act of 1882 (prompted in part by complaints from white workers), which restricted Asian immigration to merchants, scholars, and tourists. The destruction of birth records in the San Francisco earthquake of 1906 opened the door for "paper sons," Chinese immigrants who passed themselves off as sons of American-born Chinese. Lim's play focuses on the harsh conditions of the Angel Island detention center, where some immigrants were held for years; her scenes depict the cruel interrogation and refusal of immigration status, the separation of families, and the loneliness of the immigrants. The play relies heavily on Lim's compilation of factual material, documentary interviews, and statistics. It avoids privileging any one character's life story; rather, each character is presented as a type of immigrant, standing in a for a range of others. Fong's speech, for instance, references the different character types embodied by male characters in the play and links him with all immigrants, Chinese and non-Chinese, who remain undistinguished and otherwise unmemorable except in their similar motivations:

I'm not a scholar or a poet like Lee. I'm not a dreamer like Chin Gung. I'm not a hero like Lum, I'll probably never be a success. I just want a chance to make a few dollars so when I get old, I won't have to be buried in a pauper's grave. That's all I want. That's all I want. (51–52)

Each of the characters, white or Chinese, is to some extent presented as emblematic. At the same time, the play resists the collectivization of characters in favor of an insistence on individual subjectivity. This is made most explicit in the Inspector's speeches. The Inspector represents and believes in the system of exclusion, which reduces all Chinese to the status of products of the government-regulated process of rejection or admittance. But in describing one of the young men he has examined, the

Inspector imparts a sense, however fleeting, of intimate contact. In the Inspector's recognition of the "same Chinaman we deported three years ago," the statistic gains a self and becomes distinguished as an individual: "He was a smart little devil. . . . He was fast. Never flinched." Ironically, it is the Inspector's moment of recognition of the essential humanity of the immigrant and his affinity for him—"To tell the truth, I rather liked the little fella"—that prompts a hardening of his attitude. As if recognizing the implicit threat of that human connection to the system, the Inspector subsequently shores up his racist stance, changing his tone *"from amusement and near-admiration, to cold, dark detachment"*:

> But the law is the law. I have my job to do. You've got to have a system! Because if you don't, they'll take advantage and next thing you know, not only will you have droves of illegal aliens swarming into the country, but they'll be bringing over their wives, children, sundry aunts, uncles, and relatives, not to mention the little yellow ones they'll be propagating all over the U.S. (37)

It was the Chinese immigrants' poetry, roughly inscribed on the walls of Angel Island detention center, that first attracted the attention of historians and artists such as Lim. Lim collaborated with Him Mark Lai and Judy Yung to transcribe and translate these poems from the detention center, which was earmarked for demolition.[8] The poems written by the Angel Island detainees demand a similar reading as lyric emotion expressive of individual selves, as well as a community of people. Their value lies in the agreement, not tension, between the individual and the collective. In the same way, the choral effects in *Paper Angels* prompt an identification with an individual's felt experience as well as with a collective experience. The recourse to poetry suggests an emotional life that resists the new anonymity of the detainee. The old woman Chin Moo, left husbandless and alone at the end of the play, could be seen as a functionless body in America. She is the only one of the characters who is not preparing for a newly active life; one wonders about her future means of support. But her final words ("How I long to see springtime in Toisan!") belie her uselessness; they return to her past, revealing an evocative memory that fills her inner thoughts.

The creation of a subjectivity characterized by excess becomes an explicit part of the gender dynamics in Wakako Yamauchi's *The Music Lessons* and *And the Soul Shall Dance*. Yamauchi's plays foreground family problems rather than race relations; however, the racist conditions of immigration and settlement for Japanese Americans are undeniably the causes of the family problems. Both plays are set in the Imperial Valley of California in the 1930s, in the Japanese American farming communities, where relentless work, crushing debt, and fickle growing conditions create or intensify problems within human relationships. Particular moments in each play enable the actors to inform the audience of these conditions, such as the legal restrictions on land ownership. In *And the Soul Shall Dance*, Oka explains to his daughter, "In America, Japanese cannot own land. We lease and move every two, three years." In *The Music Lessons*, the personal hopelessness resulting from anti-Asian economic practices is again outlined by the characters:

> *Nakamura.* Well, first you get some names together. Good names. You can use mine. Sponsors, you know? Then you go to a produce company—in Los Angeles—put on a good suit, talk big . . . how you going to make big money for them. Get in debt. Then you pay back after the harvest. (*the futility of it occurs to him*) Then you borrow again next year. Then you pay back. If you can. Same thing next year. You never get the farm. The farm gets you. (*he drinks from the bottle*) (68)

In *The Music Lessons*, the widowed Chizuko takes on the itinerant Kaoru as her farmhand, dismissing him abruptly when her teenage daughter becomes infatuated with him. The play contrasts the poverty of Chikuzo's family and the relative prosperity and stability of the white farmers through the character of Billy, whose father works for "American Fruit growers. On salary." The physical hardship of Chizuko's situation is exacerbated by her repressed longing for a more satisfying emotional life, a life she sacrificed out of economic necessity. In *And the Soul Shall Dance,* the rift between Emiko and Oka is widened by their poverty and isolation in the harsh desert. The Murata family serves not only as the observers of Emiko's misery, but also as the commentators on the limited resources, uncertainty, and despair of both families. Yamauchi includes a moment of explicit comparison between these Japanese farmers and the white American pioneers who figure so prominently in traditional American history books. When Masako enthusiastically tells her mother about the prairie settlers in the book she is reading who "come from the East. Just like you and Papa came from Japan," her mother corrects her, "White people among white people . . . that's different from Japanese among white people." When Maskao wonders aloud why no books are written about the Japanese settlers, her mother replies, "Because we're nobodies here."

Both plays depict historical situations in which life in America tries to reduce Japanese Americans to "nobodies," both in their lack of economic and political clout and in their reduction to anonymous beings, remembered only as labor statistics. But the plays themselves resist the reduction of characters to such a system of valuation. Yamauchi's characters are attracted to excess, sometimes in the form of small, unaffordable luxuries, sometimes as greater extravagances. This excess typically manifests itself in the female characters, whose bodies and actions cannot be contained by the economic prisons intended to hold them. If, as in *Paper Angels,* the male characters refer to the need for solidarity and persistence in the task of endless labor, the female characters are wild cards, depicting that which escapes valuation within such an economy. Although the men may suffer the pangs of unrequited love, it is the women who become the true victims in a world where individual aspiration and passion are condemned.

In *The Music Lessons,* Chizuko's tragedy is explicitly linked to her appropriation of traditionally male roles. She dresses in her dead husband's clothing and manages to keep the farm afloat and the family together, but these achievements are not celebrated. Rather, she and the other characters in the play mourn the loss of the "feminine" in her life. In *And the Soul Shall Dance,* Emiko is depicted as perversely heroic for holding on to the same extravagant qualities: her memories of forbidden love, her music, her smoking, her beautiful but useless kimonos, her mad dances alone in the desert. Similarly, Oka expends his frustrated and repressed sexual energy on his daughter, buying her clothing, magazines, movies, a permanent wave. In giving this kind of redemptive value to such moments, these plays transform the ways in which we might view the female body as eroticized. Moments when Kaoru plays the violin for the women or the young Aki recites love poetry while her mother fingers a soft, flowing scarf generate their poignancy out of the harsh realities of the situation. Similarly, when Hana strokes Masako's hair to the delicate accompaniment of wind chimes, the emotional sensitivity between mother and daughter becomes an instance of resistance to the reductive nature of immigrant life. Thus, moments that display the female body, such as Emiko's dance enacting the memories of her past sexual pleasure, suggest an erotic that must be read quite differently from the stereotype of the exoticized Asian female. Here the female body seizes a moment in which there is a hope of a relation in excess of the purely economic, a luxury that defies necessity and defines the self as transcendent.[9]

Many of these plays envision eroticism and passion as a temporary escape from these conditions. This is true of Lim's *Bitter Cane,* where the extravagant love of Wing and Li-Tai must be viewed as resistance to an economy that forces men into indentured servitude and women into prostitution. Their personal and sexual relations must be viewed as something that exists outside of both economic necessity or even ethnic solidarity; Li-Tai doesn't allow Kam free sexual favors, even though he pleads for them "as a countryman." Her resistance to her own prostitution, and the refusal of both Wing and his father to be broken down by his endless work, lie in their envisioning of life ruled by passionate love outside of this economy. Such an erotic is not restricted to the feminine. The insistence on the disciplined aesthetic of Peking Opera in *The Dance and the Railroad* contrasts with the historical role of these characters as laborers. As Lone tells Ma, his art is what keeps his soul alive, even as it further tasks his body:

> *Lone.* It's ugly to practice when the mountain has turned your muscles to ice. When my body hurts too much to come here, I look at the other ChinaMen and think, "They are dead. Their muscles work only because the white man forces them. I live because I can still force my muscles to work for me." (64)

The Pitfalls of Writing History

With this idea of self as excess, we are in a position to examine Takaki's construction of Asian American history with a more critical eye. Critics such as E. San Juan, Jr., argue that Takaki, despite his painstaking scholarship and careful negotiation of political argument, ultimately resorts to liberal humanist values and is commodified by the very institutions and practices that he seeks to subvert. Because the plays so closely parallel Takaki's strategic positioning, they, too, are implicated in this criticism.

Takaki's positioning of his Asian American history as "real" voices telling true stories is worrisome, and not only because all claims to historical truth are suspect. Certainly, Takaki's presentation of these voices is self-conscious, strategic, and contestational rather than naive; he uses documents to create the sense of an authentic and therefore authoritative history precisely in order to counter previous erasures or stereotypical views of Asian Americans. However, such a compelling writing of history in "talk stories" can disguise other problems. San Juan finds Takaki's *Strangers from a Different Shore* troubling mainly in its final chapters, where it compares past and present life for Asian Americans and constructs a "balance sheet" of current gains and losses. According to San Juan, Takaki's writing of history ultimately has a "comic emplotment" that sounds optimistic even as he faithfully records contemporary instances of racism such as anti-Asian violence in the wake of Vietnam and other wars, and instances of Japan-bashing ("Beyond Identity Politics" 546). Takaki does suggest, among these more somber instances, a view of Asian Americans triumphing over racism, fighting for and to some degree winning equal status. But, as San Juan points out, Takaki suggests that success can be viewed not only in terms of Asian American participation in civil rights but also in the modest gains of middle-class economic status.

By constructing Asian American history as a story of heroic persistence and small victories, Takaki's history lends itself to an interpretation that supports the very assumptions of "natural" assimilation that Takaki has worked so hard to counter. In this interpretation, Asian Americans are yet another example of successful assimilation of an ethnic minority. Their present success undoes arguments about systematic racism, suggesting that the past can be forgotten in the kinder, gentler world of today. To conflate middle-class economic status with some measure of success on the part of Asian Americans is also to support implicitly the very economic ideology that underwrote the exploitation of Asians and other nonwhite groups in America and overseas. According to San Juan, "Takaki has superbly accomplished the articulation of the hegemonic doctrine of acquisitive/possessive liberalism as the informing principle of Asian American lives" ("Beyond Identity Politics" 546), where success is measured as a right to pursue individual fulfillment rather than a more substantive change in the system itself:

What is sought (in *Strangers from a Different Shore*) is the redemption of individual sacrifices by way of conformity to the utilitarian,
competitive ethos of a business society. . . . [Takaki's] rhetoric acti-
vates a mode of comic emplotment where all problems are finally
resolved through hard work and individual effort, inspired by past
memories of clan solidarity and intuitive faith in a gradually im-
proving future. What is this if not a pluralist society where all dis-
parities in values and beliefs—nay even the sharpest contradictions
implicating race, class, and gender—can be harmonized within the
prevailing structure of power relations? ("Beyond Identity Politics"
545–46)

To some extent, the history plays avoid this kind of pitfall because their
claims to represent Asian American history are limited and they do not
portray history as progress. If any, it is plays set in the present, such as
Hwang's *FOB* and Elizabeth Wong's *Letters to a Student Revolutionary,*
that bring out the implications of middle-class success for Asian Americans. These plays, which will be examined in the next chapter, can be
thought of as the final history plays, demonstrating all the contradictions
and perils of American success stories.

But a related "celebratory" impulse can be seen in the history plays we
have just examined, in their evocation of a history that relies on an ideal
of human transcendence. The personal stories of individual valor told in
these plays threaten to eclipse the larger social situation. Thus, the plays
could be read as privileging some aspects of a universal human condition—friendship, artistic endeavor, love—over specific social issues, with
labor practices relegated to the background of a more individualist human conflict. Certain of these plays, in their insistence on the emotional
self and the authentic voice, support a reading of history as an ultimate
triumph over the evils of the past, where the past can be known and
commandeered to fit the agendas of the present. The authentic Asian

American spirit is pictured as heroic, able to insist on self-worth and expressiveness in excess of a character's purely functional role. This perspective prompts a reading of both play and history that emphasizes feelings, values, and relationships as transcendent essences that can be separated from particular social situations. The materials of both the historical narratives and the history plays are collected or constructed, arranged, and performed as proof of the essential self and its unbreakable spirit. If Takaki uses documents, photographs, and texts as testimonials to this heroism, the history plays use their material stage in the same way. Certain Asian American history plays rely on performance as a testimony to endurance, and suggest suffering as a prelude to knowledge.

If there is a problem with these plays, and with Takaki's history, it is that the writing of such "success stories" can too easily be interpreted as a sign of success. This is again not to deny the powerful emotional satisfaction of watching or reading such histories. History of this sort is compelling in the same way that dramatic realism is: it promises a coherent subjectivity, an authentic voice, a truth within the stories. But the effects of "authenticity" lead people of color into thinking that the ability to "speak their real history" represents true empowerment and a sign of progress, even as it disguises their merger into what San Juan has called a "normative pluralism": "the subalterns submit to the status quo on the condition that they have access to 'individual freedoms,' varied life-styles, differential rewards, and so forth" ("Beyond Identity Politics" 561). The writing of these historical narratives and the production of history plays become part of the limited freedom that the subalterns are permitted in exchange for their voluntary consent to be ruled: "the ruled accept their subordinate position for the sake of a degree of freedom that indulges certain libidinal drives, sutures fissured egos, and fulfills fantasies" ("Beyond Identity Politics" 561). In other words, these histories—written and performed—become placebos offered to Asian Americans, visions of their "true" past in exchange for their continued complicity in the present.

But some history plays might in fact subvert such a process. For instance, Darrell H. Y. Lum's *Oranges Are Lucky* (first produced by Kumu Kahua and the Leeward Community College Drama Program in 1976, directed by Dennis Dubin, and recently revived by Kumu Kahua in 1996) presents stories of the past that both invite and thwart this liberal humanist interpretation.

At the eighty-first birthday party of the matriarch Ah Po, several generations of family gather at a local Chinese restaurant. While her children and grandchildren complain of life in present-day Hawaii, the old woman loses herself in memories of her passage from China to Hawaii. Ah Po's inner monologues about the past, rendered in standard English to indicate her competency in Chinese, alternate with exchanges among the younger generations in the present moment, spoken in pidgin (Ah Po also speaks pidgin with her children). At first the staging suggests both bonds and discontinuities between past and present. The younger characters rebel against old customs and appear ignorant of their own history. The older grandson Ricky rants openly against the spirit of his dead grandfather and the customs he sees as wasteful: "We burn dead people's money for you to spend in heaven, Ah Goong. We leave one bowl of food by da side of da gravestone for da caretaker of your grave and da guardian of your soul. You sucker, you sucking Ah Goong, you suck us dry with your Chinese ways." Different characters express different attitudes toward Ah Po's past experiences, treating her stories either as knowledge to be preserved or as a waste of time; when the younger grandson Dane expresses a wish to record Ah Po's stories, his aunt Esther rejects this: "Ass all old stuff, no good talk about long time ago. No use, ancient history." Yet the connectedness of past and present—the process of history—is demonstrated through the juxtaposition of Ah Po's stories and memories and the action of the present. This is expressed not only through more whimsical connections between past and present, such as Ah Po's comment that Dane should braid his long hair into "a queue like the old Chinese plantation workers," but also in deeper parallels. Ricky's rebellion against what he feels to be the crushing weight of outmoded custom has a parallel in the stories of Ah Po's youth and her arranged marriage. Ah Po's journey to America was not wholly forced on her; she welcomed it as a way out of boredom and later recalls how she declared to her husband, "I want adventures."

Oranges Are Lucky could be read as resolving years of hardship and racism with a modicum of success. The old woman is surrounded by her family, which, though culturally divided, is nonetheless intact; as she prepares to blow out her birthday candles, she says, "I wish to be American . . . da first president is George Washington." Her words resonate with irony. As part of the ritual of naturalization, they seem to indicate the old woman's acceptance of an American life as now hers. But she speaks these words as her children and grandchildren pressure her into public demonstrations of unfamiliar customs, and any celebration of her "naturalization" seems uneasy. Although the play suggests ways of celebrating the past as a progression into the present, no clear success story emerges.

Ah Po's stories do recount heroism and endurance. Her new life is in part rebellion against a traditional, rigidly classed society in which education and intellect (Chew Mung's poetry, calligraphy, and philosophy) become inhibiting; she does dismiss old prejudices against the Japanese, for example. But her break with the past is neither romanticized nor transcendent. Ah Po cannot be lauded for her heroic transcendence of circumstance. Her husband gives up his dream of running a Chinese school in Hawaii; his intellectual pursuits are crowded out by manual labor and shopkeeping. Growing fearful rather than courageous, Ah Po retreats into her own world: "I will only talk Chinese to you. I will only go to the Chinese stores. I will only eat Chinese food. Things American are no good. I do not want my children to become American. Why don't they listen to me?" The younger generation does not fulfill the dreams of their elders. Ah Po's grandchildren are not shown as exemplary: their lives are depicted as unenviable, their intellectual and community achievements unmentioned, their economic successes modest at best.

Thus, in Lum's play, history itself is pictured not as a continuous past reaching fulfillment in the present but as something that is by turns repetitive and radically disjointed from the present. The staging of Ah Po's senility reflects such an uncomfortable movement. In her memorial returns to the past, Ah Po reenacts a fragmented narrative that highlights disjuncture, dissolution, and change; the subsequent loss of connection and the rebellion of her grandchildren are testimony to this fractured history. In the play, past and present interrupt as well as continue one another. It is impossible to bind them together into a success story. Thus the play both stages the need to remember an Asian American history and suggests a necessary countering of more idealized visions of an Asian American past.

6

Asian American Doubles
and the Soul under Capitalism

The casting controversy over the 1991 New York production of *Miss Saigon* troubled many within the ranks of Asian American theater. As Asian American actors protested the casting of Jonathan Pryce as the Eurasian engineer, played in yellowface, the focus of the protest shifted away from the musical's blatantly stereotypical characters and its celebration of colonialism and toward the issue of "equal economic opportunity" for actors. Some argued that Asian Americans should be allowed to play a lead role that at the time was reserved for the white protegé of the director and producer. Cameron Mackintosh, the producer, threatened to cancel the show completely, thus depriving more Asian American actors of the chance to audition for parts. His threat was effective: the Actors' Equity Council rescinded its decision to bar Pryce, and the show was produced as scheduled.[1]

In this complex situation, the more obvious issue, namely, the promotion of stereotypes and imperialist fantasies in an extravagant theatrical production, became obscured by another set of concerns. As pointed out by E. San Juan, Jr., such events demand a reevaluation of the position that matters of artistic representation and power are somehow apart from economic interests ("Multiculturalism" 477). Although it is easy to imagine how Asian Americans might contest stereotypical depictions of Orientals generated by an artistic hierarchy that has traditionally excluded them, it is harder to imagine how they might contest a capitalist system that includes them. This chapter considers how Asian Americans are implicated in the economic system that has constructed them, and to what extent such a system redefines the bonds of race and ethnicity.

As a money- and commodity-based capitalism comes to dominate the social condition, personal relations are suppressed in favor of more impersonal and objective relations of exchange. To reproduce the means of its own production, capitalism superimposes its pervasive value system on matters of race and ethnicity as well. As Asian American drama takes its place on the world stage, it has been increasingly concerned with questions of participation by Asian Americans in "a society characterized by supposedly meritocratic competition in the 'free market'" (E. San Juan, Jr., "Multiculturalism" 471) and the tendency to measure the political progress of Asian Americans in terms of hard work and material success—that is, in terms of a consumerist lifestyle.

The myth of Asian Americans as a model minority is tied directly to such values. Such a myth can be straightforwardly disproved with statistics that take into account factors such as the level of education, number of dependents, and comparative cost of living.[2] Yet the myth persists because it is useful for affirming the values of hard work and thrift on the part of individuals, who are then rewarded with material success. Sociologist Edna Bonacich has pointed out that the very work ethic for which Asian Americans have been lauded helps to perpetuate a system of inequality. For instance, she suggests that a Korean-owned grocery store might be seen not only as an example of hard work leading to success, but also as the absorption of the immigrant family into an exploitative process: "immigrant entrepreneurship can be seen as a mechanism by which the capitalist class strengthens its own hands in the class struggle, by fragmenting the working class along ethnic lines, and increasing competition among workers. The result is lower labor standards for American

workers, excessively low labor standards for immigrants, and a perpetua-
tion of a system that knocks all workers down" ("Social Costs" 128).
Asian American professionals become "cogs in the giant crushing machine," forgetting their own complicity in an intrinsically racist as well as
hierarchical system ("Teaching Race and Class" 197). As Bonacich puts it,

> So, in being asked to join the great colorblind American rat race,
> minorities are not only being asked to negate themselves. They are
> being asked to join the very system that has oppressed them and
> continues to oppress them. They are being asked to become lieuten-
> ants of their captors. ("Teaching Race and Class" 89)

The ideology of the free market affects the perception of race and
ethnicity on another level, as issues of social inequality become transformed into those of personal identity and individual self-actualization.
Racial and ethnic identification become perceived as a matter of "lifestyle," determined to a large extent by products purchased and consumed: films, clothing, music, books, theater tickets. This emphasis on
lifestyle obscures cultural identification on a different level, separating the
upper middle class from the lower class and disguising the extent to
which the economic practices themselves are racist. Freedom becomes
envisioned in terms of economic purchasing power, and the right to possess is seen as a form of equality. Such a translation of racial politics into
these terms is doubly ironic, for although the free-market system may
disguise itself as a pure meritocracy, without regard for race or ethnic
status, it is in fact deeply rooted in the racist practices of global capitalism, which have had direct and often tragic impact on the situations of
Asians and Asian Americans.[3]

Recently, a number of critics have pointed out what they see as an
alarming trend in young Asian Americans, many of whom are less interested in working toward collective or global change for equality than in
decrying the effects of racism in hampering the fulfillment of personal

goals.[4] But their perceived selfishness and ingratitude are the result of Asian Americans being drawn into a particular ideology of consumerism and individualism, a process that can be seen in new immigrants as well as in third- and fourth-generation Asian Americans. This is not so much a problem (or consequence) of new wealth and assimilation as it is a product of the ideology of American enterprise, which re-forms human action and relationships in order to sustain and perpetuate itself.

Such lines of questioning inform the dramatic presentation of four plays that will be examined here: Charlotte Lum's *These Unsaid Things,* Arthur Aw's *All Brand New Chinese Classical Theater* (produced by Kumu Kahua in 1978, directed by John McShane), David Henry Hwang's *FOB* (first produced by Nancy Takahashi for the Stanford Asian American Theatre Project, directed by Hwang at Okada House in 1979, with subsequent productions at the 1979 O'Neill National Playwrights Conference and the New York Shakespeare Festival Public Theater in 1980), and Elizabeth Wong's *Letters to a Student Revolutionary* (which premiered at the Pan Asian Repertory Theatre in 1991, directed by Ernest Abuba). However different their dramatic styles and venues for production, these plays all highlight the inseparability of economics from the construction of race and ethnicity. Their characters show young Asian Americans attempting to define themselves through the value system which assigns worth to their activity and their bodies; their anxieties about "self" and "identity" are intimately related to their positioning within capitalism. Each play refers to the ways in which the terms of capitalism reproduce themselves through ideology; they do so by emphasizing the individual self, competition, and acquisition over the formation of community and collectivity by other means. In this sense, these plays suggest how the "American way" encourages individualism as a means of dividing and undermining potentially subversive alliances. But at the same time, the plays evoke ethnicity and race as forces that may counter such a pervasive ideology. Each play suggests the possibility of finding alternatives to such a way of life, modes of existence in which people, activities, bodies, and objects are not reduced to these terms of commodity exchange.

There is precedence for this political orientation in the history plays considered in the previous chapter. As we saw, the writers of those plays emphasized that their characters could not be reduced to mere laboring machines and could escape dehumanization through a vision, however fleeting, that was realized in passion or imagination. However, in those history plays, such an escape was envisioned as transcendent rather than critical, protective rather than transformative. Ultimately the vision of transcending an ugly situation provides only a temporary respite, as epitomized by the tragic spectacle of Yamauchi's Emiko dancing in the desert, lost in hopeless fantasies of her past. In contrast, the plays discussed in this chapter are at once less poetic and more critical. Even their more lyrical moments argue for a more distanced stance. They express the Asian American's felt need to imagine a position outside capitalism, illustrating the possibility of a space from which to critique the system, or the beginnings of human relations based on other principles.

Within the history plays, a character with a conscious will and a coherent self fights the dehumanization of a system that exploits its "Others." But in these plays, character, identity, and self are less coherent constructs. Instead, these plays emphasize a contradictory, fragmented self both constructed within capitalistic ideology and negotiating other possibilities and contradictions. Within the plays, a split consciousness, in which one character serves as a double or foil for another, becomes a theatrical focal point.

As Sau-Ling Cynthia Wong has pointed out, doubling is a consistent feature of Asian American fiction and drama. In a significant number of these works, Asian American characters see their "racial shadow" projected onto those more "Asian" than they, and violently reject this personification of their own "Asian identity" (Wong, *Reading Asian American Literature*, 109–12). Wong suggests that such a technique can give insight into a single character's psychology of projection and repression. In particular, a racial double can illustrate and personify the self-hatred of the protagonist, who rejects his or her own Asianness by projecting it onto another who is more alien. But the theatrical manifestations of doubling in these plays demand a somewhat different interpretation. Where Wong reads the double as illustrative primarily of an individual's psychological state, I read it as an enactment of larger tensions created in the very act of affirming the psychology of the individual, leading us to question what shapes ideas of Asian American selfhood and relationship. In other words, these plays are concerned not only with the psyche of a protagonist, but also with the interactions of Asian Americans caught up in myths of individual success promoted by a capitalist ideology. While illustrating the pitfalls of such an ideology, these plays also offer the possibility of alternative relationships that can withstand such myths.

Although each play performs and resolves this doubling differently, all of them call attention to the psychological tensions within characters; these are manifested in a set of splittings that are not so much indicative of "Asian versus American" as of the Asian American self under the pressures of capitalism. In particular, body doubles can be read not only as a self caught between worlds, but also as the site of ideological contests over the very nature of that self. In these terms, the split self of the Asian American character is the result of the character's existence within a system that perpetuates self-individuation and consumerism as goals and encourages the replacement of other human bonds with purely economic relations. These plays examine such situations with marked ambivalence; characters are likely to celebrate their individualism and consumerism as personal freedoms and to fight ethnic ties as bonds that constrict the liberated self. However, within each of these theatrical situations is an implicit critique, at least a warning, that the larger system, particularly in its warping of human relationships, is intrinsically flawed. In these cases, the bonds of ethnicity offer alternatives to such a system.

That these characters are markedly ambivalent or even hostile toward their doubles indicates the pervasiveness of an American individualism that sees the collective body, particularly as constituted by people of color, as a threat. When one character tries to dispose of another, the act is intended to repudiate not only the unique "Asianness" contained as an aspect of self, but also the larger notion of bonding within the Asian and Asian American collective body. By disposing of a body double, the character also repudiates the threat of a shared Asianness that offers other options; thus, the character perpetuates the system to which he or she is in thrall. Thus these plays draw attention to the antagonism between character and double to illustrate not only Asian American self-hatred but also its larger context. Significantly, they also illustrate how alternative relations, often killed or eroded by the relations of capital, might be forged anew.

Charlotte Lum's *These Unsaid Things* makes such tensions apparent. The father, mother, and daughter are each played by two actors representing the internal and external selves of these characters. Their public selves have become fossilized by patterns of abuse; their internal selves, while affectionate and respectful, never are assertive enough to mitigate the pain inflicted by this verbal violence. Lum herself speaks of this play as illustrating a universal theme rather than an ethnically marked situation. For her, the doubling of these characters, "not . . . uncaring of each other, but . . . undemonstrative in their most tender feelings," is not necessarily related to their Chineseness: "Ethnicity was not a focal point in delineating those characters. Being undemonstrative, stoic, and having generational differences are not exclusive properties of the Chinese. Indeed, the inference is that these are some ways that Chinese are so like many other human beings anywhere in the world" (*Paké* 233). In another light, however, the play complicates this assessment. It suggests through subtle details that the unhappy family situation is pressured into being by a particular set of economic circumstances, and that the "unsaid" alternatives to such a system are in fact inadequate to counter these pressures.

When the college-age daughter Lim finally decides to move out and escape from the constant bickering of her parents, she chooses an independent life of study and work as an alternative to the messy world of her family. Such a generational conflict might indeed be thought more universal, as the author suggests. But the play suggests that the family's situation arose in the first place in consequence not only of unpleasant personalities, but also of particular economic hardships. The monetary concerns of the parents fuel their isolation from one another and their habitual patterns of neglect and abuse. The father's anger is tied to his business difficulties, "cheating, pulling strings with some—kowtowing to others," and his artistic frustration, expressed through wood carvings that other family members carelessly destroy as valueless. The family is destabilized by economic need in other ways: the mother's need to do piecework at home leads to her neglecting her children. Significantly, when Lim has to make excuses to her parents for leaving, she justifies them in terms of giving up family relations for financial reasons: "I haven't been doing as good work as I wanted to and if I'm going to spend so much time and money for a college education, I may as well do it right."

In these references, the play begins to suggest how their situation within a *"low-middle class Chinese home in Honolulu"* is subject to the larger forces that mold human relationships. But the play does not go farther in its criticism of the larger system in which these characters exist. Instead, it simply depicts their insufferable lives as an existential hell, which, in Sartre's words, is other people. Implicitly, however, the references characters make to their relations, activities, and desires locate this universal situation within a specific social context. These references suggest not only how the larger economic constraints contribute to a damning situation, but also how a specifically "ethnic" relation—detailed in the scenes of family life—might be contrasted to the material one. The sharing of meals, community gossip about "old man Mau Ting," and chitchat over the price of rice in China all seem to the daughter Lim to be lacking when compared with the real feelings of praise and affection that remain unsaid. However, as the play begins to make clear, these familiar, private situations are the only alternative to the public worlds of business and education outside. Both the constant verbal and physical violence and the deep, unspoken bonds of affinity differ from the kinds of relationship Lim will have with the strangers she will live with and work for. It is the dissolution of these bonds that makes Lim's decision to seek an independent life elsewhere more poignant than triumphant.

The play shows Lim's decision to be inevitable and natural, pinning the blame on the habitual patterns of abuse, the parent's inability to "say nice things" to one another, and, at the very end, the unforgivable acts of violence recollected from the past (such as the revelation that Lim's father whipped and starved her and her siblings and slapped their pregnant mother). But within particularly resonant moments, the play touches on a much more enlightening subject of inquiry: how the doubled and con-flicted Asian American self can be seen as formed within a system that perpetuates economic relations in preference to other bonds and destroys alternative modes of kinship, dissolving them as unproductive and detri-mental to the well-being of the thoroughly liberated, fulfilled, and differ-entiated self.

These Unsaid Things inaugurates a trope that is developed further in Arthur Aw's *All Brand New Chinese Classical Theater.* Aw's use of the double also leads to an examination of how ethnicity and race are figured by capitalism. Although Aw, like Lum, stops short of explicit critique, his play intensifies the same tensions felt in Lum's work.

With its various theatrical effects—the breaking of character, onstage commentary, songs, and the disruption of linear sequences—*All Brand New* promises a radical staging. It uses two characters, Michael 1 and Michael 2, to represent the inner conflict in the protagonist; moreover, this theatrical device is explicitly linked to issues of ethnic identity. Mi-chael 2 invites the audience to "see through it all immediately and interpret these double manifestations of your protagonist—that's me—in profound ways," thus presenting the Asian American protagonist as a fragmented subject in crisis. On one level, the doubling suggests a splitting of the self into Chinese and American parts. The source of anxiety is Michael's mother, who wants him to sacrifice his personal pleasure, to marry Chinese, and to follow traditions. Michael is caught between loyalty to his family and the pull of a collective tradition, and his own desire for creative and sexual satisfaction as an individual. Both Michaels mock the stereotypes of Oriental humility, filial piety, and wisdom. Asked by David, "Whatever happened to the great oriental reverence for the elders?" Michael 1 replies, "Gave that up when we ran out of great oriental older people. Used to have great flocks of them . . . wise old people all over the place. Couldn't make it half-way down a block without being really overwhelmed by some ad-libbed words of wisdom." The Michaels act out a sarcastic rebellion against being part of this collective, against being a "full-time Chinese person."

But the depiction of Michael as a split self also suggests a profound dissatisfaction with the terms of success in America. Michael's fragmentation of self is rooted not only in his inability to find substantial worth in "traditional Chinese values," but also in an emptiness of a different kind. Having opted for thirty years of "good times," Michael finds himself trapped in the restrictions of a job that is "crappy" but "pays good," having lost his "worthwhile aims and ambitions, ideas and ideals." The lure of economic security and the gratifications available in a consumer culture lead to Michael's arguments with his other self. The white characters—hard-drinking roommate David and possessive girlfriend Jenny—similarly embody a critique of sexual and personal self-indulgence and pleasurable self-gratification.

Once this compelling tension has been introduced, however, the play does not further engage with the issues. The serious treatment is undercut by Michael's mockery of his own anxiety: "Who am I? What am I doing here? [*Uses* MICHAEL 2 *as a mirror*] I see myself but I don't see myself. It's an identity crisis . . . the sixty-fourth one, I think, but who counts?" His anxiety is dismissed as generic, "the usual everyday run-of-the-mill self-castration." But the play's failure to explore the issues further is not necessarily related to its comic irreverence. If anything, the play is cathartic in its presentation style: slapstick and farce unleash an allowable violence, a series of battles waged against the problems of interracial relationships, generational differences, and racism. It is on another level that a more fruitful consideration is neutralized, in the erasing of possible alternatives (through ethnic bonds, for example) to the individual self as imagined in capitalist America. Although Michael's dissatisfaction is clearly linked to his dual status as a member of a Chinese collectivity and an American individualized self, the relationship between the two never becomes clear. The play suggests that ethnicity never offers alternative human relationships and bonds that can truly contest and compete with the relationships of capital. In the context of Aw's play, all is absorbed into capitalistic values. Michael's "Super-Oriental" mother becomes readable only in the context of her racism, which is directed against all Caucasians, and her materialism. She wants Michael to marry well, like his brother Philip, who married what Michael abuses as a "pimple," the daughter of a Hong Kong tycoon. Michael's attraction to Jenny also seems more lust than love. The play is relentless in its stereotyping: Jenny's homophobia matches Michael's mother's "granite-hard racial hatred and petty prejudices," while the roommate David is the "symbol of white patronizing niceness."

Although *All Brand New* places ethnic difference in conflict with individual self-fulfillment, the play does not counter the ethos of utilitarian individualism in any convincing way, or propose the formation of alternative communities. Rather, all is posed in terms of Michael's preoccupation with his own identity. In this sense, Michael's Chineseness is yet another factor in his more general problem of lifestyle. Any ethnic identification is held out to be a matter of individual choice, reduced to a matter of automatic decisions, behaviors and appearances; acting Chinese or using the devices of the classical Chinese stage are matters only of personal style. The notion that ethnicity could offer a radical departure from these relations of money and loveless labor is ultimately missing.

All Brand New Classical Chinese Theater makes it difficult to envision positive collective action because the play so blatantly reduces characters to stereotype, without deliberate inquiry into the terms of reappropriation described in Chapter 4. However, within this stereotyping, we might imagine an indictment of consumerism in the way the spectatorial relationship to the stage is constructed. Throughout the play, it is the viewers' pleasure in the entertainment on stage that is made suspect. A relationship of spectator as consumer and play as commodity is explicitly evoked. Michael 2's wearing of a pigtailed Oriental cap and bowing in exaggerated humility, the bread and circuses of the boxing matches between characters, and the interruption of Michael 1's and Jenny's sex scene with a commercial all point to the supposed desire of the audience for prepackaged theater and instant gratification. So does the play's claim to offer an "All Brand New Classical Chinese Theater," a title that loudly proclaims its own marketing strategy. The parody of conspicuous consumption indicates dissatisfaction with the value system of American capitalism, under which the characters cannot be reduced to easy formulas for the self. As Michael 1 says, "We are all coming across like some TV script or pages from a comic book. And even what I just said seems faked."

FOB

David Henry Hwang's *FOB* and Elizabeth Wong's *Letters to a Student Revolutionary* more fully develop the tension inherent in the double and the critique of capitalism than do the earlier plays. In *FOB* and *Letters,* doubling services the tensions that arise as the characters try but fail to compose their own experiences in some image of the American success story. In each play, there is a "racial shadow" that can be read psychologically: the protagonists Dale and Bibi do project their own anxieties onto other characters, who serve as their foils. But the interaction of double and original does not just portray the psychological conflict of an Asian American torn between two worlds. What is revealed in these two plays is also how psychic conflict in Asian Americans derives from a system of values that rewards highly particularized notions of success, value, and human relations.

A tension between the individual and the collective is one of the earliest indications of this conflicted state. Characters such as Dale and Bibi reject the notion of ethnic identification in collectivity and overtly celebrate the individualism of the "free self." At the same time, their preoccupation with material goods is satirized; the excessive consumption indicates dissatisfaction with the value system of American capitalism. The image of individual success is also undercut by reminders of its hidden costs: ties with the family and other significant people dissolve, and personal satisfaction is not achieved. Yet these plays also suggest that racial and ethnic identification can serve as a possible mode of resistance to capitalistic values.

The possibility of redemption arises from the characters' unforeseen encounters with their doubles; the tentative kinship that forms describes a space outside a purely capitalistic and individualistic ideology. Thus these plays offer hope for the potential to contest and critique the system that has constructed them. But in showing such a possibility, the plays refrain from easy parables of psychological redemption in which the characters would learn simple lessons about the need to stick together. Although they are made newly aware of the need for ethnic identification and the possibilities of an alternative kinship and collectivity, neither Dale nor Bibi is shown as fully able to work for social change. That each of the characters (with the important exception of Karen, in *Letters*) remains firmly rooted in the system is significant, for it prevents an overly optimistic reading of their encounters with their doubles. Simple notions of self-improvement through cultural enrichment are regarded as grandiose and self-absorbed; realizing the potential within the bonds of ethnicity and race is more complicated than it seems.

Like Aw's *All Brand New Classical Chinese Theater*, Hwang's *FOB* plays out antagonisms over a series of objects: *bing*, menus, boxes, cars, and hot sauce. These battles, waged in the monologues, myths, and actions of the three characters, take on particular interest when read as symbolic of a more encompassing struggle between capitalistic individualism and other forms of human relation.

Dale opens the play by lecturing the audience on how to distinguish the American-born Chinese—ABCs—from the nameless masses "fresh off the boat"—FOBs. Dale's terms echo the stereotypes of the Asian immigrant as "yellow peril," sexually threatening, and at the same time emasculated ("Before an ABC girl will be seen on a Friday night with a boy FOB in Westwood, she would rather burn off her face"). Most important, Dale's speech emphasizes their lack of individuation: "FOBs can be found in great numbers almost anyplace you happen to be, but there are some locations where they cluster in particularly large swarms." In the speech that begins the second act, Dale suggests that individuation and material success are linked. Dale wants the power to define himself through consumption, to move from being one of "them," "a Chinese, a yellow, a slant, a gook," to being himself in terms of buying power. Thus, "making it," having those experiences that are possible only by spending money, constitutes the humanity that is separate from the Chineseness Dale fears:

My parents—they don't know nothing about the world, about watching Benson at the Roxy, about ordering *hors d'oeuvres* at Scandia's, downshifting onto the Venture Freeway at midnight. They're yellow ghosts and they've tried to cage me up with Chinese-ness when all the time we were in America. (*Pause*) So, I've had to work real hard—real hard—to be myself. To not be a Chinese, a yellow, a slant, a gook. To be just a human being, like everyone else. (*Pause*) I've paid my dues. And that's why I am much better now. I'm making it, you know? I'm making it in America. (32)

Dale's self-actualization in terms of status symbols resonates with the myth of the self-made individual, untroubled by the past or by family ties. At the same time, Dale is troubled, not necessarily by the hollowness of this material success, but by its inability to fully liberate him from "Chinese-ness." In the play, the bonds tying characters to the past and to their ethnic connections are inescapable. That Dale's hatred of FOBs is related to his suppression of a shameful family history becomes evident when he tries to project a fictional past onto Steve; this story, Steve correctly surmises, is that of Dale's own father. Sent to America to further the family business of trading in cheap goods, the father decides to stay, disappointing Dale's grandfather, "his hopes reduced to a few chattering teeth and a pack of pornographic playing cards." Dale's father embraces the dream of a materialistic, consumerist life in America. But he occupies a peculiar place within this life: when the grandfather loses all his money, Dale's father is forced to work at menial jobs, where he is exposed to the humiliation of racism. Dale is haunted by his father's betrayal of his grandfather's trust, and his notions of Chineseness are thereby affected. Throughout the play, Dale's attempts to define himself in terms of his past are contradictory. For him, "making it" in terms of material success is incompatible with being a Chinese immigrant; thus, he tries to project onto Steve his father's humiliation, forcing Steve to wipe tables and jeering, "Oh, you learn so fast. Get green card, no time flat, buddy." But he also tries to reinterpret his father's story as that of a prototypical rags-toriches tale. When he is forced to recognize Steve as a different kind of Asian immigrant, from a Hong Kong upper class that is "well-off enough to send their kids to American colleges," "kinda classy," and "already real Westernized," Dale refuses to be associated with material success. When his cousin Grace asserts, "You *are* rich," he replies, "No. Just upper-middle. Maybe," and adds, "Beside, when I was born we were still poor." He emphasizes his experience of relative poverty—"we only got one Life Saver a day"—in order to distinguish himself from "rich FOBs." The play mocks Dale's hypocrisy, satirizing on the one hand his self-conscious refusal of a limousine ride ("I mean, wouldn't you just feel filthy . . . getting out of a limo in the middle of Westwood? People staring, thinking we're from 'SC? Wouldn't you feel like dirt? . . . Where's your social conscience?") and on the other, his reluctance to eat dinner in Grace's father's small restaurant ("How can it be fun? It's cheaper"). Dale's futile attempts to define himself solely in terms of class, his guilty displacement of his father's experience, his tentative feelings for his cousin Grace, and his antagonism toward Steve all show an inability to reconcile the terms of success in America with a Chineseness that might offer an alternative relation.

The struggle in the play is not limited to the arena of Dale's psyche, although that is its most readily identifiable locus. The play offers multiple perspectives on what it means to be a Chinese American trying to make it in America. A second perspective comes from Grace. In her final first-act speech, Grace recalls the American-born Chinese girls she grew up with, who were distanced from her both by their wealth and by their superior English: "They'd just stay with themselves and compare how much clothes they all had and make fun of the way we all talked." She is no more satisfied by her associations with her white peers. Finally, she seeks contentment in isolation, although she feels an intense loneliness. Her negotiations of the American dream and ethnic community are more distanced, more critical, than either Dale's or Steve's. In her attitude toward making it in America, she at times seems as materialistic as Dale; when Steve is horrified that she would turn down a date with "Gwan Gung for your cousin," she replies, "Well, he has an X-1/9." Yet it is her immediate memories of poverty and exclusion that distinguish her from both men. Grace's stories of her mother's experience are quite different from Dale's stories about his father; as a woman, Grace's mother "starved" and was is not at liberty to quit her menial jobs, whereas Dale's father received an education. Grace's alter ego, Fa Mu Lan, tells stories of endurance and persistence in spite of suffering, and Grace's strength, which emerges slowly in the course of the play, in part comes out of her lower-class upbringing.

Steve, who supplies a third perspective in the play, easily one-ups Dale in the course of the play, for he can out-consume Dale on a number of levels; the eating contest is symbolic not only of Steve's personal prowess and his eventual success with Grace, but of his buying power as well. But his competition with Grace, constructed in terms of class, ethnicity, and gender, is another matter. Steve relies on class privilege in the opening scene of the play, in which he enters the Torrance restaurant, demanding service from Grace, the "stupid girl"; he is baffled by Grace's refusal to answer him. His pride at the beginning of the play seems directly related to his economic status; he insists "I have come as no ChinaMan before— on a plane, with money and rank." His proprietary attitude suggests that he views immigration to America as a process that leads directly to easy consumption ("This land is mine!"). Grace's symbolic defeat of Steve, as well as her gentle rejection of Dale, suggests that these class hierarchies must give way to something else. What emerges from their symbolic battles is the lesson Steve and Dale must learn: that past and present racism against Asian Americans effects a leveling on the basis of skin color that no amount of wealth or years of assimilation can atone for.

The symbolic battle between Grace and Steve comes into focus not only in the realistic action, but also in the juxtaposition of story and myth in the play. Unlike Dale, Steve and Grace ultimately find their ethnic relation through the use of legends. Notably, these are specifically Asian American rather than Asian versions of the traditional myths of Fa Mu Lan and Gwan Gung. In the preface to *FOB*, the playwright Hwang notes that the roots of the play are "thoroughly American" and the myths manifest "the existence of an Asian American literary tradition":

> Fa Mu Lan, the girl who takes her father's place in battle, from Maxine Hong Kingston's *The Woman Warrior*, and Gwan Gung, the god of fighters and writers, from Frank Chin's *Gee, Pop!* The fact testifies to the existence of an Asian American literary tradition. (3)

In using Kingston's myths, *FOB* allows its characters an alternative space in which to play. Such mythic performances are also projections, a form of doubling. Each effectively counters the demeaned, unheroic roles of the Chinese immigrant in America and allows Steve and Grace personal fantasies of power and resilience in the face of past tragedy. At the same time, myth evokes a collective tradition that holds uncertain value in America. Steve is incredulous at the reception Gwan Gung receives:

> One man—ChinaMan—wearing leisure suit—green! I ask him, "You know Gwang Gung?" He says, "Hong Kong?" I say, "No, no. Gwang Gung." He says, "Yeah. They got sixty thousand people living on four acres. Went there last year." I say, "No, no. Gwan Gung." He says, "Ooooh! Gwan Gung!" I say, "Yes, yes, Gwan Gung." He says, "I never been there before." (15)

Because they are relatively obscure in the United States, these myths exist in a space outside the realm of American leisure-suit experience. What power they have comes from the evocation of a community, one that can bind together even such unlikely persons as those in Grace's class, a dental technician and a middle-aged woman who is bored with child-rearing. If the enactments by Steve and Grace of Gwan Gung and Fa Mu Lan begin with uncertain value in America, their power as mythic alternatives becomes determined in the course of the play.

Steve's first story reinforces his proud attitude, as his Gwan Gung decides to slay villagers "for sport"; the self-indulgent brutality is stopped only by the suggestion that it might have unfortunate consequences: "This worked very well until his sword, in its blind fury, hit upon an old and irritable atom bomb." Steve is checked in his reverie by Grace. Her stories counter his fantasies of random destruction with reminders of the real cost of human life, and she hints that she will ultimately become known as "The Woman Who Has Defeated Gwan Gung." In the final act, the class and gender privilege that has given Steve his sense of identity must be "killed" by Grace's Fa Mu Lan. She exacts this penalty in retribution for his earlier carelessness, when Gwang Gung killed her family in the course of Steve's blindfolded swordplay: "Remember the day you played? Remember? Well, eat that day, Gwan Gung." Such a humbling symbolically teaches Steve that his former status, based on his spending power, no longer suffices; now that he has emigrated to America, he must learn to negotiate what it means to be Asian American.

In the final act, Steve reenacts different stories of an immigrant past as he moves toward a position of increasing humility; these stories echo not only the histories of Dale's father and Grace's mother, but also the desperate tales of poverty and sacrifice for family that first brought the Chinese to the United States. In a climactic finale, Steve is harshly reborn within this framework, in a collective ritual in which the Asian American Dale and Grace become his parents. After Grace's Fa Mu Lan stabs him through the heart with an imaginary sword, Steve takes on his final immigrant persona: that of the Chinese immigrant who, close to starvation, appeals to the white woman for work and food. It is only after this poignant monologue, and Steve's assumption of the abject figure of a starving man offering to do laundry for food, that Grace finally gives him the *bing* he demanded from her at the beginning of the play. His consumption of the *bing*, and their subsequent litany "Our hands are beauti-ful," end the ritual, staging the sacrifice of Steve's pride in return for a sacrament of a different kind. Symbolically, Steve has been made aware of his own position within the space of privilege and, more important, his blood ties to other immigrants, for whom food is a dear necessity. These are the ties from which he had earlier thought himself exempt. "Why am I made part of these deals?" he asks earlier, insisting that "Gwan Gung bows to no one's terms but his own." Through the course of their mythic battles, Grace has shown him that he is not exempt from such "deals" because "you're in the U.S. in 1980, just like the rest of us." Their working hands, earlier despised for their menial labor, now become joined in a common bond. Grace insists on their connection despite the differences of class; she must defeat him in order to join forces with him in a differ-ent war: "We are in America. And we have a battle to fight." Steve must taste death and humiliation so that he will be prepared to work collec-tively, to break down class barriers in favor of the racial community of Asian America.

The reconciliation of Grace and Steve excludes Dale, leaving him to reexamine both the items used in the play and the terms of his earlier lecture on FOBs. Within the terms of the play, the value system in which Porsches are signifiers of personal fulfillment has been abandoned, tran-scended by other bonds. Yet the ending of the play—Dale on a stage littered with objects now emptied of significance—does not fully resolve Hwang's investigation. Instead, the play leaves us with the lonely Dale, considering what our new relations—to the world of things and of peo-ple—might be in the wake of these auspicious events.

Letters to a Student Revolutionary

The character of Bibi in Elizabeth Wong's play *Letters to a Student Revo-lutionary*, like Dale in *FOB*, is initially wrapped in consumerism, an ideology that envisions freedom in terms of buying power. A more sympathetic character than Dale, Bibi nonetheless is faulted for her inability to move beyond this shallowness. Wong's play considers more fully the possibilities of other value systems and other kinds of relationships by exposing an ethnic connection, a kinship relation between Karen and Bibi, that redeems Bibi's position in the play. (Interestingly, these alternatives do not figure so much in the play's depiction of communist China, which in many ways is portrayed as alien and oppressive.)

This redeeming relation is developed through different theatrical embodiments of "the individual" and "the masses." As Bibi wanders into Tiananmen Square at the beginning of the play, marveling at the undifferentiated mass of people, she confirms the distinction she has made between the ideology of repressive conformity in communist China and her own individual freedoms as an Asian American. The chorus addresses individualism as a kind of contamination: "There is no you. There is no me. Only people. People must prevail. There is no you. There is no me. Only people." Bibi at first senses neither ethnic community nor blood ties to Chinese culture, only the repressive state of communist China, the undifferentiated compaction of desires and bodies into the "masses." This encounter in Tiananmen Square sets up a dynamic between what Bibi perceives as Chinese amorphousness and her own secure individuality:

Like in "Vertigo." Jimmy Stewart climbing the steps, looking down from the tower. *Everything* going in a woozy circle. I see me and I see me and I see me. Faces like my face, like my mother's face, like my father's face. But not really, you know. I don't fit in, not at all. (272)

Significantly, when Karen emerges from the mass, it is only to become Bibi's mirror; as she later tells Bibi: "I look at you and it is as if I look at myself in a glass." When she leaves, she vanishes once again into this mass of people, "merged with other bicycles merging together. Bibi couldn't distinguish one rider from the other." What Karen yearns for, and is taught through her correspondence with Bibi, is the doctrine of individual selfhood. Karen becomes the recipient of Bibi's "knowledge"; not only does she learn English from Bibi, but Bibi sees herself as educating and enlightening Karen about a knowledge of "self," a view made clear by the gifts that she sends. The music, books, and magazines she chooses focus on individuality—self-help books from *Dr. Spock's Baby Book* to *I'm Okay, You're Okay* and fashion magazines that shape Karen's fantasies about becoming a fashion designer, having people recognize both her and her products as "a Karen original."

But the play relates that "[t]he more she read, the more Karen grew depressed," and Bibi is no more enlightened or happy in her own life. Bibi prefers shopping in Hong Kong to touring the innumerable factories in communist China ("Now that's freedom. Shopping from dawn til dusk"). But her view of consumerism as a means of self-liberation is deceptive illusion. Bibi's fantasy of playing a movie-star role obscures the fact that hers is not true freedom, for it does not erase the distinctions of race and ethnicity. Her situation is evident in her account of going to her hairdresser, who insists on giving her a China-doll haircut: "It's like every time I go to the salon, they want to give me the same old, tired thing— the classic bob and bangs, exactly like yours. . . . They tell me, 'But oh no, you look so cute. A little China doll, that's what you are.' Make me *puke.* So I say, 'Aldo baby darling, perm it. Wave it. Frizz it. Spike it. Color it blue.'" But despite her desire to transform herself by changing her appearance, she realizes how her ethnicity is inescapably marked on her. As she tells Karen, "Sure, you come to California. And I'll set you up with Aldo. But I warn you, he'll poof and pull and snip, and you think you're going to be a new woman, but you get banged and bobbed every time." The makeover promises a change of self to the Asian American but exposes in its limitations a disguised racism.

As the play progresses, this supposed freedom of what Bibi calls "the Church of Our Lady of Retail" is handled more cynically: as Bibi tells Karen, "in America, we like to *think* we're a democracy, but we're definitely a nation of shoppers." If the play's chorus stages the Chinese government explicitly as a machine of oppression, then the play also suggests that American capitalism more invisibly but just as irrevocably molds characters to fit its needs. Bibi's successive boyfriends are described in terms that evoke the shopping catalogue or advertising language of the personals column. Significantly, Bibi loses the man of her dreams, "an Adonis in a three-piece suit, a pillar of the community, and witty but in a dry outdoorsy kind of way" in a scene at a shopping mall as the chorus chants "we are a nation of shoppers." The boyfriend dumps her as incompatible with his own lifestyle.

Bibi is consistently disappointed and unfulfilled in her endless variety of choices, and she somewhat enviously contrasts her own restlessness with Karen's lack of professional and marital choices. Bibi's training in this domain of selfhood is ineffective when real problems arise, as becomes evident when she visits the Immigration and Naturalization Service. Bibi urges those waiting in the interminable lines to stand up for their rights in the face of rudeness and racism from the government workers: "You gotta stand up for yourselves, or else your face is a doormat." Her cure for the situation, self-assertiveness, is ineffectual in the larger scheme of government bureaucracy; she is told by many who wait in line with her, "Well, get used to it, Chinita." Nor does she have a solution for the obsolescence of the endless items she buys: when her gifts to Karen break, she is unable to afford replacements.

The play suggests other problems associated both with American capitalism and Chinese communism. The execution of Karen's mother for stealing food for her children has a parallel in the later scene of Bibi's father's death, brought on by overwork. In both cases parent–child bonds are undone by the pressures of the larger economic system. Karen's mother and Bibi's father are both presented as sacrificing themselves for the nourishment of their children. The play emphasizes that economic systems and the state are inextricably intertwined; both combine mercilessly to break down family relationships.

What is most strongly contrasted in the two protagonists, Bibi and Karen, are their respective means of political action as prompted by these definitions of self and collective. Karen is able to move beyond her desire to leave China; she becomes focused where Bibi remains confused. Karen's joining the students protesting for democracy renders another vision of society, one in which an individual's freedom is inseparable from the communal good; the students are both protesting for individual rights ("We are fighting for a system that will respect the individual. The individual is not dead") and at the same time insisting that individual success should be seen in terms of a larger social good ("We must give our lives to the movement"). In becoming political, Karen's implied self-sacrifice in Tiananmen Square seems inevitable.

When Karen desires to become, like Bibi, individually fulfilled, her motives are clearly presented, but as her desires become directed toward the alternative of communal action, these motives retreat into the background. Her final moments in Tiananmen Square are portrayed not as heroic self-sacrifice but as a confused searching for her husband in an amorphous mass of human flesh. The letters exchanged between Karen and Bibi, which have glossed Karen's intentions, suddenly cease; Karen's actions again become unintelligible to Bib at the moment when Karen again blends into the masses. Karen's new sense of communal action can be understood only as the sacrifice of the individual. In the stage directions, Wong suggests using a particular image of Tiananmen Square, "*the famous photograph of the lone man standing in front of a line of tanks.*"

Again, the hoped-for alternatives to Bibi's capitalistic individualism exist less in the rendering of Karen's consciousness, which becomes unintelligible when it is no longer motivated by the desire to become individualized. Rather, the play focuses on the relation of Bibi to Karen, for this relation exposes Bibi's own ambivalences: her own social awakening, and the bonds she is capable of forming.

At the start of the play, Bibi's revolutionary tendencies are sublimated into fantasized rebellions directed against her mother. Initially she interprets the sacrifices of others (her mother's work in a sweatshop, her father's in a grocery store) as in the service of her own self-improvement: "Mom and Dad slaved so I could squander their hard work on college." She is unable to understand how the bonds of family or ethnicity could be prompted by anything other than guilt. She associates the trip to China only with a kind of consumerist ethnicity or self-actualization: "So, for thirty-five days, wherein I wished I was in the Bahamas instead, I was Kunta Kinte of the new Roots generation." But through her contacts with Karen, Bibi experiences a kind of social awakening in which the possibility of alternative relations is kindled. As Karen develops a greater sense of self, Bibi moves toward a greater recognition of kinship, if not of collectivity. As the play progresses, Bibi discards her strictly negative connections and gains a sense of responsibility for Karen. Bibi not only begins to feel the part of the "guardian angel," but to understand, with Karen's advice, her relationship with her parents. Her Chineseness becomes not only a matter of appearance and lifestyle. Bibi's changing perspective is articulated through her changing idea of the masses, the ethnicized collective, which by the end of the play is quite different from her earlier perception of the crowds in Tiananmen Square. In a scene where Bibi takes her mother to the Statue of Liberty, she is moved by her mother's response to its inscription ("Give me your tired, your poor, your huddled masses, yearning to breathe free"). The chorus joins Bibi in reciting the inscription. Bibi's moment of sympathy with her mother stems from her new recognition of herself as a product of the masses from which she so vehemently segregated herself at the beginning of the play.

Wong suggests that the bond between Karen and Bibi allows for a kinship that is both distinctive and potentially subversive. It is this alternative connection between two women that the play struggles to articulate, in an effort to understand the complex sympathy felt in the United States for the students participating in the democracy movement in China. Bibi writes to Karen in her final letter, "Please understand that I am Chinese too and I feel a deep connection to you, but what you are doing is suicide." *Letters to a Student Revolutionary*, finally, suggests the formation of an ethnic connection that is not based on family, nationalism, or economic profit. Such a connection within ethnicity offers a new possibility of action, an alternative to the kinds of relationships encouraged by the American bureaucracy or the communist state. Such a relation, though precariously embedded in other concerns, allows for the suggestion of alternatives: the vision of a better world that must accompany any critique of the system that Asian Americans now inhabit.

7

Staging "Passing" on the
Borders of the Body

As Sau-Ling C. Wong has suggested, heated debates surround the use of the terms race and ethnicity in examining literature and drama (*Reading Asian American Literature* 15). Many writers prefer the term ethnic precisely because it can imply more self-determination on the part of the individual than does the term race. Werner Sollors, for instance, in *Beyond Ethnicity: Consent and Descent in American Culture*, proposes a "voluntary or multiple-choice ethnicity" whereby ethnicity becomes "a matter not of content but of the importance that individuals ascribe to it" (35). The concept of a multiple-choice ethnicity presupposes a coherent, knowing self that "performs" its ethnicity, an actor that chooses a set of social roles. Yet the existence of historical and material categories into which bodies are placed complicates this notion of a responsible, self-determining individual who chooses to be "ethnic" or not.

It seems clear that the physical body is at the center of both the violent disputes and the conceptual fuzziness surrounding the terms ethnicity and race. These terms intersect in the complicated ways in which the physical body is inscribed with meaning, whether that meaning is chosen consciously and voluntarily or is imposed from without, through social and historical factors. In the worst cases of racism, such marking is equivalent to branding. Not only the observer's field of vision but also the individual's self-identity become indelibly marked with what Franz Fanon in *Black Skin, White Masks* describes as a fixed "corporeal schema," the "implicit knowledge . . . that each of us possesses of the position of his or her body in relation to other physical objects . . . the image each of us has of him- or herself as a body located somewhere in physical space . . . an image that each of us ordinarily constructs and needs repeatedly to reconstruct as he or she moves about the world" (111–12). Bodies are rigorously policed not only by force but also by these more ideological self-images; they are especially kept in check where any ambiguity or permeability of category boundaries might endanger the existing state of power. Every assertion that difference is consciously or willingly played out is countered by the manifest existence of more complex factors that continue to turn bodies into racialized, ethnicized, gendered, or classed signifiers. The actor's body, whether onstage or off, inescapably carries with it this set of conventional and historical meanings. Even when we are asked to see the body as neutral, as in current instances of "color-blind" casting, we cannot. As E. San Juan, Jr., reflected on the remarks made by an African American writer he met at a conference:

> But can one really invent one's identity as one wishes, given the constraints de jure and de facto enforced by the racial state? She confesses: "I can make myself up and this is the enticement, the exhilaration. . . . But only up to a point. And the point, the sticking point, is my dark female body." Identity betrays its lack in the crucible of difference. Here is where I would finally foreground the phenotypical markers, the brand of the racial stigma, as the politically valorized signifier that cannot be denied in spite of the rules of formal juridical equality. The colored body and its tropes may be the uncanny sites where the repressed—history, desire, the body's needs—returns. ("Beyond Identity Politics" 560–61)

Yet what if the terms race and ethnicity—as well as the physical markers that enact these categories on the body—were found to be inherently unstable? Several relatively recent changes of a social and legal nature, including the repeal of laws and policies that restricted immigration, interracial marriage, school integration, and naturalization, symbolically allow easier passage across the hitherto rigidly policed boundaries defined in terms of geography, social structures, and human relationships. But these historical changes have not led to complete changes in how such boundaries are constructed or perceived. When these restrictions, and the worlds they define, become more permeable, passage is not immediate or easy; rather, complex tensions, the legacy of these historical policings, arise to surround the act of crossing racial and ethnic boundaries.

Michael Awkward in *Negotiating Difference: Race, Gender, and the Politics of Positionality* has suggested that what he calls "transracial subjects" can become symbolically significant to the degree that they "manifest conceptual slippage between notions of the natural and the socially constructed, between biological determinism and cultural conditioning" (176). Their "fleshly embodiment—the assumption of traits of difference of the racial other—cuts directly to the heart of essentialist formulations of racial difference," thus intervening "upon rigid rules of racial order" (181, 182). Compared with the more paradigmatic texts of racial passing between black and white, the texts that highlight the "passing" of Asian Americans into a white society remain relatively unexplored.[1] One might argue that there is less tension involved in crossing the borders delineating Asian from non-Asian than in crossing between white and black. Yet in dramatic works by Asian Americans, the tensions of passage are overwhelming, affirming the difficult politics of such a move.

The contemporary theater affords a unique opportunity to examine not only the repression and expression of the body with respect to such a "corporeal schema" but also the desires and myths that are born out of the possibility of movement, self-determination, and reinvention. This chapter examines how certain plays configure the raced and ethnicized bodies of characters as marked within figurative boundaries, and how those boundaries might be crossed. The plays also suggest some complex responses by Asian American playwrights to the idea of "passing" through racial, ethnic, and other boundaries defined upon the body.

A theatrical fascination with traversing, sundering, or transgressing the boundaries demarcating Asian from non-Asian (especially white) is not new. For instance, one kind of passing, interracial marriage (sometimes branded miscegenation), has provided the plot for many plays. Popular New York productions of plays such as *A Japanese Nightingale* (1903), *East is West* (1918), *His Chinese Wife* (1920), *Aloma of the South Seas* (1925), and *Uptown West* (1923), as well as David Belasco's famous *Madame Butterfly* (1900), portrayed doomed love affairs between interracial couples.[2] The theatrical treatment of taboos such as interracial sex can arouse audiences and make the playwright seem politically progressive, yet result in a dramatic outcome in which racial boundaries are ultimately reinforced. Although such familiar patterns typically recur in plays by Asian Americans, there are as well a number of significant variations on these themes. Not only is there a pronounced possibility of transgressing forbidden borders, of characters passing by means of assimilation, contact, bodily disguise, or transformation, there is also a certain amount of theatrical experimentation with what these actions mean.

A subtle but significant variation is evident in an early play by Gladys Li (Li Ling-Ai), *The Submission of Rose Moy* (produced at the Arthur Andrews Theatre, University of Hawaii, Honolulu, in 1928, and first published in *Hawaii Quill Magazine* in 1927). This play establishes familiar categories that divide the characters along the lines of ethnicity and gender. The central character Rose is a Hawaiian-born Chinese college student; her father has decided to give her as a fourth concubine to the old and wealthy Kwang Wei. Rose refuses, insisting that she wants to finish her graduate education, after which she will be able to work for suffrage for Chinese women and help them "rise above the shackles of tradition that have bound our women from time immemorial, and have imprisoned their spirits." Her father is adamant, and goes to prepare the wedding plans. Rose confides in her American teacher, Mr. Donald, who offers her an introduction to his sister in Berkeley, with whom Rose can live while she studies. But just as she makes the decision to run away, her father gives her a letter left for her from her deceased mother. The letter urges her to "bow to the will of your ancestors" and "remember . . . you are a Chinese." Upon reading this edict from the maternal dead, Rose gives up her dream of education and agrees to marry at her father's request. In the final dramatic moments, accompanied by the ominous sound of gongs, Rose utters, "I am of the East—I bow. I submit to the will of my ancestors!" and faints before the ancestral tablets, while outside her American teacher waits for her, whistling "Yankee Doodle Dandy." In the stage directions, the playwright adds: "*Mr. Donald is still waiting, and he waits in vain!*"

The play employs stock characters and devices such as the delayed letter, a commandment from a dead mother, and elaborately heightened language to create dramatic tension between "Chinese" and "American," tradition and progress, patriarchy and proto-feminism. The protagonist, although her teacher insists that she is "an American-born Chinese girl," experiences "Chinese" and "American" as incompatible with one another. The play builds its moments of high drama out of the assumption that the heroine must choose between states constructed as mutually exclusive; she must choose either an enlightened "American" independence, emphasizing the "present and future," or submission to the patriarchal "Chinese" world of the "horrible past."

Rose's tragic choice is no choice at all. She has no real possibility of crossing those boundaries; destiny is portrayed as indelibly written into the blood, and Rose cannot deny the will of her ancestors. But the dramatic tension owes in part to a contemplation of a choice of identity category. Although the worlds of East and West are delineated as incompatible states, what is interesting is that the play does introduce—even if it does not develop—the theme of passing, a liminal state in which Rose's body might not be fully claimed by either world. To be sure, the play offers only rigidly exaggerated formulations. Rose first rebelliously defies her father with the impassioned words, "Give me liberty, give me freedom," but by the end of the play she has been radically transformed into "Chinese" passivity, sinking before the altar. Yet the transformation from one state to another is delayed by melodramatic equivocation. Her situation demands some qualification, which is provided by the playwright: "*Rose Moy: A Hawaiian-born Chinese college girl who is Western in ideas and ideals—and yet not entirely Western.*" Theatrically speaking, we see the body of Rose Moy poised in a state of possibility. Although there is little doubt about Rose Moy's fate (her submission is shown not as a choice but as a relinquishing of will), the play momentarily creates a space of indeterminacy where Rose need be neither fully Asian nor fully American, but might occupy both positions at the same time.

Since publication of *The Submission of Rose Moy* in 1927, the problematic of passing has been a consistent theme in plays by Asian American writers. One might even say it has become a preoccupation, as changes in immigration and naturalization laws have opened up new opportunities for the crossing of geographic and social boundaries and Asian Americans have been lauded for successful assimilation as the model minority. These changes do not necessarily lead to a state in which boundaries are freely crossed and identity can be entirely self-consciously created. On the contrary: as in *Rose Moy,* more recent plays show the boundaries of difference being reinforced; at best, crossing produces a set of difficult and sometimes frustrating contradictions. Yet the frequency and variety with which the possibility of passing is broached emphasize not only its fascination, but also its necessity.

The codified presentation of the Asian body in mainstream American theater of the nineteenth and twentieth centuries defined the body as

"Asian," not only through the exaggerated costumes, gestures, and speech, but also by emphasizing with stage makeup supposedly unmistakable physical features such as eyes, hair, and skin color. In more recent plays by Asian American playwrights, there seem to be at once an interesting subversion and a reaffirmation of these conventional stereotypes. The line between what is "Asian" and "un-Asian" suddenly blurs, allowing a reinterpretation of the body of the actor. However, the characters are not necessarily able to move freely across the borders of race without intense scrutiny or punishment. Many plays elaborate the theme of passing only to insist that such passing between racial designations is impossible, or to show the anxiety about impurity or inauthenticity that accompanies attempts at passage.

American theater has a history of turning moments of racial indeterminacy into intensely dramatic revelation, as disclosures are followed immediately by dire consequences. Moments in a number of recent Asian American plays follow this pattern. These moments suggest that those with mixed blood cannot fully pass, that they are indelibly marked by their bodies. In *The Chickencoop Chinaman*, Lee has to turn away when Tam confronts her: "But I hear something in your tongue . . . that funny red in the hair. . . . You got the blood don't ya. You're Chinese, right? A breath of the blood?" In Genny Lim's *Bitter Cane*, interraciality is evident to the discerning eye of the prostitute Li-Tai, who immediately identifies the young Wing as the son of his father, who was also of mixed race: "I knew you were your father's son before you even told me. His face was etched on yours." A thwarted racial passing is suggested for the character of Mat in Philip Gotanda's *Fish Head Soup;* in his first-act monologue, Mat reminisces about his efforts to transform himself first into an Italian Paolo, then into a Peruvian or Panamanian Joaquim, only to be brought back to his Japanese American status by the voice of his father calling his name.

Characters such as the teenage Kiyoko in Wakako Yamauchi's *And the*

Soul Shall Dance or Himiko Hamilton in *Tea* express their desire to assimilate by changing their hairstyle, as does Grace in David Hwang's *FOB* and Lee in Frank Chin's *Chickencoop Chinaman*. However, neither permanents nor wigs nor bleach can look convincing: Himiko's wig is the mark of her insanity, Lee's peroxide leaves a "telltale red," and Grace remarks that "Chinese hair looks pretty lousy when you bleach it." Although Kiyoko's permanent wave makes her happy because "all the American girls have curly hair," her new look is achieved at someone else's expense (specifically her stepmother's, whose money is stolen to pay for such alterations) and is contrasted with the "nice" straight hair of Masako, her foil in the play. Such attempts to transform the body in order to pass are depicted as painful and ugly acts that not only do not achieve the hoped-for transformation but also mark the character as insufficiently Asian.

In each of these cases, these attributes of the "true" Asian body—"natural" skin color, hair, eye shape—are presented as rigid, immovable markers of identity. Efforts to cross boundaries are violent, self-destructive, and ultimately imperfect. In these examples, the same rigidity of signification seems to operate as in the impoverished Oriental stereotypes of earlier American theater, except that the hierarchy is reversed. The Asian body with its "natural" markings creates its own borders of Asian American identity, within which the characters must stay. In David Hwang's *Family Devotions*, the young Chester is shown the image of his face by his great-uncle from China: "Look here. At your face. Study your face and you will see—the shape of your face is the shape of faces back many generations—across an ocean, in another soil." Attempts to move away from such boundaries of the body envisioned as "naturally" Asian are construed as betrayals, or at least as actions that are dangerously disruptive.

If the Asianness of the body is read as a nonpermeable boundary, passage of the Asian body through the boundaries of racial categorization requires radical violence.[3] In Gotanda's *Yankee Dawg You Die*, this violent attempt at passage takes the form of appearance-altering surgery. The young Asian American actor Bradley makes the comic but painful suggestion that the older actor Vincent Chang "holds the record for noses." Bradley scoffs at Vincent, who sells out to the latest Hollywood fashion, altering his nose to look like "Sinatra, Montgomery Clift, Troy Donahue—whatever was *in* at the time. Sort of like the 'Seven Noses of Dr. Lao.'" But it is Bradley who finally succumbs to the correcting knife of the cosmetic surgeon at the end of the play, making the feeble excuse to Vincent that "I was having a sinus problem." The nose jobs are Vincent's and Bradley's efforts to make their actor's bodies less markedly Asian, and therefore more marketable. Similarly, Bradley describes another painful alteration of the body that uses artificial means to pass from Asian to Caucasian: "My old girlfriend used to put scotch tape on her eyelids to get the double fold so she could look more 'Cau-ca-sian.' My new girlfriend—she doesn't mess around, she got surgery." As contextualized in the play, these moments present the possibility of a violent and painful surgical passing across the borders of race: a possibility that is ultimately shown to be hopeless. Plastic surgery does little to make Vincent's and Bradley's bodies more generically white and therefore suitable for better roles. Their bodies are figured by the play as inevitably raced, an obstacle to as well as the vehicle for the practice of their craft. The alternatives to Hollywood stereotype are few: Vincent's ideal of "real" acting, the impossible freedom of the neutral "color-blind" body, or Bradley's success as the iconic Asian American figure in independent films. The body cannot be seen as anything but raced within the rigid boundaries of stereotype or Other; the body *is* the boundary beyond which the actor cannot pass, even with the help of a surgeon's knife.

In many of these plays, there nonetheless remains a fascination with the possibility of passing beyond the boundaries of the rigidly marked body. Although what is most apparent are the desperate failures and the pathos of such efforts to change the body to fit a different mold, the plays introduce at least the possibility of indeterminacy. The pain associated with surgical alterations clearly marks them as negative and self-torturing, but in these moments of self-recreation there is the potential, however fleeting, for transraciality.

The *frisson* of transraciality is constituted as Tam Lum's allure in Frank Chin's *The Chickencoop Chinaman*. Chin's play relies on the violent and disruptive energy of the crossing of racial boundaries—Asian, white, or black. It subverts any secure identity or "natural" Asian character at the same time that it challenges traditional stereotypes. The character of Tam, linguistically bereft, takes on a variety of mixed dialects, accents, and mannerisms: "*jumping between black and white rhythms and accents*" and "*delivering bravatura speeches that change from W.C. Fields to American Midwest, Bible Belt holy roller, etc.*" Tam's boyhood hero is also a figure who passes, a Chinese American version of the Lone Ranger who hides his "slanty eyes" behind a mask. Although Tam's linguistic and physical mutations are mocked by other characters in the play, there is also a certain vitality to Tam that comes out of his ability to change his markings. His friend Kenji, known as "Blackjap," explains how he and Tam adopted this behavior:

Kenji. Maybe we act black, but it's not fake. Oakland was weirdness. No seasons. No snow. I was a kid missing the concentration camps . . . the country with just us, you know what I mean. Now it's blacks and Chinese all of a sudden. All changed. My folks, everybody. . . .
Lee. And you? The young prince returned from exile in the wilderness? Turned black! Presto change-o!
Kenji. I changed! Yeah! Presto! School was all blacks and Mexicans. We were kids in school, and you either walked and talked right in the yard, or got the shit beat outa you every day, ya understand? But that Tam was always what you might say . . . "The Pacesetter." Whatever was happening with hair, or the latest color, man. . . .

Sometimes he looked pretty exotic, you know, shades, high greasy hair, spitcurls, purple shiny shirt, with skull cufflinks and Frisko jeans worn like they was fallin off his ass. Me, I was the black one. "Blackjap Kenji" I used to be called and hated yellowpeople. (20)

Yet *Chickencoop Chinaman* does not celebrate these passings, for it recognizes that with destabilization of the boundaries of race there comes a disruption of authority. The racial indeterminacy of Tam, Lee, and Kenji is contrasted in the play with the open racism of Charley Popcorn and the more disturbing character of Tom, the "ornamental Oriental," both of whom try to establish Asianness as something fixed and indelible. The central preoccupation of the play, which is figured in Tam's search for a father figure, is the inability of the Chinese American male to be a proper father; and this failure is played out in a number of highly symbolic as well as literal ways. *Chickencoop Chinaman* explores the inability of the Asian male to find authority through patriarchy, inheritance, or power within a white world. Lee's marriages to husbands of different races uniquely threaten the male in search of authority; she destabilizes the already unsteady borders beyond repair and must be put in her place. Although *Chickencoop Chinaman* celebrates the energy and audacity of passing, the play nonetheless comes down on the side of a need for a masculine reordering, the establishment of secure boundaries. Despite its intense discussion, the play withholds both the promise of an authentic body marked fully as Asian and the possibility of a more fluid identity. Yet in its multiple characterizations and the theatrical excitement that these generate, it looks forward to later plays in which the passing of actors through the boundaries of the racialized body is explored further.

Tea

The Asian actor on the American stage has traditionally been confined to a limited number of situations and roles. In addition to the extra signification of its unerasable physical markers, Asianness was determined within the gendered relationships of class and sexuality; male bodies were figured as servile houseboys, loyal sidekicks, or evil villains, and female bodies as exotic love interests. As a consequence, the plots of many traditional plays were concerned with policing sexuality as it extended the borders of the body. These plays introduced interracial unions to regulate improper or illicit sex, which was ultimately prevented or allowed only with dire consequences, such as the death of one or more of the characters.[4]

The plight of five Japanese war brides living in Kansas, depicted in Velina Hasu Houston's *Tea* (first produced at the Manhattan Theatre Club in 1987, directed by Julianne Boyd), echoes such unhappy tales. The characters' geographic transplantation, interracial marriages, and bearing of interracial children are configured both seductively and tragically. But the play also complicates this traditional response to passing by staging the crossing of racial, sexual, and class boundaries not only in the stories of ill-fated characters, but also in the transformations of the actresses on the stage. Thus, the act of passing must be understood at two levels. Within the play, the characters' bodies are marked indelibly by race and sex. At the same time, the actresses constantly cross the binary divisions that mark out the narratives of the play.

Although *Tea* celebrates the interracial marriages of some of the characters, it also holds up racial difference as an impassable boundary that is drawn on the body itself. Moreover, the implicit borders of the body work to regulate the characters' attitudes toward sexuality and marriage. Interracial love is explicitly shown as a momentous event. As Teruko, speaking as her husband, a white Texan, says:

Before World War II, I never dated anything but white tomatoes. When I laid my eyes on Teri, I said to myself, "Fella, you are just about to cross the big boundary line." And I crossed it and there ain't a yellow rose in all of Texas who'll ever turn my heart like her. (190)

In post-war Japan, these female characters are attracted to the embodied differences of the American men, especially those differences marked on their skin, whether "the color of soy sauce" or "white, like a ghost." Like earlier plays, *Tea* sets up interracial unions as erotic, but sex is prevented or allowed only with dire consequences. The marriage and subsequent departure of the war brides for Kansas is linked, literally and symbolically, to death. Chiz describes leaving her father and Japan: "my heart [was] divided between two men like a dark, shameful canyon." Each of the five women suffers unhappiness in her new life, most extremely Himiko Hamilton, who eventually shoots her abusive American husband and herself. The play emphasizes the sacrifice of these women for these relationships; their bodies become, like the ghost of Himiko, "suspended between two worlds." Although some of the brides have happier marriages, they, too, are portrayed as victims of their own border-crossing. Chiz and Setsuko marry Mexican American and African American husbands who love their wives and respect their Japaneseness (Chizuye's husband, for instance, asks her to teach him how to make Japanese food). However, these two women are tragically widowed, again suggesting that interracial coupling and marriage inevitably result in the loss of personal satisfaction or the punishment of an untimely death.

The interracial unions in the play introduce the possibility of racial passing in the next generation. Yet it is emphasized that the children born of these unions are not allowed free passage between worlds; rather, their bodies are marked from both sides with indeterminacy. Each of the Amerasian children of the characters in *Tea* becomes the subject of intense visual scrutiny, as others try to mark them. Atsuko remarks, "Teruko, I saw your daughter last week. She looks Japanese (*a compliment*). That's nice. Too bad she isn't friends with my girl. My girl's always with Setsuko-san's daughter. Have you seen her? Looks Indonesian, not Japanese at all. Shame, ne." Setsuko's story is more celebratory of her daughter's status "outside" racial communities: "Back home, country papa-san says to me when my first is born, 'Bring it me for me to see.' He wants to see how ugly she is. But she is pretty, and the Japanese crowd and stare. She doesn't look Japanese, they say, and she doesn't look Negro. And I am glad because I have created something new." Yet in spite of her positive outlook, the "hybrid Japanese" children of this play are distinguished not only by their appearance and their intelligence ("teachers say they've never seen anything like it"), but by tragedy. Himiko's daughter Mieko, born in her personal "storm," is raped and murdered. Her horrible death is tied not only to the violence of men, but also, the play suggests, to "the confusion of . . . [her] Amerasian skin."

No degree of assimilation can disguise the "true" bodily identity of the five women characters, either to others or to themselves. Chiz, who in accent and dress is the most Americanized, says that she remembers "that underneath my comfortable American clothes, I am, after all, Japanese." These women are caught in an impossible state of in-betweenness, first as they are violently separated from their parents, and then as they make an incomplete transition to American language and customs. In describing their wives, the husbands are caught between incompatible war memories of killing Japs and their present love; these men are also caught in "passing," as they share the awareness of boundaries, the discrepancies between imagined life and reality. Himiko's ghost is a vivid reminder of the death that is the ultimate result of attempts to pass. An uncanny figure, Himiko is unsatisfied by her own death and unable to pass easily to the next world; she haunts the women as a reminder that their own bodies are inevitably marked.

In its portrayal of passing as inevitably tragic, the play affirms rather than negates racial, sexual, and generational boundaries. But at the same time, a similar transgression of cultural boundaries is attempted at a different level—the level of acting—with somewhat different results. A second dimension of passing is enacted by the actresses within the staging of the play. As the actresses take on the roles of their younger selves, their parents, their husbands, and their children, the boundaries of generation, gender, and race appear more fluid, and passing exceeds figurative possibility to become literal fact.

Along with *Tea*, several recent works by Asian American playwrights use characters in multiple roles to suggest the possibility of a transformative passing. Some one-actor performances such as Jude Narita's *Coming into a Passion/Song for a Sansei*, Lane Nishikawa's *I'm on a Mission from Buddha*, and Amy Hill's *Tokyo Bound* also require that the actor play a variety of roles, including both white and Asian characters. Such an intentional fluidity given to the meaning of the body on stage is very different from the traditional representation of white actors in yellowface, or even from the more recent practice of "color-blind" casting, since it ultimately insists on the instability of race as theatrical presentation, even while acknowledging the importance of race as a social construct. Again, such an exploration of passing, a passing that celebrates rather than punishes the actor's body, seems to indicate a new permeability of the borders of racial meaning as it is constructed on the stage. Cross-gender and cross-racial casting seems to promise a way out of the fixed correspondence between body and categorical type. This kind of casting in Houston's *Tea* adds another layer of meaning to the play, complicating the narrative's identification of passing with tragedy.

However, the flexibility and multiplicity of these roles-within-roles do not mean that certain essentialisms are eliminated entirely. In *Tea*, it is only the female Asian American body that is allowed to move beyond racial and gendered boundaries, to pass as the body of others. This suggests some "essential" quality of Asian American femaleness that ultimately lends itself to the acting of passing. Moreover, the multiple roles played by the actress are not indiscriminately assigned. The moments in

Tea in which the actresses play husbands and children are not fully representational; rather, the body of each actress is first and foremost her character, and only then the younger self, husband, or child that is the extension of her character. Thus, what is embodied is the indissoluble relation between members of a family, the bonds that tie each character to a notion of self. Ultimately what this conveys is not so much that the actresses' bodies are malleable and can pass effortlessly into different roles, as the symbolic containment of particular roles by Asian American female bodies. Thus, there is a dimension of *Tea* that celebrates these characters as transcendent, as able to endure, understand, and withstand the tragedy that in this play accompanies transformation. It is this encompassing endurance that is the ethos of the characters. This is echoed in the ways in which the characters reach a final understanding with one another that transcends class and racial prejudices. In the tea ceremony, their individual differences are subsumed into a choreographed expression of solidarity, reinforcing the play's concern with a community based on ethnicity and gender as a defense against the loneliness of racism.

In *Tea,* Houston investigates the tragic dimension of passing and suggests another dimension within the casting of the play. The movement of the actress from one role to another, as well as part of a collective whole, is a theatrical maneuver that to some extent disrupts the body's distinctive marking into race. Although they ultimately fall back into Japanese American characters for whom passing is an isolating and saddening experience, these characters are allowed to occupy, for a moment, the decentering space of transraciality.

Kind Ness

Although many Asian American plays associate acts of passing with punishment, others, such as Ping Chong's *Kind Ness* (premiered at the Northeastern University Division of Fine Arts and New York's La Mama

E.T.C. in 1986, directed by Chong) and Jeannie Barroga's *Walls* (premiered at the Asian American Theater Company in 1989, directed by Marian Li), present racial hybridity somewhat differently. Both plays suggest that we might more effectively move from a *recognition* of categories to a *re-formation* of perception.

Kind Ness uses the theater to confront directly how we perceive, as the narrator in scene one explains, "what is alike and what is not alike." This play not only illustrates passing—the assimilation of Buzz the gorilla into the human surburbia of the 1950s and 1960s—it also demands that we face the contradictions that are exposed in the act of passing, not only as abstract, rational questions but in our own deeply rooted histrionic responses.

The play begins with a slide show in which the audience is asked to recognize difference and similarity in various pairs of objects, images, and words. The items range from simple geometric shapes to complex and whimsical word games and associations (for example, "Woman from Este Lauder ad" is paired with "Woman from Algeria," and images of "Tupperware" are juxtaposed with "Elizabeth Taylor and Richard Burton in *Cleopatra*"). This game of recognizing "kind-ness" continues in the theatrical events and characterizations that follow. The play frequently returns to the trope suggested in the opening scene as the characters dance across the stage in various pairings or discuss their differences from one another. Each event, whether it is the playful litany of snack foods ("Ding Dongs, YooHoos, Hum Hums . . . Yo-yos and Snick Snacks and Doo-Doos and Cheese") or the final comparison of Buzz to his gorilla counterpart, relies on the audience's awareness of similarity and difference.

Viewers are also asked to make both obvious generalizations and subtle distinctions among characters along the lines of ethnic background, class, gender, and intellectual and physical ability. The blind Dot, for example, despite being "a white Jewish girl from Scarsdale," says that her "people" are soul singers such as "Blind Lemon Jefferson, Blind Willie McTell, Blind Boy Fuller." By making the acts of comparison and contrast self-conscious, the play moves from recording "instinctive" reactions to types of bodies onstage to suggesting how differences and similarities are produced. In this game of likeness and opposition, viewers are asked to reflect on the moments in which we, like the children in the play, were first taught difference and similarity.[5]

The plot of *Kind Ness* follows the assimilation of Buzz, a gorilla, into a human suburban world. Buzz's incorporation into suburban life doesn't seem impossible, particularly in comparison to the working-class Alvin's unrequited love for the wealthy Daphne, or Dot's stumbling around in a world made for the sighted. In the relative ease with which Buzz becomes a member of the human community, the play's exploration of passing becomes even more subtle. Buzz is not only assimilated but excels; he is the model minority who takes all the prizes, wins the hockey games, and gets the girl at the end of the play.

Yet the supposed success of Buzz's assimilation—the erasure of his psychological if not his physical difference—introduces its own punishment. The play's setting in an American suburb of the 1950s and 1960s evokes not open racism but a more subtle kind of discrimination, one that passes as liberal tolerance but is bent on reinforcing a difference between self and Other. The suburban parents find ways to remind the youngsters of their distinctions, asking Alvin whether his father has found work yet and telling Buzz, "Your people don't eat cheese, do they?" But paradoxically, although class, racial, and other differences are suggested in every conversation, the brutal realities of imperialism, oppression, and other kinds of racial conflict are avoided. Although Buzz openly acknowledges his history, graphically detailing the violence done to his family by human poachers, the others evade such topics. Lulu is intrigued by the photograph of Buzz's Old World mother, but becomes

embarrassed on hearing the details of her death. Such implicit reinforcing of differences is even more insidious because it allows no space for
open discussion. The tension of these unspoken barriers is released only
in the derision of childish name-calling or in the drunken stupor of
prom night, when Dot accuses the others of preferential treatment:
"You've treated me like a freak! Well, what about Buzz?! He's a fucking
monkey and you don't give him half the shit you give me!"

The world in which these characters live is a much "kinder" one than
the violent world of poachers and hunters, the Old World that Buzz has
left behind, and less openly racist in its representations than the vaudeville acts of *bwana* and gorilla that divide the scenes. Yet racism is clearly
ingrained in this world, as becomes evident in the episode when Daphne
learns that her brother has been killed in a war, presumably the Korean
War. The other human children call out a litany of racist slurs; when this
chorus is over, Buzz stands alone on stage and turns slowly in a rain of
cards, each bearing the name of a country involved in war. The differences among the characters are extended into a larger sense of difference,
as the staging comments on the relationship between individual acts of
racism and larger political conflicts. Buzz becomes the focal point of this
violence, the ultimate Other of this society.

Kind Ness also explores (in ways that are more wistful than tragic) the
complex feelings of loss associated with the successful passing of assimilation. In the final scene, Buzz, Daphne, and their baby visit the zoo, and
Buzz stares at a caged gorilla without recognition. His failure to identify
in any way with what he sees sharply highlights the problematic of successful assimilation. Buzz seems to have lost his former sense of affinity
for nonhuman beings. Where he once identified with the raw power of
other species, such as *Tyrannosaurus rex* "killing, eating, and sleeping,"
and demonstrated an awareness of his own difference, he now sees the
caged gorilla only as "big" and "ugly." And yet the scene humorously

parallels Buzz's married state with the isolation of the gorilla; Buzz receives only a casual crumb of attention from the self-absorbed Daphne, like the peanut that the barker throws to the caged gorilla.

If Buzz is biologically different from the humans, his distance from the gorilla is far greater. Yet the fact that Buzz remains linked by virtue of his appearance to the gorilla emphasizes both his own apparent lack of self-recognition and the viewer's confusion about whether difference is essential or constructed. The play spotlights how strong the bodily markers of racialization are. Buzz cannot fully pass, despite his many accomplishments. As viewers, we are invited to compare him to the real gorilla, which swings in and out of our field of vision.

Throughout the play, two small white plaques are placed in front of the playing area in order to suggest, as the stage directions indicate, that *"the audience is watching human specimens in a zoological environment."* In the final scene, the theater becomes more explicitly a kind of menagerie; moreover, we are made as aware of ourselves as viewers as we are of the different beings we hold under scrutiny. Ultimately, we are confronted not only by Buzz's ambiguous status, but also by our own propensity to compare and contrast, to categorize and to label. Buzz fascinates us because he is a transracial or, more correctly, transspecies curiosity whose passing exemplifies the limitations of our knowledge of kindness.

Walls

Michael Omi and Howard Winant use the term "racial formation" to indicate a set of historically changing and changeable political values. This term resists the "continuous temptation to think of race as an *essence,* as something fixed, concrete and objective," and the equally prevalent tendency "to see it as a mere illusion, which an ideal social order would eliminate." Instead, Omi and Winant emphasize race as *"an unsta-*

ble and 'decentered' complex of social meanings constantly being transformed by political struggle" (italics in original), meanings that cannot be subsumed by more optimistic notions of a willfully chosen "ethnic" identity (68). To use their term is to recognize that the constant perception and negotiation of difference—the issues of "racial formation"—affect not only minority groups, but all who live in the United States. In the past few decades, images of the United States as exclusively ordained for "the lovely white" have finally begun to give way. These changes, informed by activism and cultural productions by African Americans, Latinos, and Native Americans as well as by Asian Americans, are radical because they insist that identity can no longer be determined within the binary paradigm of Anglo conformity[6] versus Otherness, normalcy versus deviance.

A difficult question, one that persists even when the effects of legalized racism are no longer so apparent, is how to deal with the felt tensions of acknowledging Otherness and sameness in what is optimistically a more open society. As Michael Awkward suggests, the real problems have to do with managing racial identity, not just "the articulation of ubiquitous strategies of black being" (186). It is particularly important for Asian Americans to recognize that their political efficacy, economic well-being, representation, and identity are inextricably bound up with the relations of different communities and with the permeability of the borders that define them. It is increasingly clear that the performance of what is Asian American is more than a matter of responding to individual acts of racism or of overcoming obstacles on the path to economic success. Rather, it involves teasing out the possibility of new collectives and new identities that are still in the making. An exploration of Asian Americanness leads to considerations not only of building a pan-ethnic identity, but also the formation of alliances across racial, gender, and class lines. Such alliances may be able to combat racism, sexism, poverty, and systematic discrimination that hurt society as a whole.

Both *Kind Ness* and *Walls* suggest that it is a function of art in general and theater in particular to move us toward this point. *Walls* in particular raises the possibility of Asian Americans helping to redefine relationships among dominant and minority cultures. Even as the play acknowledges the complex ways in which racial and other differences are perceived, at the same time it envisions situations in which some understanding can take place despite these differences. The first step in forming working relationships, the play suggests, is to acknowledge rather than ignore the traumatic events of history.

Jeannie Barroga reproduces some of the controversy surrounding the design and reception of the Vietnam War Memorial, thus portraying the war as a crucial time in which an awareness of differences became inseparable from the U.S. national identity. What Barroga emphasizes (in ways that make her play markedly different from Jan Scrugg and Joel Swerdlow's book, *To Heal a Nation*, which served as inspiration for the play) is the plight of Asian American characters: the war propaganda that vilified Asians as the enemy, the failure of Asian Americans to be accepted as part of the mainstream, and the beginnings of pan-ethnic solidarity as Asian Americans banded together in the face of racism. Embedded in the play are a number of threads that relate specifically to Asian Americans and their failure to "blend in." Julie, a former antiwar protestor, warned Chinese American Dan that he could be "mistaken for the enemy" in Vietnam. Dave tells of the particular pressures on him as a Chinese American to enlist and prove his loyalty, and of his discovery of racism in the Hawaiian hospital where he worked ("Americans like me getting operated on last cause they look Vietnamese"). Vi, the Chinese American reporter, has learned to acknowledge her racial difference only when it is advantageous to present the "perfect" model minority's face. The architect Maya Lim, who thinks of herself as apolitical, learns that her being Chinese American does matter. In fighting for the integrity of her design, Maya comes to understand that she is identified with the Vietnamese as the enemy: "It's been mentioned—many times, in fact—that the fact of me as the designer of a memorial to an Asian war was upsetting. I'm a young woman, a student. And I'm Chinese American. We're all lumped together, us 'gooks.'" In the process of seeing Maya struggle with the politics involved in the war memorial's construction, Vi reaches out to help her, finally understanding the implicit racism that binds them together.

As Vi notes in her final report, present racism is linked to past wars fought in and over Vietnam. Her final statement—"There is still today, division. I myself still fight a war, one of prejudice and indifference. We are victims of that war as we are the enemy because walls do exist. Walls are still built"—directly addresses the racial prejudice against Asians and Asian Americans. But at the same time the play makes a concerted effort to show the problems of Asian Americans as only one thread in the larger weave. Instead of focusing exclusively on differences in terms of a white majority and an Asian American minority, *Walls* brings up questions about the numerous barriers that confine so many groups to minority status.

At a basic level, the "wall" is not only that which separates Asian Americans from other Americans, but also an indication of physical and emotional barriers between the characters. For the returning veterans, differences are marked out by who was present in Vietnam and who wasn't. As Stu tells Dave: "You stand there and dribble on about what you read or what you heard. But how could you know, huh? You weren't there." The play pairs characters who have this firsthand experience with those who lack it. Each of the veterans has physiological or mental scars that mark his body distinctively. This scarring is treated as another marker of difference, one parallel to race and gender. Those who have served in the war feel this significant difference to have been erased by a country that wants to forget its own ambivalence. For Scruggs, Vietnam vets have been submerged by a government that denies them and by a younger generation born after the war. His objection to Maya is not simply that she is Chinese American or that she dresses "like a hippie," but that the media prefer to focus on her rather than on the veterans: "I pick up a newspaper and see her face and how she dined somewhere in Georgetown and there's nothing about us vets, or Agent Orange, or unemployment—." Carhart is angry at what he sees to be the country's denial of honor to veterans—"Twenty years of denying we were even there"—and envisions the monument as an end to the country's secrecy.

It is the refusal to acknowledge the difference between those who served and those who did not that leads to lasting rifts between the characters. The play draws parallels between this difference and other kinds of difference whose suppression is just as damaging. Sarah insists that not only the soldiers who were present in Vietnam should be acknowledged, but also the nurses and other women who made sacrifices: "[Y]ou won't see our names up there, and you won't see our wounds. Hell, you won't even see what part of us we really lost. But we got rights to be here, all of us. We paid, just like you." Morris brings up the racism in the demographics of those sent to the front:

> *Morris.* Seventy-six percent were, what they call "lower class." You know what that means—mostly black. Breaks down to two black men to every white.
>
> *Sarah.* A numbers man.
>
> *Morris.* Hell, everybody knew that—everybody black. That's all we talked about. Can't give us jobs or a place on the bus, but they sure can find a spot for us on the front line. (254)

It is the ways in which these differences remain overlooked or suppressed that produce lasting scars. In the play, the function of the memorial is to acknowledge such differences and allow a safe space for expression of the pain and anger associated with their enactment. In foregrounding the aesthetic controversy over the design of the Vietnam War

Memorial, *Walls* asks us to consider how art can participate in such a redefinition. Art can do this, the play seems to suggest, not by escaping into a world of pure form, but by being, even in its most postmodern and abstract manifestations, the physical objects and experiential events that help establish and guide our encounters and relationships. In this sense, art becomes crucial as a means not only of addressing difference, but of envisioning ways to move beyond difference. In restaging the "art war" that occurred over the design of the memorial, the play underscores the ways in which certain aesthetic forms enable certain experiences.

The play recounts the compromise finally reached when the Fine Arts Commission approved the inclusion of a flag and a statue by Frederick Hart along with Maya Lim's memorial. Lim's geometric memorial and Hart's realistic sculpture both commemorate the veterans, but they do so in radically different ways. What distinguishes the designs is the relationship of the physical art work to physical bodies, both of the veterans and of those who were not present. Hart's statue attempts a multicultural representation of three soldiers. As Scruggs and Swerdlow observe, this statue can only remind viewers of its failure to be all-inclusive: "There was a white, a black, and Hispanic. All were young and all looked like infantrymen. Pilots, sailors, native Americans, Orientals, nurses, and other groups would not be represented" (116). Hart's attempt to depict the experience of veterans draws on physical analogy; its idealized, sculpted bodies (young, virile, male, and marked as black, white, and Hispanic) must in fact be quite different from the actual bodies of those who served. The physical body of the statue gets in the way of allowing a more inclusive representation, yet it presumes to stand in for the range of physical bodies that served in Vietnam. The statue only aggravates the highly charged symbolic difference between who was there and who was not.

Lim's design, on the other hand, allows more bodies to be included, both because of its comprehensive list of names and because of its mir-

ror-like qualities. The play celebrates the theatrical qualities of Lim's design, its ability to serve as a stage for so many bodies. The playwright
Barroga emphasizes how Lim's memorial works by including spectators
as performers, those who cry, touch the wall, leave mementos, or pay
tribute in other ways. Thus, throughout the play, the characters become
part of the "Living Park" as Terry holds up an American flag, Sarah
pushes Morris in his wheelchair up to the wall, and Stu lights candles at
the wall while other veterans form a windbreak around him. The memorial thus becomes not only the great black wall of names, but also these
performances and the bodies involved in them. The memorial restages
the body so as to reenact and refigure bodily experience. The play emphasizes how people reach out to touch the wall, as if the wall itself were
a massive body. Scruggs marvels, "it was warm. It radiated warmth. . . . I
found myself reaching out to touch it, touch the names." The wall enables contact with the past by means of a shared experience in the present. Each of the veterans establishes a connection between his living body
and those who are dead: Terry, through his marathon of flag bearing,
becomes the living monument to his friends; Stu reenacts the moment in
which he identifies with the dead veterans. Julie, Sarah, and Dave are able
to make connections with the protected space of Terry, Morris, and Stu.
Lim's memorial thus leaps over the differences established and frozen in
the past by creating a space where people can enter into a variety of more
inclusive experiences.

The stories told throughout the play indicate an anxiety about community, exemplified in relationships between the Vietnam War and the
Asian American movement. But as the play progresses, Barroga constructs a vision of America as a social body that renders these differences
permeable in the face of a common set of wounds. Sarah tells the veteran
Morris that "you and me is color," but in fact the idea of color as a
common bond exceeds black and white. The most intense relationship,
both physically and emotionally, is that between African American Dave

and Asian American Stu, while the relationship of Julie, Dan, and Jerry suggests equally strong bonds of love and friendship. Like a mirror, the wall absorbs its viewers into an image of the ideal body politic: all-embracing, all-inclusive. As individual bodies pass into the warm, black, reflective body of the memorial, their differences are not erased but subsumed into a larger image of America as multiple and varied. It is not just to ease casting problems that Barroga suggests that the roles of Julie, Rich, Carhart, and Jerry might be "*any race.*" The real issue in *Walls* is not the identity of any individual character but the character of a social body. In Barroga's play, the dividing lines of experience and color increasingly bleed into one another. The ending is carefully choreographed in a harmonious and totalizing vision where the characters seem to "mirror" a multiethnic, multigendered, multi-abled America.

In each of the plays discussed in this chapter, characters wrestle with the perceived limits of the body and its inability to pass beyond the barriers of race and ethnicity as categories defining and confining the body. It is not until *Walls* that one sees envisioned onstage a pluralistic society into which Asian Americans can fit as one of many others. Here, symbolic walls are rendered permeable, and passing becomes the natural state rather than a transgressive act. After the scarring of the larger social body, the reenactment of pain reminds our bodies how, despite other differences, they are more alike than different.

Omi and Winant's *Racial Formation in the United States* persuasively argues that although race is always important in politics and culture, its meaning is never irrevocably fixed. How race is embodied can and does change. Thus, individuals and groups of people can work to rearticulate race, reconfiguring what it means and how these meanings manifest themselves. Such a possibility is helpful not only in understanding the importance of acts of passing in these plays, but also in imagining what moral we might extract from them. The continued fascination with passing is first a mark of how strongly race cannot be denied: as Omi and

Winant point out, race cannot be disregarded for presumably more fundamental categories of sociopolitical identity such as ethnicity, class, or nation. Rather, racial categories persistently figure in our formation of individual and group identity. But neither does this continued importance mean that any one system of racial order must necessarily remain in place. The different visions in each of these plays mark out how conceptions and meanings of race can themselves change with time, place, and event. In what further ways the plays themselves manifest or help to effect these changes is a question that still deserves debate.

EPILOGUE

If race and ethnicity are changing social formations, then theater can assist us in understanding certain dimensions of these formations and their contexts. Through the medium of the stage—the use of space, the actions of the body, the shaping of the viewer's perception—the plays that I have chosen for this study all explore various ways of enacting what is "Asian American." These plays are important not only for understanding the history and culture of Asian Americans; they are also crucial to any study of contemporary American theater, for they fuse new perspectives on race, ethnicity, and other kinds of difference with innovations in theatrical form. To look at them critically is to require that we reassess the terms in which we discuss, interpret, and value theater and drama.

The structure of this book has cut across some of the boundaries established by traditional dramatic criticism—boundaries between amateur and professional, mainstream and minority, writing and production—in favor of exploring race and ethnicity as defining and shaping modes of dramatic presentation. I chose such a structure for a number of reasons. My first intent was to correct the systematic denial of racial, ethnic, and other kinds of difference that has infected much of theater history and dramatic criticism until the past few decades. Theater studies have only begun to respond to the need for new scholarship and theoretical methods that would address how such differences matter, and in turn to reassess connections between the theater's cultural representations and political change. Second, I have followed the lead of the plays themselves, many of which suggest that race and ethnicity establish a common ground that can eclipse distinctions based on gender, class, and other differences. This is a problematic assumption, and one that has rightly received much critical attention.[1] It is clear that many of the examples of Asian American drama I have discussed share in the values of the Asian American movement—its push for political and cultural visibility, its fight against racist representation, the call for the formation of a panethnic community. Theater work by Americans of Asian descent, particularly in the past three decades, has participated in this legacy in the writing and production of plays, and in the establishment of theaters. Yet those who work in this theater must keep in mind that the term Asian American, like any other indicator of individual and collective identity, must constantly question its own prejudices, exclusions, and hierarchies, and allow for change. Thus the plays discussed here cannot be thought of as *representing* Asian America—as standing in for the life experiences of individuals or groups of people who are transcendently marked by race and ethnicity. Rather, the plays deserve attention for their *performing* of various impulses and actions that signify different modes of consciousness, desire, and imagination necessarily limited by time, space, and scope.

Future studies of Asian American theater and drama could fruitfully move in one of several directions. An obvious continuation of the present study would be the ongoing examination of new plays and productions by Asian Americans. Works such as Ping Chong's *Deshima, Undesirable Elements,* and *Chinoiserie,* and Chay Yew's *Whitelands* trilogy have received mainstream recognition both in America and abroad; new as

well as more established writers such as David Henry Hwang, Philip Gotanda, and Jessica Hagedorn continue to produce work for screen and
stage. Yet the study of new works should be conducted in parallel with
other projects, among them more primary research on earlier plays and
on theaters. For instance, a study of early works for the theater written by
Asian Americans in Hawaii would help provide a firmer historical and
social context for our contemporary notions of what is Asian American.
There is also much to be done in writing the histories of specific Asian
American theaters; such a study might yield an entirely different sense of
Asian American cultural production than a literary examination of play-
scripts and playwrights. In any research on Asian American theaters, particular attention must be paid to community theater as well as to commercial stages. A broader notion of theatrical participation is crucial in
understanding how Asian America theater might reshape itself to fit
newer immigrant and refugee communities who are currently excluded.

A related task might be to move in the direction of a comparative
study. The theoretical approaches and critical issues of this book and
others[2] help describe and interpret how dramatists of color have presented the performances of race and ethnicity. It would be most produc-
tive to extend some of the insights found in these studies to a comparison of how other ethnic and racial minorities, as well as Asian
Americans, "stage" themselves.

All of these studies would not only provide readings of plays by artists
of color, but would also need to address the larger critical framework in
which these plays might be read. They would need to explore the range
of a playwright's participation in the larger questions of what it means to
signify race or ethnicity on the stage. They would need to address the
ongoing marginalization of artists of color by in the academy and in
mainstream theater. They would share common worries about the relationship of artistic and intellectual production to politics: Do works for
the theater, and books written about them, sustain the larger process of

reform and change, or do these works divert attention from the real issues with illusions of artistic progress? Finally, these studies would need to cope with how such racial and ethnic terms as Asian American might still prove viable, given the constantly changing nature of lived experience.

NOTES

Chapter 1

1 The term Asian American as used in this book is broadly conceived to include persons who were born and have lived in Canada as well as the United States.

2 For reasons of time I was unable to include in this book discussions of plays published in the most recent of these collections. Edward Sakamoto's *Hawai'i No Ka Oi: The Kamiya Family Trilogy* (Honolulu: University of Hawaii Press, 1996), Philip Kan Gotanda's *Fish Head Soup and Other Plays* (Seattle: University of Washington Press, 1995), and *Contemporary Plays by Women of Color*, ed. Roberta Uno and Kathy Perkins (London: Routledge, 1996), were published after completion of this study.

3 Jessica Hagedorn's *Teenytown* (1988), written with Laurie Carlos and Robbie Mc-Cauley, appears in *Out From Under: Texts by Women Performance Artists*, ed. Leonora Champagne (New York: Theatre Communications Group, 1990). *Contemporary Plays by Women of Color*, ed. Kathy Perkins and Roberta Uno (London: Routledge, 1996), includes plays by Elizabeth Wong, Diana Son, Louella Dizon, Bina Sharif, and Brenda Wong Aoki. *Mrs. Chang*, by Han Ong, appears in "The New American Theater," ed. by John Guare, CONJUNCTIONS 25 (1995).

4 Sau-Ling Cynthia Wong provides a useful summary in *Reading Asian American Literature*, p. 4. See also Abdul R. JanMohamed and David Lloyd, "Introduction" to *The Nature and Context of Minority Discourse* (Oxford: Oxford University Press, 1990).

5 See John Guillory's discussion in Chapter 1 of *Cultural Capital: The Problem of Literary Canon Formation* (Chicago: University of Chicago Press, 1993).

6 "By experiencing their bond to people never actually seen, consumers of electronic

media can be affected by traditions to which they have no ancestral connection" (Shohat 17).

7   See chap. 3 of James Moy's *Marginal Sights,* and Ronald Takaki, "The 'Heathen Chinee' and American Technology," chap. 10 in *Iron Cages.* David Henry Hwang reverses such depictions in a interchange in *The Dance and the Railroad:*

> *Lone.* I am a white devil! Listen to my stupid language: "Wha che doo doo blah blah." Look at my wide eyes—like I have drunk seventy-two pots of tea. Look at my funny hair—twisting, turning, like a snake telling lies. (*To Ma*) Bla bla doo doo tee tee.
>
> *Ma.* We don't understand English.
>
> *Lone.* (*Angry*) Bla bla doo doo tee tee!
>
> *Ma.* (*With Chinese accent*) Please you-ah speak-ah Chinese?
>
> *Lone.* Oh. Work—uh—one—two—more—work—two—
>
> *Ma.* Two hours more? Stupid demons. As confused as your hair. We will strike! (81–82)

8   Although differences are made between Chinese and Japanese (Dr. Rudolph G. Liszt insists that "Chinese eyes slant more . . . Japanese hair is sparser"), these are the only such "types" mentioned. Philippe Perrottet makes a revealing remark, "The only oriental types that we shall discuss are Chinese and Japanese, which have great deal in common facially. More subtle variations on the eastern face, such as Koreans or Mongolians, do not mean very much to a western audience, and it is doubtful if the differences could be clearly shown in make-up on a European face" (*Practical Stage Make-Up* [London: Studio Vista, 1967, rev. 1975]).

9   For instance, Yoti Lane insists that "It will almost always be necessary to wipe out the natural mouth" (*Stage Make-Up* [Minneapolis: Northwestern Press, 1950], p. 81).

10 Lee Baygan, for instance, illustrates this "believable" appearance with images of a coolie and a geisha (*Makeup for Theatre, Film and Television*). For further examples of caricature and "yellowface" illustrations, see Rudolph G. Liszt, *The Last Word in Make-up,* 1975; Charles S. Parsons, *A Guide to Theatrical Make-up* (London: Sir Isaac Pitman and Sons, 1932), pp. 77–79; and *Denison's Make-Up Guide for Amateur and Professional* (Chicago: T.S. Denison and Co., 1932), p. 21. An interesting and unusual development is marked by Richard Corson's 1981 edition of *Stage Makeup,* which contains directions for "Orientals who wish to play Caucasians" and uses photographs of Randall Kim in the role of Titus Andronicus (Englewood Cliffs, NJ: Prentice-Hall, 1981, p. 105).

11 "[W]hy should we in the Sight of Superior Beings, darken its People? why increase the
Sons of Africa, by Planting them in American, where we have so fair an opportunity,
by excluding Blacks and Tawneys, of increasing the lovely White . . .?" Benjamin
Franklin, "Observations Concerning the Increase of Mankind" (1751), in *The Papers of
Benjamin Franklin*, ed. Leonard W. Larabee (New Haven: Yale University Press, 1959),
vol. 4, p. 234. For an analysis, see Takaki, "Reflections," and *Iron Cages*.

12 In his 1950 guide to stage makeup, Yoti Lane noted that "Of all make-up the transformation of Europeans into Orientals is one of the most difficult. Producers realize this
and with the passing of time seem to have practically eliminated the necessity for its
use . . . the musical comedy is one of the few fields left for the presentation of Oriental
types" (Lane, *Stage Make-Up* [Minneapolis: Northwestern Press, 1950], p. 80).

13 Bruce A. McConachie, "The 'Oriental' Musicals of Rodgers and Hammerstein and the
U.S. War in Southeast Asia," *Theatre Journal* 46 (1994): 385–98.

14 Significant scholarly attention is only now being paid to these earlier professional and
amateur Asian American performers. Arthur Dong's 1989 documentary *Forbidden City*
(distributed through the National Asian American Telecommunications Association,
San Francisco) records the experiences of the "Chop Suey Circuit." Robert Cooper-
man has documented theatrical performances by interned Japanese Americans in
"Barrack 408: Theater at the Tule Lake Relocation Center" (paper delivered at the
Modern Language Association convention, Chicago, December 1995).

15 Hamamoto notes that "At the height of his box-office popularity in 1920, Hayakawa
earned $7,500 per week. His earning power placed him among such elite silent-era
film stars as Francis X. Bushman, Rudolph Valentino and Mary Pickford, all of whom
Hayakawa counted as both friends and professional peers" (Hamamoto, *Monitored
Peril*, 251).

16 Some examples are performances of William's *The Glass Menagerie* (1990) and
Sondheim's *Into the Woods* (1992) and *Merrily We Roll Along* (1995) by East West
Players, Shakespeare's *Merchant of Venice* (1992) by the Asian American Theater Company, and Chekhov's *Three Sisters* (1988), Ibsen's *A Doll's House* (1993), and Noel Cow-
ard's *Private Lives* (1995) by the Pan Asian Repertory Theatre. See also the interview
with Tisa Chang in William H. Sun's "Tradition, Innovation, and Politics: Chinese and
Overseas Chinese Theatre Across the World," *TDR* 38, no. 2 (Summer 1994): 15–71.

17 For instance, the 1994–95 season for the Asian American Theater Company featured
Persimmon Lips, written and performed by SHAG, Asian Pacific Women's Collective.
Theater Mu's 1995 New Eyes Festival included readings from Justin Chin's *Orientalitus*,
and currently East West Players plans a 1997 run of Chay Yew's *Whitelands* trilogy.

Sharon Lim-Hing's *Superdyke, the Banana Metaphor and the Triply Oppressed Object* appears in *Piece of My Heart,* ed. Makeda Silvera (Toronto: Sister Vision Press, 1991) and in *A Certain Terror: Heterosexism, Militarism, Violence, and Change,* ed. Richard Cleaver and Patricia Myers (Chicago: Great Lakes Region American Friends Service Committee, 1993).

18   See Ping Chong's comments in "Writing Home: Interviews with Suzan-Lori Parks, Christopher Durang, Eduardo Machado, Ping Chong and Migdalia Cruz," *American Theatre* (October 1991): 40–42.

19   Michael Omi, introduction, in Philip Kan Gotanda, Fish Head Soup *and Other Plays* (Seattle: University of Washington Press, 1995), p. xxvi.

20   Information on Asian American theaters and plays has only recently begun to be archived. Some materials from the Pan Asian Repertory Theatre can be found in the New York Library of the Performing Arts. Material on East West Players (Los Angeles) is now archived in the UCLA University Research Library in Arts and Special Collections. The Asian American Theatre Company (San Francisco) has begun an archive at the University of California, Santa Barbara.

Roberta Uno has done extensive work on plays by Asian American women. In addition to publishing the anthologies *Unbroken Thread* and *Contemporary Plays by Women of Color* (co-edited with Kathy Perkins), she has put together a collection of unpublished scripts, interviews, and production material from 1924 to 1992. This material is available at the University of Massachusetts Special Collections in Amherst, Massachusetts.

The Hamilton Library at the University of Hawaii at Manoa hosts the collections *College Plays 1937–1955, University of Hawaii Plays 1958–1969,* and *Theatre Group Plays 1946–1969,* indexed in *An Index to Original Plays in Sinclair Library 1937–1967,* by Edward A. Langhans and Fay Hendricks (Honolulu: University of Hawaii Press, 1973). Aditional plays can be found in *University of Hawaii Plays 1970–1992* and *Theatre Group Plays 1970–1981.*

Chapter 2

1   I do not suggest "guilt by association" through the use of a Eurocentric dramatic form in preference to traditional Asian staging. I am asking what difficulties can be found in the form of theatrical realism itself when considered as political or strategic theater.

2   Some of the earliest examples of dramatic writing by Asian Americans were produced

by Willard Wilson's playwriting classes in the University of Hawaii's English Department. Wilson gives his writing student a specifically mimetic task: to "look around . . . to attempt to present life as it has impinged upon him and as he sees it." See Wilson, *College Plays* (Honolulu: University of Hawaii Press, 1946–47), vol. 2, p. 3; quoted in Uno, *Unbroken Thread,* p. 5.

3   Frank Chin, "Confessions of the Chinatown Cowboy," *Bulletin of Concerned Asian Scholars* 4 (Fall 1972): 60.

4   "The humor turns black. . . . The two most beguiling characters die suddenly and nightmarishly. Is this a warning? Is this what happens to a family that is warped by isolation? Is it time to stop hanging onto shreds of strange traditions somebody brought from China?" Maxine Hong Kingston, foreword to Hwang, FOB *and Other Plays,* p. ix.

5   Significantly, Hwang has described this play as "a farce which then turns into a spiritual tragedy at the end" (DiGaetani, 163).

6   For some accounts of critical reviews, see Dorothy Ritsuko McDonald's introduction to The Chickencoop Chinaman *and* The Year of the Dragon: *Two Plays by Frank Chin,* and Douglas Street's *David Henry Hwang.*

Chapter 3

1   This nationalist movement might be described as the second phase, where, in the call for total revolution, "immigrants reassert ethnicity in all its autonomy." R. Radhakrishnan, "Is the Ethnic 'Authentic' in the Diaspora?" in *The State of Asian America: Activism and Resistance in the 1990s,* ed. Karen Aguilar-San Juan (Boston: South End Press, 1994), pp. 219–234. In the same volume see also Lane Ryo Hirabayashi and Marilyn C. Alquizola, "Asian American Studies: Reevaluating for the 1990s," pp. 351–364.

2   "The Chinese do not need a Freud to find the books and myths containing the keys to the most deeply rooted, most fully grown Chinese subconscious." Frank Chin, "Come All Ye Asian American Writers of the Real and the Fake," in *The Big Aiiieeeee!: An Anthology of Chinese-American and Japanese-American Literature,* ed. Jeffrey P. Chan (New York: Penguin, 1991), p. 33.

3   See, for instance, Elizabeth Abel, "Race, Class, and Psychoanalysis? Opening Questions," in *Conflicts in Feminism,* ed. Marianne Hirsch and Evelyn Fox Keller (New York: Routledge, 1990), pp. 184–204.

4 This extends what is suggested by Teresa de Lauretis in her reading of Freud: "Normal sexuality . . . would designate the achievement, on the part of the subject, of the kind of sexual organization that a particular society and its institutions have decreed to be normal." "Freud, Sexuality, and Perversion," in *Discourses of Sexuality: From Aristotle to AIDS,* ed. Domna C. Stanton (Ann Arbor: University of Michigan Press, 1992), p. 232.

5 See "Fetishism," in *The Standard Edition of the Complete Psychological Works,* trans. James Strachey (London: Hogarth Press, 1953), vol. 21, pp. 152–157.

6 See Wei, 75–77.

7 From Alvin Eng's title song, "Rock Me Goong Hay," quoted in "Taking It Personally," ed. Janice Paran, *American Theater* (October 1991): 65.

Chapter 4

1 This scene refers to James Shigeta's performance in Samuel Fuller's 1959 film, *The Crimson Kimono.* For a reading of this film, see Marchetti, chap. 7.

2 According to Darrell Y. Hamamoto, "For most Asian Americans, Bruce Lee struck a blow against white racism with each high-velocity punch he delivered." See Hamamoto, *Monitored Peril,* p. 61.

3 For one example of such a reading, see Chalsa Loo, "*M. Butterfly:* A Feminist Perspective."

4 David L. Eng's article targets Asian American as well as American homophobia in criticizing a limited, heterosexual reading of the play's relationships. Eng argues instead for a reading of the play in which Gallimard is the closeted Caucasian homosexual, the "Rice Queen." See Eng, "In the Shadows of a Diva," pp. 93–111.

Chapter 5

1 For an analysis of metaphors of the social order as a biological organism and the Asian American's exclusion from the body politic, see Robert C. Yamashita and Peter Park, "The Politics of Race: The Open Door, Ozawa and the Case of the Japanese in America," *Review of Radical Political Economics,* 17, no. 3 (1985): 135–56.

2 Takaki provides two dramatic examples. Native Americans were relocated to reservations in part because they were held to be groups, not individuals; moreover, the reservation system itself was designed to "civilize" Indians and prepare them for entry

into white American society. Second, racial distinctions became the basis for policy in the decision to relocate Japanese Americans to internment camps during the Second World War. Japanese American men of draft age were forced to answer loyalty questions and to swear "unqualified allegiance to the United States of America" over other foreign powers. As Takaki notes, young men of Italian or German ancestry were not subject to such a test. See Takaki, "Reflections," pp. 29–30.

3   See Robert E. Park, "Human Migration and the Marginal Man," *American Journal of Sociology* 33, no. 6 (May 1928): 890; Robert E. Park, "Racial Assimilation in Secondary Groups with Particular Reference to the Negro, in *Papers and Proceedings, Eighth Annual Meeting of the American Sociological Society, 1913* (Chicago: 1914), vol. 8, p. 71.

4   See Edward K. Strong, Jr., *The Second-Generation Japanese Problem* (Stanford: Stanford University Press, 1934).

5   By contrast, Sucheng Chan's *Asian Americans: An Interpretive History* (Boston: Twayne, 1991) focuses "primarily on collective behavior and the organization of society—especially the economy—and not on individual aspirations or achievements," even while she also posits "members of minority groups as agents of history—men and women who make choices that shape their lives, even when these may be severely limited by conditions beyond their control" (pp. xiii–xiv).

6   I include both books that present oral history, such as Joann Faung Jean Lee's *Asian American Experiences in the United States: Oral Histories of First to Fourth Generation Americans from China, the Phillipines, Japan, India, the Pacific Islands, Vietnam, and Cambodia* (London: McFarlane and Co., 1991) or that seem to figure fiction as oral history, such as *Growing Up Asian American: An Anthology*, ed. Maria Hong, with an afterword by Stephen Sumida (New York: William Morrow, 1993).

7   Some important recent scholarship describes the close ties between patterns of Asian American immigration and experience and labor. See Evelyn Hu-DeHart's comments in "From Area Studies to Ethnic Studies: The Study of the Chinese Diaspora in Latin America," in *Asian Americans: Comparative and Global Perspectives* (Pullman: Washington State University Press, 1991), pp. 5–16. See also Herbert Hill, "Race and Ethnicity in Organized Labor: The Historical Sources of Resistance to Affirmative Action," in *Ethnicity and the Work Force*, ed. Winston A. Van Horne (Madison: University of Wisconsin Press, 1985), pp. 19–64; Robert C. Yamashita and Peter Park, "The Politics of Race: The Open Door, Ozawa and the Case of the Japanese in Amer-

ica," *Review of Radical Political Economics* 17, no. 3 (1985): 135–56; and Lucia Cheng and Edna Bonacich, eds., *Immigration under Capitalism: Asian Workers in the United States before World War II* (Berkeley: University of California Press, 1984).

8   See Him Mark Lai, Genny Lim, and Judy Yung, *Island: Poetry and History of Chinese Immigrants on Angel Island, 1910–1940* (Seattle: University of Washington Press, 1980).

9   In *Reading Asian American Literature,* C. Sau-Ling Wong shows how these key themes of luxury and necessity can be traced through Asian American literature.

Chapter 6

1   See Krieger, "Miss Saigon and Missed Opportunity," pp. 839–66. See also Cecilia Pang and Elizabeth Wong, "The 'Miss Saigon' Diaries," *American Theatre* (December 1990): 40–43.

2   See Keith Osajima, "Asian Americans as the Model Minority: An Analysis of the Popular Press Image in the 1960s and 1980s," in *Reflections on Shattered Windows,* ed. Okihiro et al., pp. 165–174; and "The Model Minority Myth: Asian Americans Confront Growing Backlash," *The Minority Trendsletter* 1, no. 2 (September–October 1987): 5–7. See also Barringer, Gardner, and Levin, *Asian and Pacific Islanders in the United States,* chap. 3: "Incomes: The Question of Parity."

3   See E. San Juan, Jr., "Multiculturalism," p. 547.

4   See in particular Karin Aguilar-San Juan's introduction and Glenn Omatsu, "The 'Four Prisons' and the Movements of Liberation," in *The State of Asian America,* ed. Karen Aguilar-San Juan, pp. 1–18 and 19–70.

Chapter 7

1   An exception might be the important work done on the Eurasian writers Sui Sin Far (Edith Maude Eaton) and Onoto Watanna (Winnifred Eaton); see Amy Ling, "Creating One's Self: The Eaton Sisters," in *Reading the Literatures,* ed. Shirley Geok-lin Lim and Amy Ling; and Annette White-Parks, *Sui Sin Far/Edith Maude Eaton: A Literary Biography* (Urbana: University of Illinois Press, 1995). See also the account of sculptor Isamu Noguchi's voluntary internment in Robert Maeda, "Isamu Noguchi: 5-7-A, Poston, Arizona," *Amerasia* 20, no. 2 (1994): 61–76.

2   Readings of a number of these plays, including *East Is West* (1918), by Samuel Ship-

man and John B. Hymer, *His Chinese Wife* (1920), by Forrest Halsey and Clara Be-
ranger, *Aloma of the South Seas* (1925), by John B. Hymer and Leroi Clemens, and
Uptown West (1923), by Lincoln Osborn, were given in a lecture by Randy Barbara
Kaplan, "Asian Temptations, White Love: 'Dangerous Liasons' on the Broadway Stage,
1900–1930," delivered at a Five College Asian American Studies Faculty Seminar at
Smith College, December 1993. *A Japanese Nightingale* was an adaptation of the 1901
novel of the same name by Winnifred Eaton.

3   For a descriptions of offstage parallels, see Wei, *The Asian American Movement*, pp.
45–46.

4   Anna May Wong's suggestive comment on her own film career was, "When I die, my
epitaph should be she died a thousand deaths. That was the story of my film career.
Most of the time I played in mystery and intrigue stories. They didn't know what to
do with me at the end, so they killed me off." "Anna May Wong Dies at 54," *New York
Herald Tribune*, 5 February 1961, quoted in Moy, *Marginal Sights*, p. 86.

5   "*Kind Ness* was obviously a work that is very close to me. I had the image of a gorilla,
that's how the whole thing started. I thought of the Archie comic books, how much
more quintessentially American can you get than Archie comics? Since I grew up on
the '50s and '60s that was a good time for me to set it in and certainly the comics
make me think of that too. I wanted to do a kind of prototypical, USA suburbia, the
scene of the typical American melting pot situation. I don't think they ever specify the
ethnic types in Archie comics but I broke it down to have one Irish Catholic, one
French-Canadian kid, one Jewish girl, one rich Mayflower family and Buzz, the gorilla. Often people ask me the question, why did you use the gorilla? Why didn't you
use just another ethnic group? I always say, it gives much more distance to have a
gorilla, instead of another person. Also, you can see how they treat him as 'other'
much more clearly." See Chong, "Notes," p. 65.

6   See Milton M. Gordon, *Assimilation in American Life* (New York: Oxford University
Press, 1964), pp. 88–114.

Epilogue

1   See, for instance, the special issue "Thinking Theory in Asian American Studies,"
Amerasia 21, nos. 1–2 (1995).

2   See, for example, Tejumola Olaniyan, *Scars of Conquest/Masks of Resistance: The Inven-
tion of Cultural Identities in African, African-American, and Caribbean Drama* (Oxford:

Oxford University Press, 1995); and Diane Taylor and Juan Villegas, eds., *Negotiating Performance: Gender, Sexuality and Theatricality in Latin/o America* (Durham, N.C.: Duke University Press, 1994). See also Karen Shimakawa, "'made, not born': National Abjection and the Asian American Body on Stage (Ph.D. diss., University of Washington, 1995).

WORKS CITED

Anderson, Benedict. *Imagined Communities: Reflections on the Origins and Spread of Nationalism*. London: Verso, 1984.

Aguilar-San Juan, Karin. *The State of Asian America: Activism and Resistance in the 1990s*. Boston: South End Press, 1994.

Aw, Arthur. *All Brand New Classical Chinese Theatre*. In *Kumu Kahua Plays*, ed. Dennis Carroll. Honolulu: University of Hawaii Press, 1983.

Awkward, Michael. *Negotiating Difference: Race, Gender, and the Politics of Positionality*. Chicago: University of Chicago Press, 1995.

Barringer, Herbert R., Robert W. Gardner, and Michael J. Levin. *Asians and Pacific Islanders in the United States*. For the National Committee for Research on the 1980 Census. *The Population of the United States in the 1980s: A Census Monograph Series*. New York: Russell Sage Foundation, 1993.

Barroga, Jeannie. *Walls*. In *Unbroken Thread: An Anthology of Plays by Asian American Women*, ed. Roberta Uno. Amherst: University of Massachusetts Press, 1993.

Bascara, Victor. "Hitting Critical Mass (or Do your parents still say 'Oriental,' too?)." *Critical Mass: A Journal of Asian American Cultural Criticism* 1, no.1 (Fall 1993): 3–38.

Baygan, Lee. *Makeup for Theatre, Film, and Television*. New York: Drama Book Publishers, 1982.

Berson, Misha, ed. *Between Worlds: Contemporary Asian-American Plays*. New York: Theatre Communications Group, 1990.

Bhabha, Homi. "Of Mimicry and Man: The Ambivalence of Colonial Discourse." In *The*

Location of Culture. London: Routledge, 1994. First published in *October* 28 (Spring 1984): 125–33.

———. "The Other Question." *Screen* 24 (November 1983): 18–36.

Bonacich, Edna. "The Role of the Petite Bourgeoisie Within Capitalism: A Response to Pyong Gap Min." *Amerasia* 15, no. 2 (1989): 195–203.

———. "The Social Costs of Immigrant Entrepreneurship." *Amerasia* 14, no. 1 (1988): 119–28.

———. "Teaching Race and Class." In *Reflections on Shattered Windows: Promises and Prospects for Asian American Studies.* Pullman: Washington State University Press, 1988.

Bonacich, Edna, and Lucie Cheng, eds. "Introduction: A Theoretical Orientation to International Labor Migration." Chap. 1 in *Labor Migration Under Capitalism: Asian Workers in the United States Before World War II.* Berkeley: University of California Press, 1984.

Brustein, Robert. "A House Divided." *American Theater* (October 1991): 44–46, 140–43.

Butler, Judith. "Endangered/Endangering: Schematic Racism and White Paranoia." In *Reading Rodney King/Reading Urban Uprising,* ed. Robert Gooding-Williams. New York: Routledge, 1993.

Campomanes, Oscar V. "Filipinos in the United States and Their Literature of Exile." In *Reading the Literatures of Asian America,* ed. Shirley Geok-lin Lim and Amy Ling. Philadelphia: Temple University Press, 1992.

Chan, Jeffrey Paul, Frank Chin, Lawson Fusao Inada, and Shawn Wong, eds. *Aiiieeeee!: An Anthology of Asian American Writers.* New York: Penguin, 1974, 1983, 1991.

Chan, Jeffrey Paul, Frank Chin, Lawson Fusao Inada, and Shawn Wong, eds. *The Big Aiiieeeee!: An Anthology of Chinese American and Japanese American Literature.* New York: Penguin, 1991.

Chan, Sucheng. *Asian Americans: An Interpretive History.* Boston: Twayne, 1991.

Chin, Frank. The Chickencoop Chinaman *and* The Year of the Dragon: *Two Plays by Frank Chin.* Seattle: University of Washington Press, 1981.

———. "This Is Not an Autobiography." *Genre* 18 (Summer 1985): 109–30.

Cho, Fiona. "Daddy, I don't know what you're talking." *Critical Mass* 1, no. 1 (Fall 93): 57–61.

Chong, Ping. *Kind Ness.* In *New Plays USA 4.* New York: Theatre Communications Group, 1988.

———. "Notes for 'Mumblings and Digressions: Some Thoughts on Being an Artist, Being an American, Being a Witness. . . .'" *MELUS* 16, no. 3 (Fall 1989–90): 58–68.

Chock, Eric, ed. *Paké: Writings By Chinese in Hawaii.* Honolulu: Bamboo Ridge Press, 1989.

Chow, Rey. *Women and Chinese Modernity: The Politics of Reading Between West and East.* Minneapolis: University of Minnesota Press, 1991.

Diamond, Elin. "Mimesis, Mimicry, and the 'True-Real.'" In *Acting Out: Feminist Performances,* ed. Lynda Hart and Peggy Phelan. Ann Arbor: University of Michigan Press, 1993.

DiGaetani, John L. "Interview with David Henry Hwang." In *A Search for a Postmodern Theater: Interviews with Contemporary Playwrights.* New York: Greenwood, 1991.

Dolan, Jill. "In Defense of the Discourse." *TDR* 33, no. 3 (Fall 1989): 58–71.

———. *The Feminist Spectator as Critic.* Ann Arbor: University of Michigan Press, 1988.

Du Bois, W.E.B. "Krigwa Players Little Negro Theatre." *The Crisis* 32 (July 1926): 134–36.

Eng, David L. "In the Shadows of a Diva: Committing Homosexuality in David Henry Hwang's *M. Butterfly.*" *Amerasia* 20, no. 1 (1994): 93–111.

Fanon, Franz. *Black Skin, White Masks,* trans. Charles Lam Markmann. New York: Grove Press, 1967.

Glazer, Nathan. *Affirmative Discrimination: Ethnic Inequality and Public Policy.* New York: Basic Books, 1975.

Gledhill, Christine. "Pleasurable Negotiations." In *Female Spectators: Looking at Film and Television,* ed. E. Deidre Pribram. London: Verso, 1988.

Gooding-Williams, Robert, ed. *Reading Rodney King/Reading Urban Uprising.* New York: Routledge, 1993.

Gotanda, Philip Kan. *Yankee Dawg You Die.* In *New American Plays* 1. Portsmouth, N.H.: Heineman, 1992.

Hagedorn, Jessica. "Asian Women in Film: No Joy, No Luck." *Ms.* (January–February 1994): 74–79.

Hall, Stuart. "New Ethnicities." In *Black Film, British Cinema. ICA Conference* (February 1988): 27–31.

Hamamoto, Darrell Y. *Monitored Peril: Asian Americans and the Politics of TV Representation.* Minneapolis: University of Minnesota Press, 1994.

Houston, Velina Hasu. *Tea.* In *Unbroken Thread: An Anthology of Plays by Asian American Women,* ed. Roberta Uno. Amherst: University of Massachusetts Press, 1993.

Hwang, David Henry. "A Conversation with David Henry Hwang." In *Bearing Dreams, Shaping Visions: Asian Pacific American Perspectives,* ed. Linda A. Revilla, Gail M. Nomura, Shawn Wong, and Shirley Hune. Pullman: Washington State University Press, 1993.

————. *The Dance and the Railroad.* In *FOB and Other Plays.* New York: Penguin, 1990.

————. *Family Devotions.* In *FOB and Other Plays.* New York: Penguin, 1990.

————. *FOB.* In *FOB and Other Plays.* New York: Penguin, 1990.

————. *M. Butterfly.* New York: Penguin, 1988.

Iko, Momoko. *Gold Watch.* In *Unbroken Thread: An Anthology of Plays by Asian American Women,* ed. Roberta Uno. Amherst: University of Massachusetts Press, 1993.

Jameson, Fredric. "On Negt and Kluge." *October* 46 (Fall 1988): 151–77.

JanMohamed, Abdul R., and David Lloyd "Introduction: Toward a Theory of Minority Discourse: What Is to Be Done?" In *The Nature and Context of Minority Discourse.* Oxford: Oxford University Press, 1990.

Kim, Elaine. *Asian American Literature: An Introduction to the Writings and Their Social Context.* Philadelphia: Temple University Press, 1982.

Kondo, Dorinne K. "*M. Butterfly:* Orientalism, Gender, and a Critique of Essentialist Identity." *Cultural Critique* (Fall 1990): 5–29.

Krieger, Lois L. "Miss Saigon and Missed Opportunity: Artistic Freedom, Employment Discrimination, and Casting for Cultural Identity in the Theater." *Syracuse Law Review* 43 (Summer 1992): 839–66.

Li, Ling-ai (Gladys Li). *The Submission of Rose Moy.* In *Paké: Writings By Chinese in Hawaii,* ed. Eric Chock. Honolulu: Bamboo Ridge Press, 1989.

Lim, Genny. *Bitter Cane.* In *The Politics of Life: Four Plays by Asian American Women,* ed. Velina Hasu Houston. Philadelphia: Temple University Press, 1993.

————. *Paper Angels.* In *Unbroken Thread: An Anthology of Plays by Asian American Women,* ed. Roberta Uno. Amherst: University of Massachusetts Press, 1993.

Lim, Shirley Geok-lin, and Amy Ling, eds. *Reading the Literatures of Asian America.* Philadelphia: Temple University Press, 1992.

Liszt, Rudolph G. *The Last Word in Make-up.* New York: Dramatist's Play Service, 1975; 1942.

Loo, Chalsa. "*M. Butterfly:* A Feminist Perspective." In *Bearing Dreams, Shaping Visions: Asian Pacific American Perspectives,* ed. Linda A. Revilla, Gail M. Nomura, Shawn Wong, and Shirley Hune. Pullman: Washington State University Press, 1993.

Lowe, Lisa. "Heterogeneity, Hybridity, Multiplicity: Marking Asian American Differences." *Diaspora* 1, no. 1 (Spring 1991): 24–44.

Lum, Charlotte. *These Unsaid Things.* In *Paké: Writings By Chinese in Hawaii,* ed. Eric Chock. Honolulu: Bamboo Ridge Press, 1989.

Lum, Darrell H. Y. *Oranges Are Lucky.* In *Kumu Kahua Plays,* ed. Dennis Carroll. Honolulu: University of Hawaii Press, 1983.

Marchetti, Gina. *Romance and the "Yellow Peril": Race, Sex, and Discursive Strategies in Hollywood Fiction.* Berkeley: University of California Press, 1993.

Moy, James S. "David Henry Hwang's *M. Butterfly* and Philip Kan Gotanda's *Yankee Dawg You Die:* Repositioning Chinese American Marginality on the American Stage." In *Critical Theory and Performance,* ed. Janelle G. Reinelt and Joseph R. Roach. Ann Arbor: University of Michigan Press, 1992. Originally published in *Theatre Journal* 42 (March 1990): 48–56.

———. "The Death of Asian on the American Field of Representation." In *Reading the Literatures of Asian America,* ed. Shirley Geok-lin Lim and Amy Ling. Philadelphia: Temple University Press, 1992.

———. *Marginal Sights: Staging the Chinese in America.* Iowa City: University of Iowa Press, 1993.

Mulvey, Laura. "Visual Pleasure and Narrative Cinema." In *Narrative, Apparatus, Ideology,* ed. Philip Rosen. New York: Columbia University Press, 1986. Originally published in *Screen* 16, no. 3 (Autumn 1975).

Mura, David. *Turning Japanese: Memoirs of a Sansei.* New York: Doubleday, 1991.

Newman, Harry. "Casting a Doubt: The Legal Issues of Nontraditional Casting." *Journal of Arts Management and Law* 19, no. 2 (Summer 1989): 55–62.

Okihiro, Gary. *Margins and Mainstreams: Asians in American History and Culture.* Pullman: Washington State University Press, 1994.

Okihiro, Gary Y., Shirley Hune, Arthur A. Hansen, and John M. Liu, eds. *Reflections on Shattered Windows: Promises and Prospects for Asian American Studies.* Pullman: Washington State University Press, 1988.

Omatsu, Glenn. "The 'Four Prisons' and the Movements of Liberation: Asian American Activism from the 1960s to the 1990s." In *The State of Asian America: Activism and Resistance in the 1990s,* ed. Karin Aguilar-San Juan. Boston: South End Press, 1994.

Omi, Michael, and Howard Winant. *Racial Formation in the United States: From the 1960s to the 1980s.* London: Routledge, 1986.

Revilla, Linda A., Gail M. Nomura, Shawn Wong, and Shirley Hune, eds. *Bearing Dreams, Shaping Visions: Asian Pacific American Perspectives.* Pullman: Washington State University Press, 1993.

Roof, Judith. *A Lure of Knowledge: Lesbian Sexuality and Theory.* New York: Columbia University Press, 1991.

Rosen, Philip. *Narrative, Apparatus, Ideology: A Film Theory Reader.* New York: Columbia University Press, 1986.

Said, Edward W. *Orientalism.* New York: Vintage, 1979.

San Juan, E., Jr. "Beyond Identity Politics: The Predicaments of the Asian American Writer in Late Capitalism." *American Literary History* 3, no. 3 (Fall 1991): 542–65.

———. "Multiculturalism vs. Hegemony: Ethnic Studies, Asian Americans, and U.S. Racial Politics." *The Massachusetts Review* 32, no. 3 (Fall 1991): 467–78.

Scruggs, Jan C., and Joel L. Swerdlow. *To Heal a Nation: The Vietnam Veterans Memorial.* New York: Harper and Row, 1985.

Shimakawa, Karen. "'Who's to Say?' Or, Making Space for Gender and Ethnicity in *M. Butterfly.*" *Theatre Journal* 45, no. 3 (October 1993): 349–62.

Shiomi, R. A. *Yellow Fever.* Toronto: Playwrights Canada, 1984.

Shohat, Ella. "The Struggle Over Representation: Casting, Coalitions, and the Politics of Identification." In *Late Imperial Culture,* ed. Román de la Campa, E. Ann Kaplan, and Michael Sprinker. London: Verso, 1995.

Silverman, Kaja. *The Acoustic Mirror: The Female Voice in Psychoanalysis and Cinema.* Bloomington: Indiana University Press, 1988.

Sollors, Werner. *Beyond Ethnicity: Consent and Descent in American Culture.* New York: Oxford University Press, 1986.

Steele, Shelby. "The Memory of Enemies." *Dissent* (Summer 1990): 326–32.

Street, Douglas. *David Henry Hwang.* Boise: Boise State University Western Writers Series, 1989.

Takaki, Ronald. *Iron Cages: Race and Culture in 19th Century America.* New York: Oxford University Press, 1990.

———. "Reflections on Racial Patterns in America." In *From Different Shores,* ed. Ronald Takaki. New York: Oxford University Press, 1987.

———. *Strangers from a Different Shore: A History of Asian Americans.* New York: Penguin, 1989.

Trinh, Minh-ha. *Woman, Native, Other: Writing Postmodernity and Feminism.* Bloomington: Indiana University Press, 1989.

Uno, Roberta. *Unbroken Thread: An Anthology of Plays by Asian American Women.* Amherst: University of Massachusetts Press, 1993.

Wei, William. *The Asian American Movement.* Philadelphia: Temple University Press, 1993.

White, Hayden. *Tropics of Discourse: Essays in Cultural Criticism*. Baltimore: Johns Hopkins University Press, 1978.

Wong, Elizabeth. *Letters to a Student Revolutionary*. In *Unbroken Thread: An Anthology of Plays by Asian American Women*, ed. Roberta Uno. Amherst: University of Massachusetts Press, 1993.

Wong, Sau-Ling Cynthia. *Reading Asian American Literature: From Necessity to Extravagance*. Princeton: Princeton University Press, 1993.

———. "Ethnicizing Gender: An Exploration of Sexuality as Sign in Chinese Immigrant Literature." In *Reading the Literatures of Asian America*, ed. Shirley Geok-lin Lim and Amy Ling. Philadelphia: Temple University Press, 1992.

Wong, Yen Lu. "Chinese-American Theatre." *The Drama Review* 20, no. 2 (June 1976): 13–18.

Worthen, William. *Modern Drama and the Rhetoric of Theatre*. Berkeley: University of California Press, 1989.

———, ed. *The HBJ Anthology of Drama*. Fort Worth, Tex.: Harcourt Brace, 1993.

Yamauchi, Wakako. *The Music Lessons*. In *Unbroken Thread: An Anthology of Plays by Asian American Women*, ed. Roberta Uno. Amherst: University of Massachusetts Press, 1993.

———. *And the Soul Shall Dance*. In *Between Worlds: Contemporary Asian-American Plays*, ed. Misha Berson. New York: Theatre Communications Group, 1990.

———. *12-1-A*. In *The Politics of Life: Four Plays by Asian American Women*, ed. Velina Hasu Houston. Philadelphia: Temple University Press, 1993.

Yoshikawa, Yoko. "The Heat Is on *Miss Saigon* Coalition." In *The State of Asian American: Activism and Resistance in the 1990s*, ed. Karin Aguilar-San Juan. Boston: South End Press, 1994.

INDEX

References to photographs of productions are printed in boldface type.

Ah Sin, 10–12, 96

And the Soul Shall Dance (Yamauchi), 31, **129**, 143, 153–55, 195–96

Angel Island Theater Company (Chicago), 15

Aoki, Brenda Wong, 4; *The Queen's Garden*, 18

Asian American movement, 16, 20–21, 23, 79, 218

Asian American Tactical Theatre, 17

Asian American Theater Company (San Francisco), 15; *The Dance and the Railroad*, **125–26**; *FOB*, **130**; *Tea*, **133**; *The Year of the Dragon*, **121**; *Yellow Fever*, **122**

Aw, Arthur, *All Brand New Chinese Classical Theater*, 166, 171–74

Awkward, Michael, 191, 209

Barroga, Jeannie, *Walls*, 33, **135**, 205, 208–15

Belasco, David, *Madame Butterfly*, 13, 110, 192

Bhabha, Homi, 29–30, 89, 94–97, 109–10, 113–14, 120

Bitter Cane (Lim), 143, 148, 149–50, 155–56, 195

Boublil, Alain, *Miss Saigon*, 13

Brustein, Robert, 4

Charlie Chan, 11–12, 51

Chickencoop Chinaman, The (Chin), 17, 18, 28–29, 62–81, 83, 84, 148, 195, 196, 198–99

Chin, "Charlie," 25

Chin, Daryl, 36

Chin, Frank, 19, 21, 61; *The Chickencoop Chinaman*, 17, 18, 28–29, 62–81, 83, 84, 148, 195, 196, 198–99; *The Year of the Dragon*, 18, 24, 27–28, 35, 44–51, 56, 58, 60, **121**

Chong, Ping, 4, 18, 33, 36, 218, 224 n. 18; *Kind Ness*, 204–8, 229 n. 5

Chow, Rey, 28, 58–59

Chu, Louis, *Eat a Bowl of Tea*, 45

Dance and the Railroad, The (Hwang), 31, **125–26**, 143, 146–47, 148, 149–50, 157, 222 n. 7

Dolan, Jill, 26–27, 36–40, 42–43, 58
Du Bois, W.E.B., 8

East West Players (Los Angeles), 15, 92;
    12-1-A, **124**
Eng, Alvin, *The Goong Hay Kid*, 87

Family Devotions (Hwang), 24, 27–28, 35,
    44–45, 51–56, 60, 196
Flower Drum Song, 14, 46
FOB (Hwang), 32, 57, **130**, 148, 166, 174–83
Forbidden City (San Francisco), 13, 223 n.
    14
Fu Manchu, 10–11, 96

Gold Watch (Iko), 31, 143–44, 146, 147, 148
Gotanda, Philip Kan, 4, 23, 219, 221 n. 2;
    Fish Head Soup, 195; *Yankee Dawg You
    Die*, 14, 29–30, 58, 91–94, 98–108, 119–
    20, 148, 196–97
Group Theater (Seattle), 18

Hagedorn, Jessica, 4, 11, 18, 36, 97, 219,
    221 n. 3
Hayakawa, Sessue, 14, 102, 223 n. 15
Hayashi, Eric, 99–100
Hill, Amy, 25; *Tokyo Bound*, 203
Honolulu Theatre for Youth, 20
Houston, Velina Hasu, *Tea*, 33, **133–34**, 147,
    199–204
Huie, Karen, *Columbus Park*, 18
Hwang, David Henry, 4, 65, 219; *The
    Dance and the Railroad*, 31, **125–27**, 143,
    146–47, 148, 149–50, 157, 222 n. 7; *Family
    Devotions*, 24, 27–28, 35, 44–45, 51–56,
    60, 196; *FOB*, 32, 57, **130**, 148, 166, 174–
    83; *M. Butterfly*, 18, 25, 29–30, 44, 92–
    94, 98, 105–20

Iko, Momoko, *Gold Watch*, 31, 143–44, 146,
    147, 148
In the Alley (Sakamoto), 21

Kim, Randall: as Tam Lum, 16–17; as Titus
    Andronicus, 222 n. 10
Kind Ness (Chong), 204–8, 229 n. 5
Kingston, Maxine Hong, 57, 65–66
Kumu Kahua (Honolulu), 15, 20; *Tea*, **133**;
    Yellow Fever, **122**

Letters to a Student Revolutionary (Wong),
    32, **131–32**, 166, 174, 182–88
Li, Gladys Ling-Ai, *The Submission of Rose
    Moy*, 33, 192–94
Lim, Genny, 19; *Bitter Cane*, 143, 148, 149–
    50, 155–56, 195; *Paper Angels*, **128–29**,
    143, 151–53 155–56, 195
Lum, Charlotte, *These Unsaid Things*, 166,
    169–71
Lum, Darrell, *Oranges are Lucky*, 32, 160–
    62

M. Butterfly (Hwang), 18, 25, 29–30, 44,
    92–94, 98, 105–20
Madame Butterfly (Belasco), 13, 110, 192
makeup books, 12, 222 nn. 8, 9, 10, 223 n. 12
Miss Saigon (Boublil and Schönberg), 13,
    91, 110; protests over casting, 15, 163
Mixed Blood Theater (Minneapolis), 18
Miyamoto, Nobuko, 19, 25
Moy, James, 10, 27, 40–43, 58, 93–94
Mulvey, Laura, 37–40, 42–43, 58
Music Lessons, The (Yamauchi), 143, 153–55

Narita, Jude, 25, 41–42, 203
New World Theater (Amherst), 18; *The
    Dance and the Railroad*, 127; *Letters to a
    Student Revolutionary*, 132; *Walls*, 135

Nishikawa, Lane, 25, 81, 203
Northwest Asian Theater Company (Seattle), 15

Omi, Michael, on racial formation, 7–8, 17, 208–9, 215–16
Ong, Han, 4, 24, 221 n. 3
Oranges Are Lucky (Lum), 32, 160–62

Pan Asian Repertory (New York), 15; And the Soul Shall Dance, 129; FOB, 130; Letters to a Student Revolutionary, 131
Paper Angels (Lim), 128–29, 143, 151–53
Paraiso, Nicky, 25
Parsloe, C. T., 11–12
Pom Siab Hmoob Theatre (Minneapolis), 18

Reunion (Toshigawa), 21
Roof, Judith, 39

Sakamoto, Edward 4, 221 n. 2; In the Alley, 21
Sam, Canyon, 25
San Juan, E., Jr., 150, 164, 156–59, 190
Schönberg, Claude-Michel, Miss Saigon, 13
Shepard, Sam, Buried Child, 54–55
Shiomi, R. A., Yellow Fever, 28–29, 62–63, 81–88, 122–24
Silk Road Theater (New York), 15
Sollors, Werner, 189
Submission of Rose Moy, The (Li), 33, 192–94

Takaki, Ronald, 3, 31–32, 145–49; arguments with Nathan Glazer, 137–43; on Chinatown 45; critique of, by E. San

Juan, Jr., 156–59; on railroad strike, 146–47
Tea (Houston), 33, 133–34, 147, 199–204
Teatro Ng Tanan (San Francisco), 17
Theater Mu (Minneapolis), 15; Mask Dance, 18; Paper Angels, 128–29; River of Dreams, 24; Yellow Fever, 122
These Unsaid Things (Lum) 166, 169–71
Tong, Winston, 18, 36
Toshigawa, Bessie, Reunion, 21

Umeki, Miyoshi, 14
Uyehara, Denise, 25

Winant, Howard, on racial formation, 7–8, 17, 208–9, 215–16
Wong, Anna May, 14, 102, 115, 229 n. 4
Wong, Elizabeth: Kimchee and Chitlins, 18; Letters to a Student Revolutionary, 32, 131–32, 166, 174, 182–88
Wong, Sau-Ling Cynthia, 64, 167–68, 189, 221 n. 4

Yamauchi, Wakako, 19; 12-1-A, 31, 143–45, 146, 147; And the Soul Shall Dance, 31, 129, 143, 153–55, 195–96; The Music Lessons, 143, 153–55
Yankee Dawg You Die (Gotanda), 14, 29–30, 58, 91–94, 98–108, 119–20, 148, 196–97
Year of the Dragon (film), 97, 99
Year of the Dragon, The (Chin), 18, 24, 27–28, 35, 44–51, 56, 58, 60, 121
Yellow Fever (Shiomi), 28–29, 62–63, 81–88, 122–24
Yep, Lawrence, Pay the Chinaman, 87
Yew, Chay, 18, 218

Also in the *Asian American History and Culture* series:

Sucheng Chan, ed., *Entry Denied: Exclusion and the Chinese Community in America, 1882–1943*, 1991

Gary Y. Okihiro, *Cane Fires: The Anti-Japanese Movement in Hawaii, 1865–1945*, 1991

Yen Le Espiritu, *Asian American Panethnicity: Bridging Institutions and Identities*, 1992

Karen Isaksen Leonard, *Making Ethnic Choices: California's Punjabi Mexican Americans*, 1992

Shirley Geok-lin Lim and Amy Ling, eds., *Reading the Literatures of Asian America*, 1992

Renqiu Yu, *To Save China, To Save Ourselves: The Chinese Hand Laundry Alliance of New York*, 1992

Velina Hasu Houston, ed., *The Politics of Life: Four Plays by Asian American Women*, 1993

William Wei, *The Asian American Movement*, 1993

Sucheng Chan, ed., *Hmong Means Free: Life in Laos and America*, 1994

Timothy P. Fong, *The First Suburban Chinatown: The Remaking of Monterey Park, California*, 1994

Chris Friday, *Organizing Asian American Labor: The Pacific Coast Canned-Salmon Industry, 1870–1942*, 1994

Paul Ong, Edna Bonacich, and Lucie Cheng, eds., *The New Asian Immigration in Los Angeles and Global Restructuring*, 1994

Carlos Bulosan, *The Cry and the Dedication*, edited and with an introduction by E. San Juan, Jr., 1995

Yen Le Espiritu, *Filipino American Lives*, 1995

Vicente L. Rafael, ed., *Discrepant Histories: Translocal Essays on Filipino Cultures*, 1995

E. San Juan, Jr., ed., *On Becoming Filipino: Selected Writings of Carlos Bulosan*, 1995

E. San Juan, Jr., *The Philippine Temptation: Dialectics of U.S.–Philippine Literary Relations*, 1996

Deepika Bahri and Mary Vasudeva, eds., *Between the Lines: South Asians and Postcoloniality*, 1996

Velina Hasu Houston, ed., *But Still, Like Air, I'll Rise: New Asian American Plays*, forthcoming